AF538924

Internationalization of Higher Education

Internationalization of Higher Education

Prof. Surinder Pal Singh

RANDOM PUBLICATIONS
NEW DELHI (INDIA)

Internationalization of Higher Education

ISBN 978-93-5111-473-4

Published in 2015 in India by

RANDOM PUBLICATIONS

4376-A/4B, Gali Murari Lal, Ansari Road
New Delhi-110 002
Phone : +9111-43580356, 011-23289044, 011-43142548
e-mail: sales@randompublications.com,
info@randompublications.com, randomexports@gmail.com

Reprint 2021

Type Setting by : Friends Media, Delhi-110089
Printed at : Replika Press Pvt. Ltd.

Preface

Higher education has become increasingly international in the past decade as more and more students choose to study abroad, enrol in foreign educational programmes and institutions in their home country, or simply use the Internet to take courses at colleges or universities in other countries. This growth is the result of several different, but not mutually exclusive, driving forces: a desire to promote mutual understanding; the migration of skilled workers in a globalised economy; the desire of the institutions to generate additional revenues; or the need to build a more educated workforce in the home countries, generally as emerging economies.

Cross-border higher education has developed differently across countries and regions. By and large, student mobility has been policy-driven in Europe and demand-driven in the Asia-Pacific region, while North America has mostly been a magnet for foreign students. On the other hand, delivering foreign educational programmes and institutions so that students can study at a foreign college without leaving home has been largely driven by educational institutions themselves. It has been made easier by institutional frameworks which grant substantial autonomy to higher education institutions and by the policies adopted by receiving countries. But the growth and diversification of cross-border education raises a number of questions for governments and higher education institutions.

In addition to making clear theoretical distinctions between different forms of globalization and internationalization, this book offers an intelligent and comprehensive account of higher education's efforts to respond to the challenges of globalization. It deserves a place on the bookshelf of any student, scholar, university manager, or government policy maker who has an interest in globalization and higher education internationalisation; it will provide inspiration and serve as a useful source of reference.

Author

Contents

1

Globalization and Internationalization

The historically international nature of universities is playing out in new and dynamic ways, while the trend is extending broadly and rapidly across the higher education sector. Pushed and pulled along by the forces of globalization, internationalization presents many exciting opportunities to higher education institutions and systems. At the same time, real risks and challenges are inherent in this complex and fluid environment. At stake are issues of competitiveness and relevance, requiring new kinds of strategic thinking and acting with regard to the international dimension by all types of higher education actors.

Concepts and Definitions

Although closely related and frequently used interchangeably, the terms *globalization* and *internationalization* in higher education refer to two distinct phenomena. Globalization typically makes reference to "the broad economic, technological, and scientific trends that directly affect higher education and are largely inevitable in the contemporary world." Internationalization, on the other hand, has more to do with the "specific policies and programs undertaken by governments, academic systems and institutions, and even individual departments to deal with globalization".

A give and take between globalization and internationalization has been evident to many higher education observers, but one of the key distinctions between the two concepts is the notion of control. Globalization and its effects are beyond the control ofi any one actor or set of actors. Internationalization, however, can be seen as a strategy for societies and institutions to respond to the many demands placed upon them by globalization and as a way for higher education to prepare individuals for engagement in a globalized world. Indeed, internationalization has been conceived in many quarters as a necessary "process of integrating an international, intercultural, or global dimension in the purpose, functions, or delivery of postsecondary education". This process consists largely of two main spheres of action, commonly characterized as "internationalization at home" and "internationalization abroad".

Internationalization at home typically consists of strategies and approaches designed to inject an international dimension into the home campus experience-for example, by including global and comparative perspectives in the curriculum or recruiting international students, scholars, and faculty and leveraging their presence on campus. Internationalization abroad, on the other hand, calls for an institution to project itself and its stakeholders out in the world. Key examples include sending students to study abroad, setting up a branch campus overseas, or engaging in an interinstitutional partnership.

Beyond the umbrella concepts of internationalization and globalization, a variety of other terms are used-such as, the international dimension, international education, international programming, international and/or interinstitutional cooperation, international partnerships, cross-border education, borderless education, and regionalization. The varied terminology refers to the breadth of experiences in this area and to the distinctive approaches to internationalization taken by different higher education systems and institutions around the world.

Key Manifestations

The internationalization of higher education is notable for the multiple ways in which it has manifested itself around the world. Although each local, national, and regional context presents unique characteristics, several broad trends can be identified globally. These developments include mobility of people, programs, and institutions; the rising prominence of collaborative research; evolving curricula as well as approaches to teaching and learning; an increasingly heightened sense of the interconnectedness of the higher education enterprise across the globe; and the growing pervasiveness of the phenomenon of internationalization across institutions and broader systems of higher education.

The mobility of students and scholars has characterized the university since its earliest days in medieval Europe. In the last decade, however, the numbers of students studying outside their home countries have increased exponentially. By 2025, research undertaken for DP Pty Ltd in Australia suggests that roughly 7.2 million students may be pursuing some higher education internationally, an increase of 188 percent over the 2006 UNESCO estimate. In some parts of the world, international student mobility has become a central issue in higher education.

For example, a recent study on the impact of the ERASMUS student-mobility program, launched in 1987, indicates that the initiative "has had a leading role in internationalisation policies in higher education at national, European and international level[s]", and affected a wide range of other policies and practices in European higher education.

No less important but harder to track and comprehend are the mobility trends of academics-researchers, scholars, and teaching staff-who spend some period of time working outside of their home countries. The burgeoning number of international agreements between tertiary institutions often includes long- and short-term faculty exchange components. International scholarship and fellowship programs, along with other collaborative projects, move countless numbers of scholars around the globe each year to conduct research abroad, while professional and scholarly meetings and conferences keep many academics on the move abroad.

In some cases, academic superstars have been actively recruited from one country to another in an attempt to shore up prestige and academic output in the receiving institutions, while severe human-resource crises have resulted from the large-scale flight of academics (commonly known as "brain drain") from poorer and less stable countries (notably in sub-Saharan Africa) to more welcoming and resource-rich environments in the North.

International mobility has not been limited to people; the last decade has seen a veritable explosion in numbers of programs and institutions that are operating internationally. It is extremely difficult to gauge the exact number of overseas operations, given the many different manifestations of cross border provision. These include fully fledged "sister" institutions of existing universities (such as New York University in Abu Dhabi), branch campuses of parent institutions (a common model for many of the foreign players setting up shop in the regional hubs in such places as Dubai, Qatar, and Singapore), and collaborative arrangements (such as the one between the University of Nottingham and Zhejiang Wanli Education Group-University, which allows for the operation of the University of Nottingham Ningbo, China). Also prevalent are single programs or narrow fields of study being offered overseas by one institution or jointly by two or more. This area of activity has also seen significant growth in numbers of new kinds of providers, notably for-profit companies and those operating actively in the online environment. There is also a notable degree of fluidity and uncertainty in this area.

A sense of opportunity and also of urgency has been felt by many institutions keen to engage internationally, but the fact that cross-border arrangements come and go with some frequency speaks to the many complexities and challenges inherent in moving programs and other institutional activities abroad. It is also critical to acknowledge that the international flow of educational programming is highly unequal, moving largely in a North-South direction. However, there are exceptions to this rule, including the presence of Pakistani and Indian institutions in Dubai's "Knowledge Village," for example.

The effects of internationalization on higher education can also be seen in the way that the core activities of universities, specifically teaching and research, have been shifting in recent years. The demands of the global knowledge society have placed pressure on higher education to focus more heavily on particular kinds of activities, approaches, and outcomes. Research production in key areas-such as information technology and the life sciences-has risen on national development agendas and for the prestige of individual institutions, and has therefore become a very high priority for many universities around the world.

Much of the world's best research can only be carried out through international collaborative efforts, given the size and complexity of the issues and/or the cost of materials and the investments of time and personnel needed to carry studies through to completion.

Meanwhile, global business trends have put a premium on producing young professionals with particular kinds of credentials and skills. The best example of this may be the American-style MBA degree, which is now offered in countless countries around the world. At the same time, an arguably global interest in developing students who are skilled communicators, effective critical thinkers, dynamic problem solvers, and productive team members in diverse (increasingly international and intercultural) environments is changing the way that teachers teach and students learn in many contexts, as well as the specific content to which students are exposed. Recent debates on the role of humanities and the liberal arts in East Asia, for example, provide a good example of shifting or expanding curricular considerations in light of globalization and internationalization.

The last 10 years have clearly witnessed a profound and deepening sense of interconnectedness within the higher education enterprise across the globe. Universities, the knowledge they produce, the academics they employ, and the students they graduate are directly and intimately connected to the global knowledge economy. What happens in institutions and systems in one part of the world has effects far beyond the immediate environment. The international ranking exercises that have taken on such prominence in the last decade are a prime example of how universities no longer operate in a vacuum, nor even simply a local or national context, but instead sit to a great degree on a world stage.

Ultimately, one of the most critically important characteristics of internationalization to emerge over the last decade is its pervasiveness. The phenomenon is apparent at all levels of the higher education enterprise around the world, affecting individual institutions, regions within countries, and national systems of higher education.

At the institutional level, internationalization can be perceived in the way that large numbers of universities have adopted expanded missions, in many cases embracing service to a community that extends beyond local and national boundaries and aiming to produce "global citizens" with "global competencies." The establishment of international program and support offices, and the designation of staff time for these kinds of activities, has also become extremely commonplace in tertiary institutions across the globe.

In some countries, internationalization seems quite prominent at a regional level. In Spain, for example, universities in the various Autonomous Communities-such as Catalunya and Andalucía, to cite just two cases-have banded together to promote their respective regions as destinations for internationally mobile students. In the United States, more than 20 individual states-from California to Oklahoma, Indiana to Massachusetts-have adopted state-level resolutions in support of international education. Although the state-level initiatives in the United States are largely symbolic actions with little to no substantial impact in practice, the symbolism itself is notable evidence of the rising importance of the international dimension.

Meanwhile, internationalization of higher education has reached the national agenda in a wide range of countries. Qatar, Singapore, and the United Arab Emirates stand out as examples of countries taking rather dramatic steps to promote internationalization as a matter of national policy. Their strategies have focused on the recruitment of prestigious foreign universities to establish local campuses, with the goal of expanding access to the local student population and serving as higher education "hubs" for their regions.

Economic development and prestige enhancement are often key motivating factors there. Other countries, like the United Kingdom, Australia, and Canada, have adjusted visa and immigration requirements to attract foreign students to their higher education systems, motivated significantly by the desire to maintain economic competitiveness and realize substantial financial gains by enrolling large numbers of full-fee-paying internationals. In the United States, for example, it is estimated that international students and their families contributed nearly $15.5 billion to the US economy during the academic year 2007-2008 Globally, one estimate indicates that the world's international students represent a $45 billion "industry".

In addition to income generation, educational, political, and cultural motivations have also become relevant. Many countries in Europe have pursued foreign policy agendas focused on capacity building. These agendas include cooperative activities within the higher education sector, particularly in the developing world and frequently in partnerships that include countries with which there are former colonial ties.

Internationalization has also reached prominence at regional and international levels. The Bologna process and Lisbon strategy in Europe are the clearest examples of international engagement at this level, with the Bologna process drawing more than 40 countries into a "European higher education area."

It is hoped that the European higher education area (EHEA) will achieve a common, Europe-wide framework of understanding around tertiary education and lifelong learning, with significant cross-border intelligibility of degrees and qualifications, and a high level of quality, attractiveness, and competitiveness on a global scale. Indeed, the regional focus in Europe appears to have served as the key point of reference for regionalization efforts elsewhere in the world. For example, the Latin American and the Caribbean area for higher education initiative aims to strengthen cooperation in the region in order to achieve objectives such as:

> ... the harmonization of curricula and institutional reforms, interdisciplinarity, mobility and academic exchange (intraregional mobility of students, researchers and teachers), the implementation of joint agendas for the generation of research with social relevance and priority in the framework of the training needs of human resources at the highest level of scientific and technological innovation, dissemination of knowledge and culture, and offering an increasing range of services to government and productive sectors of our nations.

A focus on regionalization can also be seen in the establishment of such entities as the African Network for Internationalisation of Education, and in the development of the African Union Harmonisation Strategy. Similar concepts are being explored in Asia, as evidenced by the November 2008 meeting organized by the Southeast Asian Ministers of Education Organization Regional Centre for Higher Education and Development entitled "International Conference on Raising Awareness: Exploring the Ideas of Creating Higher Education Common Space in Southeast Asia."

And the 2006 Catania Declaration-signed by education ministers from Algeria, Egypt, France, Jordan, Greece, Italy, Malta, Morocco, Portugal, Slovenia, Spain, Tunisia, and Turkey-puts forth an agenda designed to "activate a structured cooperation in order to promote the comparability and readability of higher education systems" across much of the Mediterranean region). The inclusion of higher education in the World Trade Organization's General Agreement on Trade in Services (or GATS) regime is another clear reflection of the way in which the international dimension of higher education has achieved a global profile.

Opportunities, Challenges and Risks

For some analysts, the impact of globalization on higher education offers exciting new opportunities for study and research no longer limited by national boundaries, while others see the trend representing an assault on national culture and autonomy. It is undoubtedly both. At the very least, with 2.8 million students, countless scholars, degrees, and universities moving about the globe freely there is a pressing need for international cooperation and agreements.

Perhaps the "healthier" consequence of economic globalization and the subsequent pressure on higher education to function internationally has been the necessity for effective (and more transparent) systems of accountability, shared benchmarks, and standards for ethics and quality. Nations can no longer penalize students and scholars who have earned credentials and experience from another country. When individuals cannot enjoy the benefits of education outside of the country where it was acquired, the resulting waste of talent is unacceptable. Yet multiple stakeholders need internationally recognizable benchmarks and standards to properly evaluate unfamiliar foreign qualifications, and these agreements are not reached easily.

At the same time, it is critically important to recognize that some of the forces that currently influence internationalization in higher education are not necessarily compatible with local needs for development and modernization, and opening borders puts diverse motivations for educational development into conflict.

Opportunities

During the last decade, international engagement has risen visibly on institutional and national agendas around the world, even in the face of competing priorities. There are political, logistical, and educational dimensions to this momentum. The growing ease of international travel and a rapidly expanding IT infrastructure have opened many new possibilities to higher education. New models for online learning make education and resources more readily available to individuals who reside in locations physically distant from universities. Information technology provides researchers with a broader reach for scholarly collaboration. These expanded opportunities for collegial engagement across borders-whether mediated through technology or not-hold the promise of much-needed capacity-building in research in contexts where this is lacking. Joint-degree programs, "twinning" efforts, and other approaches to cross-border education-to the extent that these operate in environments with appropriate regulatory and quality assurance oversight- extend the resources of individual universities without significant additional investment, again providing the promise ofi expanded capacity-building for underresourced institutions and systems.

Stakeholders in a variety ofi regions across the globe are moving toward a shared language and framework that facilitate the mobility ofi more and more students during their studies and after graduation. International exposure and experience are commonly understood as mechanisms to provide more graduates and scholars with perspective and insight that will increase their capacity to function in a globalized society.

Internationalization in many contexts has moved from being a marginal, occasional, or ad hoc activity to a more centrally administered, carefully organized, and thoughtful component ofi institutional action. Indeed, in recent years, there has been real movement in universities around the world from reactive to proactive stances in relation to internationalization.

An opportunity now exists for many higher education systems and institutions to move to implement more strategic lines ofi action in regard to the international dimension. These are likely to include very targeted efforts to fashion institutional agreements with strategic partners, leverage the resources of new or existing networks, or develop new approaches to international engagement at more regional rather than global levels. Student mobility is expected to continue as an area of significant dynamism, while growth and innovation in international collaborative research activities also show important potential.

A widespread focus on internationalization-at individual, institutional, and governmental levels-does present real opportunities for stakeholders to move from rhetoric to action in ways that were not conceivable just a decade ago.

Challenges

The necessity of internationalizing higher education-to keep pace with both economic and academic globalization-presents many challenges at institutional and policy levels.

To be meaningful and sustainable, internationalization requires access to some amount of resources (human and financial) as well as their effective deployment and management. For the world's poorest countries and most resource-deprived institutions, the opportunities to engage internationally can be extremely limited or fraught with worrisome trade-offs.

In Africa, for example, the reliance on massive amounts of foreign funding for research and other activities have long placed African universities at a disadvantage on several levels, not the least of which is having to cope with a foreign donor's unpredictable and shifting priorities, as well as serious disconnects between non-local-funder priorities and local needs and interests. The financial dimension of internationalization is also an issue for higher education actors, rich and poor, in the current global financial crisis. Finding and leveraging appropriate resources is a major task moving forward, particularly in contexts where the international dimension is viewed as an optional action area, rather than as an integral component of the academic enterprise and administrative apparatus.

The mobility of higher education programming presents other serious challenges. New providers are crossing national borders with great ease. Some of these initiatives are done at the invitation of the host government, as in the cases of Singapore and Qatar; others are driven by the interests of the provider. These new cross-border programs typically follow the structure of the provider's home country and may or may not be compatible with the education system, cultural norms, or labor-market requirements of the host country. It is often the case that neither the host nor home country has the capacity to monitor the quality, ethics, or conditions of the education being provided. These circumstances increase the urgency of international standards, oversight, and qualifications frameworks.

Perhaps the most disconcerting characteristic of globalized higher education is that it is currently highly unequal. Philip Altbach's observation that "existing inequalities are reinforced while new barriers are erected" aptly describes a world in which the influence of Northern, and largely English-speaking paradigms for producing knowledge and setting scientific and scholarly agendas, dominate. The elite universities in the world's wealthiest countries hold a disproportionate influence over the development of international standards for scholarship, models for managing institutions, and approaches to teaching and learning. These universities have the comparative advantage of budget, resources, and talent sustaining a historic pattern that leaves other universities (particularly in lesser-developed countries) at a distinct disadvantage.

African universities, for example, have found it extremely challenging and complex to enter the global higher education stage; they barely register on world institutional rankings and league tables, produce a tiny percentage of the world's research output, and were long undermined by a powerful global policy discourse that downplayed the role of higher education in development for the world's poorest countries.

The dominance of a specific language or languages for scholarship represents yet another challenge in a globalized world. There is a distinct advantage in using a common language; learning this one language provides access to most of the world's research and teaching materials. Yet, the use of a single language has inevitably limited access to knowledge and also hinders the pursuit of scholarship in other languages. In places like Africa, the use of nonnative languages also carries with it the heavy history of colonialism and has the potential to affect quality in contexts where faculty, students, and researchers are generally unable to operate with high levels of fluency.

Finally, the students and scholars most likely to take advantage of the range of new opportunities in a globalized higher education environment are typically the wealthiest or otherwise socially privileged. The enormous challenge confronting higher education involves making international opportunities available to all equitably. It is also an urgent necessity to collect and analyze more accurate data on international student and scholar mobility, particularly concerning the developing world. For example, in Africa, "countries are hampered by a crippling lack of data in developing an effective strategy with a clear direction for identifying and supporting international education as an important component of higher education in the current global context".

An open and honest assessment of the dark side of the international student and scholar experience-particularly as concerns racism and xenophobia is also an enormous challenge.

Risks

In terms of a global perspective, "commercialization of higher education," "foreign degree mills," and "brain drain" stand out as key risks of internationalization. Cross-border education, specifically, presents particular kinds of threats, including

> … an increase in low quality or rogue providers; a decrease in public funding if foreign providers are providing increased access; non-sustainable foreign provision of higher education if profit margins are low; foreign qualifications not recognized by domestic employers or education institutions; elitism in terms of those who can afford cross-border education; overuse of English as the language of instruction; and national higher education policy objectives not being met.

However, risk assessment does vary by region of the world and according to the relative strength and standing of specific higher education institutions and systems. Research suggests that the overall perception of risk associated with internationalization is higher in the developing world and that different regions of the world are concerned with different aspects of the phenomenon. For example, Latin America, the Caribbean, and the Middle East have been identified as parts of the world that are more sensitive to the possible "loss of cultural identity" through international engagement, while problems associated with "elitism" as a side effect of internationalization are more present for developing and middle-income countries than for more developed economies.

It is clear, however, that if current trends of globalization and internationalization continue, the distribution of the world's wealth and talent will be further skewed. The global migration of talent makes it possible for wealthier nations and institutions to attract and retain human capital desperately needed elsewhere. Philip Altbach observes that 80 percent of the students from China and India who go abroad do not return home immediately after obtaining their degree, while 30 percent of highly educated Ghanaians and Sierra Leoneans live abroad. A flow of talent South to North and North to North has continued to dominate in the last decade. However, exceptions to this rule have also emerged in recent years. The rising numbers of foreign students opting to study in places like China, Singapore, Qatar, and Abu Dhabi represent notable variations on the traditional paradigms of international student mobility. Furthermore, Pawan Agarwal, et al. note "a growing South-South movement which indicates the emergence of regional hubs." This kind of role is clearly played, for example, by South Africa, which hosted some 52,579 international students in 2004, of which approximately 68 percent "came from the Southern African region," and a total of 86.6 percent "came from the South or from the developing world". New manifestations of South-South flow among academics must also be acknowledged. A primary example here is the recent recruitment of a large number of Nigerian academics to Ethiopia to help staff a rapidly expanding Ethiopian higher education sector.

> Still, wealth and power continue to exert powerful influence.
>
> We are now in a new era of power and infuence. Politics and ideology have taken a subordinate role to profits and market-driven policies... As in the Cold War era, countries and universities are not compelled to yield to the terms of those providing aid, fostering exchanges, or offering Internet products, but the pressures in favor of participation tend to prevail. Involvement in the larger world of science and scholarship and obtaining perceived benefits not otherwise available present considerable inducements. The result is the same-the loss of intellectual and cultural autonomy by those who are less powerful.

The success of the most prestigious universities in attracting the world's talent cannot be blamed entirely on the influence these universities possess. There are "push factors" as well. Limited access to resources and political constraints may drive scholars from their home country. Governments wishing to retain talent will have to confront the dilemma that results from allowing political expedience to inhibit scholarly activity.

National autonomy in regard to education is certainly at risk and closely related to the concerns about the increasing commodification of higher education. The failure of the most recent round of the General Agreement on Trade and Services (GATS) to sign a treaty that would liberalize "trade" in higher education is most likely only temporary.

It is perhaps most clear in the context of GATS that the principles of free trade and the social needs of nations come into conflict. Should a GATS treaty be signed, or regional trade agreements take hold in more substantive ways, it would most likely contribute to the influence of for-profit providers of education and educational services whose products are rarely adapted to local priorities or need and undermine the ability of individual countries to regulate these entities. Given the complexity of issues involved in international trade discussions relevant to higher education-and the myriad stakeholders pursuing different agendas with regard to these matters-an urgent need arises for "the higher education sector [to] be informed and vigilant about the risks and benefits and, more importantly, about the need for appropriate policies and regulations to guide and monitor current and future developments". Failure to develop capacity at a national level to understand and effectively deal with these developments is a serious risk, particularly for less-developed countries.

Nontrade initiatives for international cooperation also present complex side effects, leaving smaller and/or poorer nations potentially more vulnerable in these arrangements. Rinne notes that the birth of "a new class of deterritorialized transnational policy actors" creates tension with the long-held paradigm of higher education as an enterprise at the service of national interests.

The forces of globalization have exerted an enormous influence over higher education in the last decade, and internationalization has emerged as the primary response to this phenomenon. Barring major unforeseen developments that would derail current trends, the international dimension in higher education appears to be here to stay and will likely continue to rise in prominence on the agendas of individual institutions and national and regional systems of tertiary education around the world. Internationalization presents many new and exciting opportunities for cooperation within the academic enterprise and can be a powerful tool for the enhancement of quality and the insertion of innovation across many dimensions.

At the same time, many significant risks and challenges must be faced in a costly, fast-paced, competitive global higher education environment. As with many other aspects of higher education, the phenomenon is playing out against a backdrop of inherent inequity around the world. The need to understand and harness the benefits of internationalization, while minimizing the risks and costs, is of central importance moving forward.

Access and Equity

The importance of equal access to higher education was emphasized repeatedly in the declarations that emerged from the 1998 World Conference on Higher Education. UNESCO reaffirmed Article 26(1) of the Universal Declaration of Human Rights proclaiming, "Everyone has the right to education... higher education shall be equally accessible to all on the basis of merit." Increasing the participation and role of women in higher education was emphasized, but the declaration included many other factors and conditions that have resulted in inequitable patterns of participation.

Much progress has been made. While many countries have enrolled upwards of 50 percent of the age cohort (and therefore reflect the extent of massification during the last few decades), too many countries still enroll only a small percentage of the cohort. Poorer nations are likely to enroll fewer students than wealthier nations. Additionally, even as enrolment has expanded, participation has rarely been representative of the society as a whole. Within most nations, access to higher education is often (still) the privilege of specific segments of society.

Many nations have attempted to address inequities with aggressive policies (e.g. affirmative action or reservation policies for admission), innovative financing schemes, and tutoring programs, but it is always clear that these patterns are not easily erased and the challenge remains of making higher education truly accessible to all.

New providers, new delivery methods, the diversity of postsecondary institutions, and the ease of international mobility should (in theory) make higher education available to more people. While this has indeed been the case, the diversity of opportunities has also helped to underscore those pernicious issues that hamper progress.

Massification and Uneven Gains Worldwide

Participation in postcompulsory education has expanded exponentially throughout the world during the last several decades. Globally, the percentage of the age cohort enrolled in tertiary education has grown from 19 percent in 2000 to 26 percent in 2007. Still, while the actual number of participants grows, the proportion of the age cohort varies from region to region and traditional patterns of unequal enrolment persist. Not surprisingly, the most dramatic gains have taken place among upper-middle and upper-income countries. In low-income countries tertiary-level participation has improved only marginally, from 5 percent in 2000 to 7 percent.

In Africa the challenge is to increase participation for the entire age cohort. With only 5 percent of the age cohort enrolled, sub-Saharan Africa has the lowest participation rate in the world. Countries in the region struggle with limited capacity, overcrowding, limited infrastructure, inadequate management, poor student preparation, and high cost Distance learning has made higher education significantly more accessible, particularly in rural Africa, but lack of infrastructure and the cost to individuals and institutions to acquire new technology combine to moderate progress.

China and India have recognized the need for increasing their respective pools of talent to support continued economic growth. Yet China enrolls 23 percent of the age cohort, while India enrolls only 12 percent. Demand has grown too rapidly for either country to respond with the necessary infrastructure or with an adequately prepared professoriate.

Despite steady increases in tertiary enrolment in Latin America, participation for the region is still less than half of the enrolment in high-income countries. Cost is still a significant barrier to access. Enrolment in the region struggles against obstacles common to much of the developing world. Although tuition is low (compared to higher-income countries) or free at many public universities in the region, attendance still entails significant private cost (education-related costs, living expenses, opportunity cost) that average 60 percent of gross domestic product per capita. Few countries offer grant or loan programs to make education feasible for lower-socioeconomic sectors of society.

What Does Access Mean?

In its simplest form, greater access to higher education means making it possible for more individuals to enroll. Despite many policy initiatives in recent years, broader postsecondary participation has not benefited all sectors of society equally. Research has demonstrated that the challenge is complicated by a large number of variables.

Truly providing equal access to higher education means overcoming the social and economic inequities within each nation and the corresponding disparities that result.

> Inequalities in higher education participation are evident throughout the life course and include differences in terms of time (and age), place, gender, ethnicity, first language, parental (and sibling) social class, parental

> education, type of school attended, housing tenure, health/disability, criminal activity, learning difficulties, family structure and religious background. Multiple social disadvantages can result in initial education and, subsequently, participation in other forms of learning. Parental income and education are particularly influential. Occupational status and family size are also relevant... Quality of life factors (such as infant health) are important for understanding disengagement from education rather than participation within it.... The question is raised as to whether policymakers should seek to reduce inequality in education directly, or seek to reduce the wider inequalities that are reflected in education.

These issues are not unique to England by any means. To what extent can access to higher education ever be equal without corresponding policy to address the social conditions that disadvantage some population groups while benefiting others?

Accommodating a more diverse population and broadening access create many new tensions between societies and institutions. Universities are under a great deal of pressure to meet the complex and often contradictory expectations of the societies they serve. Prejudice, discrimination, and disadvantage did not begin within the university. Yet, the university is obliged to address these and other challenges embedded in diverse contemporary societies. In the current economic climate universities are facing extreme budget pressure precisely when they are being asked to provide new services to address the needs of ever more diverse students. "Today universities are required to promote equity, fairness and justice, on the one hand, and maintain efficiency, quality and public accountability, on the other".

Historically, underserved populations tend to be less well-prepared for higher education than many of their peers. Countries often tend to equate open admission with equal access but low rates of completion raise doubts about whether access alone is sufficient. Greater diversity also raises concerns about quality and forces societies to address the tension between equity and excellence in admission.

A commitment to broader participation ultimately requires each society to insure that all of its young citizens have both the prerequisites (academic and economic) and ongoing support to participate successfully, as well as equal opportunity to apply their knowledge and skill in the labor market upon graduation. The goals must be understood as more than access, and also attend to opportunities for progress and success For expanded access to have meaning, systems must be in place to insure the success of the new populations enrolling.

The unequal distribution of wealth and resources worldwide also determines the extent to which nations can address these problems. The scope and complexity of the challenge are enormous. While advances are being made, there is still much to be accomplished.

Geography

Geography is easily underestimated as a factor that contributes to unequal participation in higher education. Tertiary institutions are not distributed evenly throughout a nation. Rural populations are more likely to be more distant from postsecondary institutions than urban populations. Indigenous peoples are even more likely to live in remote areas, compounding the challenge of improving the participation rate of these groups.

While new technology should, in theory, help bridge this gap, rural areas are less likely to have the necessary modern infrastructure, and rural families are unlikely to have the equipment necessary to participate in distance programs. Furthermore, traditional-age students (particularly children of parents without postsecondary education) will not possess the discipline and self-motivation to make distance technology a viable alternative to presential learning.

Geography, combined with other factors, contributes to the disadvantage of specific populations. For example, aboriginal people in Australia have less access to even secondary schools in their home community, let alone tertiary institutions. Secondary completion was only 32 percent of the age cohort in 1998, complicating the challenge of increasing participation in higher education.

Similarly, in Mexico where the national gross enrolment ratio has grown from 14 percent in 1995 to 26.2 percent in 2005, participation in poor urban areas was only 11 percent and in poor rural areas only 3 percent. Since the early 1990s, the Ministry of Education has invested in the development of additional educational services in underserved areas with some success. Ninety percent of the students that have enrolled are the first in their family to pursue higher education; 40 percent live in economically depressed regions.

Wealthier countries have been able to close the distance somewhat. The rapid expansion of the community college system in the United States put postsecondary institutions within the geographic reach of most of the American population, but this was a result of massive investment. Other high-income countries (the Republic of Korea, for example) still host most of their universities (and certainly their most prestigious) in their major cities. Developing countries do not have the resources necessary for the development of new universities in remote areas. As a result, low secondary school completion rates in rural areas, coupled with the lack of guidance and the expense of relocating (for those students who do complete secondary school and wish to continue), conspire to depress continuance for rural populations.

More to Access Than Meets the Eye

Greater participation rates in higher education do not (by themselves) open the same opportunities equally to all. Research shows repeatedly that disadvantaged populations once enrolled are less likely to continue to degree completion. In addition, these groups also attend particular types of institutions and programs of study. These programs are typically those that offer fewer opportunities for employment and further study.

The small percentage of the age cohort of aboriginal people in Australia who enroll in tertiary education are more likely to be concentrated in basic-entry university programs and vocational education institutions, earning not only fewer but lower-level credentials.

Even where gross enrolment ratios are high, inequities persist. The United States demonstrates impressive enrolment capacity, infrastructure, and funding, but participation by racial and ethnic minorities is disappointing.

Although minority enrolment doubled during the last quarter of the 20th century, closer inspection of the data reveals that participation rates for minority students continue to lag behind. Data reported for 2006 show 41 percent of the white age cohort enrolled at a college or university compared to 32 percent of young black adults and 24 percent of Hispanic students. Not only are enrolment rates uneven, but data show a graduation gap, where white students continue to graduate in larger numbers than their minority peers.

Community colleges have made tertiary education more accessible (geographically and economically) to more individuals in the United States since the 1940s, but research shows that the likelihood that community college students will continue on to a four-year degree is largely determined by the socioeconomic status of the student's family, regardless of race or ethnicity.

A recent comparative study of 15 countries (mainly in the North and mostly upper-income countries) found that the expansion of higher education has allowed larger proportions of all social strata to attend. Yet the study also concluded that despite greater inclusion, the privileged classes have retained their relative advantage in nearly all nations.

In France, for example, overall participation in higher education is quite high. Yet, France has a hierarchical system of tertiary education where enrolment in elite institutions often provides access to unique postgraduate opportunities. Despite significant increases in broad-based participation in higher education in general, the elite-postsecondary-track graduates are still more likely to be male and to be children of highly educated.

Opportunities for tertiary-level education have also expanded significantly in the Republic of Korea, but these new places have been opened in lower-status institutions (including those that do not lead to postgraduate education). These new institutions are most likely to absorb lower-income students. Wealthier students have the option and advantage of private tutors to help them prepare for university entrance examinations and, as a result, compete more successfully for limited places in elite universities.

Other developed countries have similar challenges to overcome in order to reach the goal of rewarding merit equitably.

Affirmative Action, Positive Discrimination, Quotas, and Reservation Programs

Widening participation in higher education has been seen as a force for democratization, but this is only the case when participation is representative of the population as a whole. Most countries ration admission to higher education in some way, typically on the basis of an examination. Merit is assumed to make opportunity available equally if all aspirants are evaluated by the same criteria. Yet, because of the many influential variables alluded to above, this is not the case. Traditional beliefs about meritocracy tend to reproduce privilege and exclusion.

Providing higher education to all sectors of a nation's population means confronting social inequalities deeply rooted in history, culture, and economic structure that affect an individual's ability to compete. To address the problem, many countries have implemented policy initiatives to rectify past wrongs. But obliging societies to change behavior and values is no simple matter. Advocates of human rights find themselves challenging cultural and religious traditions that countries may not readily discard. Many conservative Islamic cultures reject the notion that women should have access to the same education available to men. Traditional Indian culture accepts a notion of caste, which does not assume that opportunity will be dispensed equally. Policy does not easily change attitudes.

Nevertheless, programs labeled "affirmative action" or "reservation programs" are being used throughout the world to compensate for patterns of past discrimination. These programs represent "positive discrimination" or "reverse discrimination" in other words, they give priority to groups once discriminated against over other social groups. These groups reflect differences of gender, race, ethnic groups, economic sectors, and/or religion.

Women have made important strides in gaining access to higher education, but they are distributed unevenly. In the OECD countries (with the exception of the Republic of Korea, Switzerland and Turkey) women now account for more than 50 percent of the enrolment. According to UNESCO data, women persist longer in most countries, with the notable exception of the African region. Still, the ratio of women to men tends to be higher in vocational and intermediate degree programs in many member countries, although this appears to be changing. UNESCO data show that, worldwide, women represent roughly half of the enrolment, but closer inspection shows similar unevenness in their distribution across fields of study. For example, women represented 21 percent of the enrolment in engineering, manufacturing, and construction (average of all reporting countries) in 2000 and only improved to 23 percent of the enrolment in those fields by 2007. In contrast, women represented 65 percent of the enrolment in education in 2000, and this grew to 68 percent in 2007.

Initiatives designed to address inequities are inevitably perceived as unfair by at least one sector of society and invariably controversial. Initiatives in Ghana, Kenya, Uganda, and the United Republic of Tanzania have lowered admissions cutoffs for women to increase female enrolment. This kind of strategy can prove to be a mixed blessing if women, once admitted to university, are perceived as being academically inferior to men.

Simply admitting more women through affirmative action programs overlooks a significant part of the problem. The intersections of gender, poverty, and higher educational opportunities have been examined in Ghana and the United Republic of Tanzania. The research has shown that disadvantage is often the result of combinations of characteristics; when gender is intersected with socioeconomic status, participation rates of poorer women are extremely low in both African countries.

In many societies, social class and status also need to be addressed. Although India has expanded tertiary enrolment significantly during the past two decades, participation has not increased equally across all sectors of society. The Indian government now obliges universities to reserve a set percentage of the spaces in the incoming class for "socially and educationally backward classes".

Modest improvement has occurred, but the gross enrolment ratio of lowers castes, rural populations, and Muslims lag behind the general population. Muslims in India are underrepresented in higher education but are not included in the new reservation program. Most of the lower castes gaining access to tertiary study are clustered in less expensive bachelor of arts programs where graduates encounter limited job prospects, reinforcing the premise that increasing participation alone does not achieve social equity.

India's initiative to address issues of equitable access highlights many of the challenges of pursuing social integration with policies targeted at higher education. Most of the underrepresented groups in higher education also have a lower secondary-level completion rate. The reservation program places pressures on universities that they are not prepared to address among them the need to either decrease the number of places available to the "general (non-reservation) students" or increase the total number of places. With limited human resources and budget, expansion is quite difficult.

In Brazil, enrolment in higher education has been skewed toward more prosperous white, able-bodied citizens. State legislatures in Brazil have mandated that universities reserve space for disabled and Afro-Brazilian students. The disabled are often overlooked in discussions of access and equity and are perhaps almost universally underrepresented in postsecondary institutions, certainly the case in Brazil. Brazil is a largely mixed-race country, and the challenge of determining who qualifies as Afro-Brazilian has been considerable.

Strategies being tried worldwide are moving more members ofi underrepresented groups into higher education. Yet, without a commitment to cultivate respect and understanding for these relative newcomers, many professors and peers may not welcome these students: "The non-beneficiaries have a general tendency to devalue the accomplishments of the students and faculty belonging to the reserved category".

Completion Rates

Social equity will not be achieved through access to further education alone. In order to fully enjoy the benefits ofi higher education and to contribute to the society and economy in which they live, individuals need to complete their program ofi study. True progress depends on high levels ofi completion for all population groups.

As already noted above, students ofi color in the United States have a much lower completion rate than white students. In Argentina, where secondary school graduates have free and open access to public universities, the completion rate (based on the ratio ofi graduating to entering students) is less than 24 percent. The interpretation ofi access has to go beyond merely getting more students "through the door." Mechanisms to support success are essential, yet they are rarely in place and where they do exist inadequately address the needs ofi the new diverse populations enrolling.

Only limited data are available about completion rates, especially in developing countries. This is important data for the continued improvement ofi greater inclusion.

Costs and Financing

Cost remains an enormous barrier to access, obviously affecting some social sectors more than others. As more countries "privatize" public as well as private institutions, more direct cost is being passed along to students. Even where universities refrain from charging tuition or other enrolment fees, students have to bear indirect costs such as living expenses and (often) the loss of income. For students who reside in rural or remote areas, access to higher education may require the additional expense of relocating.

In order to mediate cost as an obstacle many countries offer scholarships, grant and/or loan programs. These financing schemes (when available) lower the "net cost" of pursuing higher education. These programs are demonstrating some degree of success but cannot by themselves remove economic barriers. Financing schemes make good policy but they are not always embraced by the individuals they are designed to help.

In fact, the price of higher education acts as a serious deterrent in several ways: the price constraint and whether the individual believes that the total price outweighs the benefits ofi a particular educational choice; a cash or liquidity constraint, where an individual cannot obtain sufficient funds to cover the immediate cost of education; and debt aversion or a reluctance to incur debt in order to obtain an education. These issues weigh more heavily on students from poorer backgrounds.

Furthermore, although research consistently demonstrates that tertiary education has significant positive impact on the life earnings of an individual, these benefits are not always as apparent (or convincing) to historically underserved populations without family members or other role models who have demonstrated the benefits of higher education. Finally, poorer students are less likely than wealthier students to confidently make long-term investments or to trust long-term outcomes.

Based on research in several countries, the availability of grants (non-repayable subsidies), as opposed to loans, has been described as an important positive influence on the retention of lower-income students. Fear of debt tends to be a greater deterrent for students from poorer backgrounds since there is less financial "backup" in the case of unemployment or underemployment after graduation (a common condition in the developing world).

Many countries offer loan schemes designed specifically for tertiary study that have had success in increasing access. Income-contingent loan schemes (where repayment plans are tied to postgraduation earnings) and other innovative approaches have gained popularity in Australia, New Zealand, and South Africa and increasingly elsewhere, but are still more attractive to middle- and lower-middle-class students. By tying the repayment schedule to income, students can be more confident of managing their loan burden after graduation in a broader range of circumstances.

Mexico has also introduced loan programs to make the private sector more accessible to a broader spectrum of families. In Mexico, the private sector is absorbing much of the expanding enrolment demand, but since this sector is tuition-dependent, cost becomes a serious obstacle to students from low-income families. The national association of private universities (Federación de Instituciones Mexicanas de Educación Superior) has launched a loan program to bridge the economic gap. But in order to be viable, loans can only be made to families that sign a collateral agreement, a condition that automatically limits the reach of the program. Yet the Canton and Blom assessment demonstrates that the loan program still opens the possibility of postsecondary education to many individuals who otherwise would not have considered it.

Chile has introduced a new loan program that targets students from lower-income families. Although the loan program is not tied to postgraduate income, the payment schedule is adjusted so that students pay less upon graduation and more at subsequent stages of the loan period, based on the assumption that income improves over time. Chile has addressed the problem of collateral by making the tertiary institution the guarantor of the loans for the students it enrolls.

Without question, financial assistance is key to expanding access to new populations. Research is still inconclusive on the most effective way to ameliorate cost as a deterrent to low-income groups, but the need to address economic barriers to higher education remains critically important.

Teaching and Retaining More Diverse Students

Expanded enrolment that encompasses historically underrepresented populations presents many new challenges to the institutions enrolling them. The previous academic preparation of these new students will be uneven at best, deficient at worst. If the objective of expanded access is to graduate this new cohort as well as to enrol it, then new systems for academic support and innovative approaches to pedagogy will be necessary.

One of the challenges of the diversity lies in the gulf between traditional teaching and the expectations of the new student cohort, with student-learning needs proving to be as diverse as the group itself. Faculty are more inclined to see this as a "student problem" than a teaching problem and expect students to adapt. A number of issues have been observed:

> As universalization progresses, most new students are simply less interested in the kind of education provided by existing higher education institutes or are simply less academically gifted. In order to attract these students, new tactics need to be introduced.

Mexico has taken the innovative step of creating new "intercultural universities" that are grounded in indigenous philosophies, cultures, languages, and histories. This creates and environment where the new student population is less likely to be received as an "outsider."

Hockings, et al. have studied how university teaching influences student engagement in classrooms in a range of subjects (biosciences, business, computing, history, and health and social care) in different types of English postsecondary institutions. They explored social, cultural, and educational diversity and difference among the student population and the pedagogic practices that actively embrace or limit the potential for student learning. They suggest that some pedagogies do not engage the diverse interests or meet the needs of all students, while alternative pedagogic approaches appear to create inclusive learning environments and increase academic engagement.

In order to engage previously underrepresented students and hence retain them, efforts to align the curriculum and teaching approaches to their needs, interests, learning styles, and previous experience will be critical.

There is little question that participation in higher education has expanded dramatically during the last decade. Although there have been greater gains in wealthier nations, the improvement has taken place everywhere and seems to benefit all social strata. The nearly equal participation of women in higher education in so many countries is cause for celebration.

Experience has shown that expanded access to higher education alone does not fully address the issue of social equity. Institutions must consider the conditions required for successful completion as well, which means new services, innovative pedagogy, financing schemes, career advising, and more factors. Successful inclusion also requires strategies to develop respect among diverse cultures studying together.

What has become increasingly apparent is that access to higher education cannot be separated from a host of other social and economic issues. Simple solutions cannot solve complex problems. Ultimately, equitable participation in tertiary education across all sectors of society is inextricably linked to other educational, social, and economic conditions beyond higher education. Rates of completion for secondary education must be improved. Success at the secondary level (like tertiary study) is too often linked to income and parental education and profession(s).

The cost of education must be addressed to enroll and retain lower-income students. Even students who enroll at tuition-free public institutions incur expense that might prove to be a fatal barrier to the successful completion of a postsecondary degree. Making loans available does not necessarily remove financial barriers. Students from lower-income families are more hesitant to assume the risk of debt and more likely to forego income in order to study. Creative solutions will be required to overcome cost as an obstacle to participation.

In their report, Bloom, et al. emphasize that improved access to higher education will not provide advantages to individuals or societies unless corresponding macroeconomic development takes place to insure productive work for new graduates. Research is limited and, subsequently, not conclusive but indicates that there may be corresponding inequalities that follow disadvantaged groups into the labor market.

As nations attempt to increase participation for underrepresented groups, each initiative seems to reveal additional underlying challenges. As with other aspects of the ongoing revolution in higher education, the goal of access for all populations seems less audacious than it did a decade ago, but the pursuit of the goal has underscored the depth and breadth of the problem. Increased access alone for men and women to higher education will demonstrate limited success unless it is part of a larger, more far-reaching socioeconomic development strategy.

References

Adelman, C. 2009. *The Bologna Process for U.S. Eyes: Re-learning Higher Education in the Age of Convergence*, Institute for Higher Education Policy, Washington

Barrow, C. 2008. *Globalization, Trade Liberalization, and the Transnationalization of Higher Education.* 18 November 2008 presentation at Boston College,

Chestnut Hill, MA. Canton, E. and Blom,A. 2004. *Can Student Loans Improve Accessibility to Higher* Education and Student Performance: An Impact Study of the Case of SOFES, *Mexico*, World Bank, Washington DC.

D'Antoni, S. 2008. *Open Educational Resources: The Way Forward*, UNESCO, International Institute for Educational Planning, Paris.

2

Quality Assurance and Accountability

By the 1998 UNESCO World Conference on Higher Education, quality assurance was already a concern of nearly all nations, most of which had implemented schemes to evaluate the quality of institutions and programs in higher education. These systems vary enormously in focus, reach, objectives, and impact.

Over the last decade, greater attention has been focused on "convergence" or making different national quality assurance schemes and frameworks more comparable or complementary to one another. Increasingly, nations are relying on quality assurance schemes used in other nations as guarantees of quality both to validate the domestic higher education system in its own right and to support all kinds of cross-border activity-student mobility, joint-degree programs, validation of professional qualifications, and others.

Cross-border intelligibility can be very useful, but "convergence" also introduces risks and challenges. Nations are often stretched to design quality assurance schemes that reflect international practices, while preserving objectives and practices that take into consideration unique local needs and limitations.

Quality assurance has become a rapidly growing concern in a context of ongoing change in higher education around the world. At the same time, defining and measuring quality usefully has become more difficult. As the higher education landscape has become more complex, so have the expectations of individual institutions. In addition to educating, tertiary-level institutions have assumed (and been assigned) a broader social role-including resolving social inequities, providing appropriately trained labor, contributing to regional and national economic growth, and producing marketable research. Meanwhile, institutions are also obliged to operate more efficiently and transparently. Against these broad and shifting expectations, different constituencies judge the quality of higher education in various ways.

Today, "customers" or "stakeholders" have a considerable influence in determining the perception and measures of quality. Fee-paying students, professional bodies, employers, politicians, and funding agencies are all voicing their particular expectations of what a degree or diploma should represent. New terms such as "transparency," "performance indicators," and "outcome measures" now figure prominently in the discussion. Yet, despite near universal agreement that the quality of higher education must be assured, concern for institutional autonomy, national culture, and the importance of relevance to local contexts further complicate the discussion.

Defining exactly what quality looks like is especially problematic in the midst of significant expansion and internationalization. The massive growth in enrolment at the end of the last century and the subsequent diversity of both students and institutions add many layers of complexity to quality assurance efforts. Additionally, globalization, regional integration, and the ever-increasing mobility of students and scholars have expanded the need for internationally recognized standards or benchmarks to help guide the comparison and evaluation of academic and professional qualifications.

Quality in higher education was once assured (in most countries) by the regulation and oversight of provincial and/or national ministries of education. National higher education systems were restricted in size and scope so national standards were plausible and could be applied efficiently to a limited number of institutional types. The current diversity of institution types and providers-along with increasingly international orientations of these actors-has made this kind of evaluation less practical, while making broader and more flexible criteria necessary. A near universal shift has occurred from ex ante regulation (establishing standards and limitations beforehand) to ex post evaluation (measuring and evaluating performance after the fact) with ex post evaluation usually being conducted and coordinated by new parastatal agencies taking into consideration expanded criteria for judging institutional performance. The rapidly expanding private sector presents additional challenges to government agencies.

Quality assurance agencies, new and old, responsible for monitoring institutional and program quality, are under pressure from multiple constituencies to address evermore complicated expectations. Preoccupation with quality is now universal, and few countries, if any, have opted out of the quality assurance movement. However, like all issues addressed in this report, the pursuit of quality plays out differently in various regions and countries.

Defining Quality

At some point, every essay that is written about quality assurance addresses the challenge of defining what *quality* actually means in higher education. The general understanding of quality has evolved with each passing decade and continues to adapt to changing contexts and exigencies. At the 1998 UNESCO world conference it was already clear that the range of activities to be evaluated was expansive:

> Quality in higher education is a multidimensional concept, which should embrace all its functions, and activities-; teaching and academic programmes, research and scholarship, staffing, students, buildings, facilities, equipments, services to the community, and academic environment.

A decade later the definition provided in a UNESCO-CEPES report reflects the increasing complexity of the higher education environment:

> Quality in higher education is a multi-dimensional, multi-level, and dynamic concept that relates to the contextual settings of an educational model, to the institutional mission and objectives, as well as to the specific standards within a given system, institution, programme, or discipline.

In practice, the issue of quality is addressed more usefully as a process than an idea. Quality assurance is viewed as a process where key elements of higher education are measured. It is in this process that the concepts of performance, standards, norms, accreditation, benchmarks, outcomes, and accountability overlap to form the foundation of the quality culture emerging in higher education everywhere. The differences in exactly what is measured and how reflect the way different nations and cultures interpret quality.

Process of Quality Assurance

Even without a concise definition of quality in higher education, a pattern for evaluating higher education has been established in most of the world. In a break from the past, this new pattern tends to rely on peers rather than government authorities to conduct the evaluation process.

Most quality assurance schemes begin with a self-study or self-review of the institution or program being evaluated. The self-study obliges an institution to undertake a thorough examination of its own practices, resources, and accomplishments with an eye toward measuring performance against mission and identifying ways to improve.

The process is described by the Australian Universities Quality Agency as a "systematic and independent examination to determine whether activities and related results comply with planned arrangements and whether these arrangements are implemented effectively and are suitable to achieve objectives". The process usually includes an evaluation or inspection of the effectiveness of the internal quality systems.

An important trend in quality evaluation is that institutions are now more often evaluated against their own self-defined mission and less often against an institutional model defined by a regulatory agency. This approach has become increasingly necessary and important with the growing diversity of institutions and delivery systems. The framework that regulators then use for judging the quality of an institution may reflect one or more of the following criteria-quality as excellence, quality as fitness *for* purpose, and quality as fitness *of* purpose, quality as enhancement or improvement.

Another trend has been a modification in the role of government and parastatal agencies. In many cases, the regulatory function of many of these agencies has shifted to a validating role. In other words, as quality has come to be seen as a continuous process of assessment and improvement, coordinating bodies are focusing on whether institutions have adequate mechanisms in operation to support this dynamic process.

This approach to quality assurance as described above forms the underpinnings of most schemes in practice today. But, as they say, the devil is in the details. Evaluations in different systems focus on specific elements of higher education. These processes may be similar, yet the language and terminology of quality assurance are used and often understood differently in each language and culture. In a study undertaken by the European Network for Quality Assurance in 2006, it became apparent that for quality assurance schemes to function across national boundaries the vocabulary of quality needs to maintain its meaning as it crosses cultural boundaries. The report emphasizes that assumptions should not be made lightly as nations move toward new international agreements. Glossaries, such as "Quality Assurance and Accreditation: A Glossary of Basic Terms and Definitions", endeavor to clarify the vocabulary of quality. The importance of terminology in reaching shared understandings and agreements cannot be underestimated.

Limitations of National Programs

External independent mechanisms for evaluating the quality and performance of higher education in the United States have been in place since the early part of the 20th century. This was not the case elsewhere where oversight belonged exclusively to governments until the end of the last century. In the early 1990s, fewer than half of the countries in Europe had established new quality assurance agencies, but by 2004 nearly every country had created an agency charged with the oversight of quality assurance for the higher education sector, although with widely varying mandates, responsibilities, and authority. National quality assurance schemes are the essential building blocks of international conventions but are not sufficient by themselves.

At the same time that national programs to monitor quality assurance were being implemented throughout the world, many new cross-border models for higher education were being created. These new models (foreign providers, private nonprofit and for-profit universities, and online delivery) are often excluded from national quality assurance schemes although they account for an increasing number of university students. The explosive growth of both traditional institutions as well as new providers in higher education raises new questions in regard to standards of quality in this ever more diverse environment.

The need for some basis for the comparison of the quality of programs and of qualifications at the international level has become more urgent as a result of the increasing number of internationally mobile students, now projected to reach 7.5 million by 2025. Local systems for quality assurance are simply no longer adequate.

National programs to evaluate quality will be essential to international conventions, but they vary considerably in focus and method. Some national schemes are more narrowly focused than others-sometimes evaluating only public universities or specific degree programs. In addition, quality assurance mechanisms are still relatively new in much of the world; institutions and individuals are participating at varying levels of sophistication and experience. National schemes and international conventions are now evolving simultaneously, with each effort influencing the direction of the other.

Managing Mobility

With students and programs moving across borders with increasing ease, a pressing need has emerged for common reference points. The comparability of educational qualifications has become a key issue in international discussions.

National schemes may well build the foundation for quality assurance. However, without incorporating internationally recognized benchmarks and frameworks, there is no means of comparison. As greater mobility is both inevitable and generally considered desirable, international agreements that encourage the mutual recognition of programs and credentials have become more significant. At a practical level, this policy means finding a way to define and validate the level and quality of postsecondary qualifications for individuals who reside and/or work in a country other than where their education was completed.

The Lisbon Recognition Convention in 1997 emphasized that it is a student's *right* to receive fair recognition of his or her educational qualifications within the European region. Lisbon also stressed the importance of national centers staffed with experts who can perform this kind of evaluation. The increasing diversity of the higher education landscape makes the comparison of qualifications particularly challenging and underscores the need for at least some shared guideposts to allow individuals to enjoy the academic and professional benefits that their credentials merit.

Since the late 1970s, UNESCO regional meetings in Africa, Asia, Europe, Latin America, and the Middle East have facilitated the elaboration of conventions that commit signatories to common policy and practice, easing the mobility of individuals within each region. These conventions emphasize the value of shared terminology and evaluation criteria to make mutual recognition of partial or completed studies more efficient and transparent. Additionally, by making national institutions of higher education more widely accessible to students and faculty within each region and increasing the "portability" of diplomas and certificates, higher education can become a vehicle for the retention of talent and, as a result, contribute to regional development.

The Bologna Process reflects enormous progress in regard to the integration of higher education in Europe, going further than other regions by creating a common degree structure, qualification frameworks, and implementing new requirements to make the achievement reflected by each level of educational attainment more transparent.

Supranational conventions are continuing to be developed, reviewed, and revised. Ultimately the international recognition of academic and vocational credentials will require new channels of discussion between regions, nations, and institutions, but above all, it will require trust.

Evaluating Qualifications

As already indicated, higher education can be evaluated in many different ways and at many levels. Institutions can be evaluated in their entirety according to the qualifications of professors, the extent of library resources, research output, and other factors. Professors can be evaluated on the basis of their research productivity or success in securing grants. Students can be evaluated in terms of grades or accomplishments. The evaluation of educational qualifications has special significance in that these credentials serve as a kind of international currency, affording the holder different levels of opportunity depending on how the qualifications are valued.

How educational qualifications are evaluated is a newer dimension of the quality assurance conversation. Historically, the emphasis has been on the content covered in the course of the degree program. In some cases, the broader academic experience is evaluated, taking into consideration complementary coursework and extracurricular activities. New criteria (such as relevance to the labor market) are being added to the assessment of qualifications. Increasingly, attention is being paid to competencies developed in the course of study. In Europe, the Educational Qualifications Framework aims to define qualifications in terms of the depth of knowledge, skills, and competencies they represent. The "Tuning Project" underway in Europe and Latin America and recently launched in three American states attempts to further define these competencies within specific fields of study. Determining what a qualification should represent, once earned, is a fundamental piece of the quality puzzle, but this discussion is still in its early stages.

Finally, there is always the risk of qualifications without any validity whatsoever. With many new providers offering options for postsecondary study, it is sometimes difficult to distinguish legitimate institutions from diploma or degree mills that make credentials available for purchase. Diploma mills have exploited the need of many individuals for easy access to a degree or certificate, given the advantages that advanced study offers in the labor market. The existence of this type of fraud increases the urgency of international mechanisms for quality assurance as they potentially demean the value of educational credentials. Diploma mills all too often blend in with new, legitimate nontraditional providers.

In the interest of educating and protecting stakeholders, UNESCO has launched the "Portal of Higher Education Institutions" online to guide individuals to sources of information to help them distinguish legitimate from bogus documents and institutions.

Growing Emphasis on Outcomes

Historically, quality assessments relied on quantitative data such as full-time professors with advanced degrees, volumes in a university library, papers published by faculty, or student-professor ratios. In recent years, there has been a growing emphasis on the "outcomes" of higher education. In other words, evaluators are looking for new data and indicators to demonstrate that students have mastered specific objectives as a result of their education. The experience of implementing outcome-based learning is still limited to a small number of institutions in a few countries, but this dimension of evaluation is growing rapidly.

OECD has introduced an initiative to assess learning outcomes on an international scale. The Assessment of Higher Education Learning Outcomes (AHELO) project was launched in 2006 to build the capacity for evaluating teaching and learning. The project is still under development with a target-launch-date in 2016. The approach focuses on the following aspects:

- *Physical and organizational characteristics:* observable characteristics such as enrolment figures or the ratio of male to female students
- *Education-related behaviors and practices:* student-faculty interaction, academic challenge, emphasis on applied work, etc.
- *Psychosocial and cultural attributes:* career expectations of students, parental support, social expectations of higher education institutions, etc.
- *Behavioral and attitudinal outcomes:* students' persistence and completion of degrees, continuation into graduate programs or success in finding a job, student satisfaction, improved student self-confidence, and self-reported learning gains claimed by students or their instructors.

The desire to measure student learning and learning outcomes requires sophisticated instruments and skilled staff, although there is limited availability of both. There are two primary instruments in use in the United States. The National Survey of Student Engagement surveys students to measure their degree of academic involvement and compiles results to achieve an institutional score that reflects how well the university does at creating a learning environment. The Collegiate Learning Assessment tests general skills such as communication and critical thinking. In this case also, data are compiled to produce an institutional score.

While the trend toward a greater attention to learning and learning outcomes has been very positive, there is still only limited attention to teaching quality. Effective and varied pedagogy deserves a more prominent place in the future discussions, as does the impact on teaching quality of such large percentages of part-time professors in so much of the world.

So Many Players

Discussions are taking place at many levels by innumerable international organizations to address the need for a shared understanding of quality. Although an international agency with overarching authority for recognizing and accrediting institutions and programs might be helpful, the politics and logistics of implementing a scheme at this level make it unlikely for the present. Practical considerations suggest (at least for the short term) that evaluation will continue to be managed locally and that adequate information about these processes must be easily available and transparent in order to satisfy the needs of international stakeholders.

There has been a veritable explosion of new agencies taking on roles for different aspects of quality assurance and, as a result, there is a need to evaluate and certify these authorities so as to trust their work in this area. There are unethical agents entering the quality assurance arena as well. "Accreditation mills," like diploma mills, easily confuse stakeholders by mimicking the terminology of legitimate agencies and institutions.

The discussions and negotiations related to the Bologna Process placed Europe in the vanguard of coordinating national and regional efforts for quality assurance. The establishment of the European Association for Quality Assurance in Higher Education (ENQA) in 2000 brought together many of the national quality assurance agencies in the region and created an important forum to engage member countries in transnational quality assurance projects.

Membership is ENQA confirms the legitimacy of an agency, but in 2008, European ministers responsible for higher education established the European Quality Assurance Register (EQAR) as an additional mechanism for coordinating the efforts to improve quality within Europe. The registry will offer a list of accreditation agencies that comply with the European Standards and Guidelines for Quality Assurance (ESG).

The six regional accrediting bodies in the United States that accredit postsecondary institutions operate independently and determine their own standards and procedures. Degree programs are accredited separately by professional associations in different fields. The Council for Higher Education Accreditation (CHEA) serves as clearinghouse and umbrella organization for legitimate accrediting bodies in the United States.

Other organizations are attempting to coordinate quality assurance activities on an international level, many with support from the World Bank. These organizations have formed on the basis of common interests or geographical proximity. APQN, the Asia-Pacific Quality Network was established in 2003 to provide training and support to quality assurance efforts in the region. RIACES, the Iberoamerican Network for Quality Assessment and Assurance in Higher Education, was established in 2004 as a forum for cooperation in Latin America and the Caribbean. ANQAHE, The Arab

Network for Quality Assurance in Higher Education was established in 2007 for the same purpose.Of the new organizations promoting quality assurance activities on an international level, INQAAHE the International Network for Quality Assurance Agencies in Higher Education has the broadest reach. Founded in 1991, this network is an association of organizations or an umbrella organization, whose members are regional, state, and professional quality assurance agencies. The organization plays several key roles, acting as a liaison between international organizations such as the World Bank, UNESCO, and OECD and their members; providing support to new quality assurance agencies; offering forums where members can share experiences and information; and encouraging cooperation among members.

Inevitably, participants in the quality assurance movement end up with multiple memberships in overlapping organizations, which may facilitate international dialogue but may also lead to an excessive number of annual meetings, duplication, and confusion, not to mention budgetary strain.

International Validation and Rankings

"Consumers" of education (students, parents, employers) are demanding some kind of certification of institutions and the qualifications they award. Mechanisms for establishing international comparability of qualifications are still new and largely untested. In the long run, the establishment of qualifications frameworks and endeavors like the Tuning Project are likely to have enormous international impact. In the interim, some universities look to accreditation agencies based in other countries to validate the quality of their degree programs and provide some level of international credibility.

Despite sensitivities about the importance of national culture in higher education, a number of quality assurance agencies operate outside their countries (or region) of origin with increasing frequency. Specialized program accreditors such as the US-based Association to Advance Collegiate Schools of Business (AACSB) and the Accreditation Board for Engineering and Technology (ABET) as well as the European Quality Improvement System (EQUIS) are now evaluating and accrediting universities throughout the world (OECD, 2004). US regional associations regularly receive requests for accreditation from foreign institutions, and each organization responds differently, in accordance with its own guidelines. The effect of the increasing reach of these agencies is likely to be greater standardization of programs and an endorsement with growing international recognition and influence, with prejudice toward the paradigms used in the North.

In the absence of other forms of international certification, university rankings have helped many individuals to order the vast international higher education landscape. Once only the scourge of the United States, international rankings now position universities through the world on long, eagerly awaited lists. Few educators would defend rankings as a reflection of quality, but where a university falls in the rankings is often interpreted as a measure of its quality by the larger public. Furthermore, rankings have the perverse effect of sometimes persuading university administrators to divert effort and resources to develop characteristics that will affect its position in the rankings and, not necessarily, its quality.

Both the number of published rankings and their influence have grown. The Shanghai Jiao Tong University rankings, first published in 2003, have had (perhaps) the greatest international impact. This ranking emphasizes research output which gives it greater credibility within the academic community than rankings shaped by student surveys or staff-student ratios. Moving universities into the top level of the Shanghai Jiao Tong rankings has even become a goal of national policy in several countries.

Capacity Building

During the last few decades, acceptance of quality assurance schemes has grown considerably. Where they were once seen in many countries as an affront to institutional and national autonomy, there is greater recognition of the value of this process in meeting the challenges that globalization has presented to higher education.

Yet, as with nearly all aspects of the quality assurance movement, participants and stakeholders must trust the process. This means well-planned and well-executed self-studies, audits, and peer evaluations. As this process is new in so many countries, few people possess the knowledge, skill, or experience to implement it. The shortage of human resources prepared to undertake and manage complex activities, like self-studies and peer reviews, has become a serious challenge to building successful quality assurance programs worldwide.

UNESCO has partnered with the World Bank to create the Global Initiative for Quality Assurance Capacity (GIQAC), which will be another supranational agency that will include members of many of the regional and international quality assurance networks. The World Bank will allocate significant funding during the next few years to provide technical assistance to governments, agencies, and universities (especially in developing nations) to "establish, develop, or reform QA systems, processes, and mutual recognition arrangements" as well as provide specialized training and support exchanges for quality assurance professional staff.

Influence of Free-Trade Negotiations

Professional bodies responsible for validating the quality of university programs and, often, licensure have also been actively involved in developing frameworks for the mutual recognition of qualifications, frequently in conjunction with free-trade negotiations.

Agreements between nations are encouraged but not always easy to establish. Within the North Atlantic Free Trade Agreement (NAFTA), Canada and Mexico have agreed to recognize engineering qualifications as long as the engineer has the specified education, examinations, and experience; only Texas has approved the agreement in the United States. Requirements for architecture have been recognized by Canada and more American states but not Mexico.

Reciprocal recognition between the Canadian Institute of Chartered Accountants and its counterpart institute in New Zealand resulted from agreement on guidelines for professional qualifications and a model curriculum. These agreements are being accomplished very slowly, field by field, country by country.

The GATS negotiations are likely to have future bearing on the portability of professional qualifications. These negotiations have been extremely controversial. The encouragement for giving more latitude to market forces to shape higher education could result in more for-profit institutions bypassing nascent international quality-control mechanisms. The terms of fair trade do not necessarily translate into good educational policy or practice, yet pressure on nation states to liberalize "trade in educational services" is likely to increase. Developing countries, unable to meet growing demand for access to higher education, are most vulnerable to the entrance of for-profit providers and least well positioned to regulate their activities.

Quality assurance in higher education has risen to the top of the policy agenda in many nations. Initially, nations scrambled to set up agencies and establish standards, procedures, and schedules. Many countries are still in this early stage of design and implementation. Countries with more experience are now wrestling with the deeper issues and complexities of quality assurance in higher education. Diversity has certainly created a richer environment of institutions, students, and opportunities but it presents enormous challenges for establishing appropriate standards or benchmarks that can be compared from one institution to another and from one country to another.

There are risks as well as benefits in the growing quality movement. International practices (often developed in North America and Europe) influence the development of quality assurance schemes everywhere but may not always be the most useful for evaluating higher education in developing countries. The process must focus on realistic objectives and appropriate goals for each local environment. If not, quality assurance will swiftly become a political or bureaucratic process with limited value.

Much depends on the quality of higher education-with both private good and public good to be gained. Yet quality remains difficult to define and subsequently problematic to measure. Furthermore, quality will have different meanings in different environments.

Postsecondary education has to prepare graduates with new skills, a broad knowledge base, and a range of competencies to enter a more complex and interdependent world. Agencies throughout the world are struggling to define these goals in terms that can be understood and shared across borders and cultures.

Since the 1980s there has been extensive and ongoing discussion within nations, within regions, and across the globe, to find new ways of assuring the many stakeholders involved that quality is being evaluated and monitored. What has resulted at the very least is an explosion of new agencies and a sufficient number of new acronyms to boggle the mind-INQAAHE, GIQAC, ENQA, ECA, EQAR, QAA, CHEA, NOQA, among others.

Schemes for quality assurance are now accepted as a fundamental part of providing higher education, but national, regional, and international efforts need to be integrated. One very important question moving forward is whether this integration will lead to the dominance of a "Northern" model for quality assurance that disregards the diverse conditions of higher education worldwide. The need for international cooperation is clear, but the dialogue is really only just beginning.

References

Etzkowitz, H. and Leydesdorff, L.A. 1997. *Universities and the Global Knowledge Economy: A Triple Helix of University-Industry-Government Relations*. London and New York, Pinter

Fallis, G. 2007. *Multiversities, Ideas and Democracy*. Toronto, University of Toronto Press.

Guri-Rosenblit, S. 2009. *Digital Technologies in Higher Education: Sweeping Expectations and Actual Effects*. New York, Nova Science

Johnstone, S.M. 2005. Open educational resources serve the world. *EduCause Quarterly*, Vol. 28, No. 3, pp. 15.

3

Financing Higher Education

The financing of higher education in the first decade of the 21st century has been dominated by two phenomena. First, higher education is increasingly important to economies, individuals, and societies striving for democracy and social justice. Second, the cost of higher education is rising significantly. Massification, driven by demographics and the higher percentage of students completing secondary school and desiring higher education, is driving up unit costs for instruction and research. The overall cost pressure is growing at rates beyond which most countries' public revenue streams can keep pace. This is a critical trend, given that public revenue has traditionally accounted for some, if not all, of the higher education expenses in a majority of the world's countries.

These developments would be challenging under the best of circumstances. However, the current global economic crisis exacerbates financial concerns in higher education across the globe. The situation is characterized by slowing economic growth in many developing countries, contracting economies in many high-income countries, and "sharply tighter credit conditions." "Coming on the heels of the food and fuel price shock," and spreading rapidly through tightly interconnected trade and banking channels around the world, the effects of the crisis "are likely to cut into government revenues and governments' ability to meet education, health, and gender goals". Although the extent, nature, and duration of these circumstances will vary from country to country, higher education around the world is sure to feel the negative impact of these developments.

Worldwide Trends in the Financing of Higher Education

Eight trends sit at the heart of this analysis. Each of these trends has economic, political, and social roots as well as consequences. In turn, these trends, while varying by context, form the setting for higher education's widespread financial austerity and policy solutions. In summary, these trends are:

1. *The increasingly knowledge-based economies of most countries:* higher education in many places is increasingly viewed as a major engine of economic development. In countries with more broadly based innovation systems, these elements are clearly recognized as a key contributor to the advancement of cutting-edge knowledge.
2. *An increasing demand for higher education by individuals and by families for their children:* this increase in demand may go well beyond the capacity that knowledge economies can absorb, even leading to high numbers of unemployed and underemployed college and university graduates. However, the extent of this rapidly rising demand for higher education is due in part to increased competition for good jobs and employers' use of higher education degrees as a screening device for allocating the best jobs.
3. *Unit, or per student, costs that rise faster than infation rates:* this cost increase is magnified by rising enrolment pressures that drive the total higher education cost in most countries beyond rates of inflation.
4. *The inability of government tax revenues to keep pace with rapidly rising higher education costs:* this failure results from the difficulty most economies face in raising taxes both cost-effectively and progressively, as well as the increasing competition from other political and social public needs.
5. *Increasing globalization:* among many other things, globalization contributes both the increasing demand for higher education and the inadequate government revenue to support it. The declining tax revenue is partly a function of production and capital in one country being transported to areas of lower wage/lower tax jurisdictions.
6. *The increasing reliance in almost all countries on nontax revenues:* known as cost-sharing, parents and/or students are increasingly responsible for tuition and other fees that contribute to higher education

revenue requirements. Tuition fees are emerging even in Europe, which was long the bastion of free public higher education, and are increasingly found even in former Communist or Socialist countries. Tuition fees are also ideologically and politically contested even where they play a relatively minor role in the total expenses incurred by parents and/or students. Tuition fees serve as a flash point in the larger political contests arising from the inability of governments to meet the needs of all the people.

7. *The increasing importance of financial assistance:* student-loan schemes are especially important and more cost-effective for maintaining higher education participation and access in the face of increasing parent and student expenses.
8. *An increasing liberalization-that is, a free market and private sector orientation-of economies:* this liberalization is leading many governments to respond to higher education's financial challenges by corporatizing and privatizing public universities, implementing new public management tools for public university budgets and financing, and encouraging private colleges and universities.

The worldwide surge in private higher education over the last several decades is a significant development, and the financing models for this sector have implications for institutional stakeholders, including students and the broader society. In most cases around the world, private tertiary institutions depend on tuition revenue. Tuition dependence means that these colleges and universities must manage their enrolments and expenditures extremely carefully and that they are often financially unable to weather unexpected enrolment downturns. Because they rely on tuition, these institutions often target only those student populations that can afford to pay fees, which can "exacerbate class or other divisions in society".

A small number ofi cases around the world possess other sources of funding for private higher education apart from tuition. In places where private universities may be owned by individuals or families (such as in Colombia, the Republic ofi Korea, and Japan), the personal wealth ofi the owner(s) may be a significant financial resource for such institutions. The United States stands out as an unusual example ofi a context where private institutions enjoy significant financial contributions from alumni as well as individual and corporate donors. American students attending accredited private colleges and universities may also bring public support with them, in the form of federally administered student grants and loans. Government support for private higher education also exists in India, and to a lesser extent in places like the Philippines and Japan. For the most part, though, private higher education institutions around the world are responsible for generating their own resources. Indeed the active generation of profit is now a critical activity in the corporate and for-profit higher education sectors, which have grown considerably over the last decade in a wide variety of contexts.

Higher Educational Austerity

The immediate effect of these trends on the financing of higher education (again, varying by country) is a state of austerity in universities, postsecondary education institutions, and national higher education systems. These nearly universal-and growing-higher education conditions have affected:

- *Universities and other postsecondary education institutions:* overcrowded lecture halls; restive and otherwise unhappy faculty; insufficient or outdated library holdings, computing, and Internet connectivity; a deterioration of physical plants; less time and support for faculty research; and a widely assumed loss in the quality of both teaching and learning as well as research
- *National systems of higher education:* capacity constraints; the inability to accommodate all graduates who are eligible for and desire further study; faculty "brain drain" as the most talented faculty move to countries with fewer financial troubles; and an inability to compete in the global knowledge economy
- *Students:* tuition fees where there used to be none, in addition to the rising costs of student living; the need to work while studying, go into debt, or both, for those fortunate enough to find a place at all.

This downturn has been most crippling in sub-Saharan Africa but is serious throughout the developing countries, as well as in many of the so-called *countries in transition* - such as those emerging from the former Soviet Union. In Europe and Latin America, as well, there is serious overcrowding and students are unable to find seats in lecture theaters. Teaching is often reduced to didactics and rarely includes discussion and opportunity to ask questions. Other manifestations include the loss of secure faculty positions and faculty morale and students leaving higher education with burdensome levels of debt. These downward trends can be seen in countries as affluent as the United States, the United Kingdom, Sweden, and Canada.

Beyond this sheer austerity, and especially noticeable in countries that have moved toward the political right, is a diminution of trust in government and in the public sector generally, including (perhaps especially) public universities. This distrust of government goes beyond insufficiency public budgets and results in a loss of the esteem in which public universities were once held.

Policy Solutions on the Cost Side

In response to these financial pressures and demands for accountability, universities and national systems have sought solutions. Solutions on the cost side include increasing class sizes and teaching loads, deferring maintenance, substituting lower-cost part-time faculty for higher-cost full-time faculty, and dropping low-priority programs. These solutions are difficult, academically problematic, and heavily contested, especially by the faculty and their political allies, who frequently reject the claims that public revenues are insufficient and who may not understand the academic priorities of their governments or university leaders.

Cost-side solutions are most injurious to participation and accessibility when they limit the capacity of public institutions and force increasing numbers of young men and women into higher-priced (and often lower-quality) private colleges and universities. Some students may be required to pay higher fees than others, even when enrolled in the same public university. Students who lack family resources for private instruction and/or living expenses may be forced earlier into the workforce.

Strategic cost-side solutions, on the other hand, use available resources more wisely to support academic quality, capacity, social equity, and the needs of students, employers, and society alike. The management of governmental agencies and the norms of civil service employment-which prize employment continuity above all else-are generally incompatible with many strategic cost-side solutions to the financial problems common among universities and other institutions of higher education. Typical issues with government agencies include laws, contracts and political considerations that forbid terminating staff, hiring part-time or temporary workers, contracting out services, carrying unspent funds forward from one fiscal year to the next, or shifting available funds from one budget category to another.

A clear shift has occurred in government laws and regulations dealing with public universities in the last decade or two in many Canadian provinces and virtually all American states, in some European countries (notably the Netherlands and the United Kingdom), and very recently in China and Japan-all in the direction of greater managerial autonomy and flexibility. These efforts have frequently transformed public universities from simple governmental agencies into public corporations, giving the management new authority and sometimes corporate-style governing boards coupled with new accountability requirements. These new developments for greater managerial autonomy and flexibility-essentially moving toward managerial models associated with private enterprise-are collectively referred to as new public management and are designed to maximize the university's teaching and research outputs for the public as well as to provide incentives for maximizing nongovernmental revenue. Universities, for example, rather than the ministry or the state budget office, may be given authority to:

- establish wage and salary policies (formerly reserved for the ministry or parliament and government financial, personnel, and civil service bureaucracies);
- reallocate expenditures from one category to another in response to institutional priorities (formerly generally forbidden);
- carry forward unspent funds from one fiscal period to the next, thus encouraging savings and institutional investment and discouraging spending for no reason other than avoidance of loss or the appearance of an excessive budget;
- enter into contracts with outside agencies and businesses expeditiously and competitively (formerly too frequently politicized and prolonged); and
- receive and own assets and sometimes even borrow and incur debt (not allowed in ordinary government agencies).

Cost-side solutions to financial shortfalls-after deferring expenditures on new plant, equipment, and facilities maintenance-may seek to lower the average per-student costs of instruction by increasing average class size, increasing teaching loads, and substituting lower-cost junior or part-time faculty for higher-cost senior faculty. All such solutions are painful and are typically resisted by faculty and staff and their political allies. However, the gap from the diverging trajectories of higher education costs and available revenues is simply too wide to be closed by further cuts in expenditures alone, even with some of the more radical cost-side solutions like mergers and distance education. Finally, in many or even in most countries, the low- hanging fruit of easy expenditure cuts and other efficiency measures have long since been taken, leaving only the most difficult and educationally problematic solutions on the cost-side. In short, higher education in almost all countries must turn to nongovernmental revenues to supplement the increasingly insufficient revenue available from governments.

Policy Solutions on the Revenue Side

Revenue supplementation as an alternative to cost cutting and as a preferred route to financial viability may take the form of faculty and institutional entrepreneurship, as in the selling of specialized and marketable teaching or scholarship, the renting of university facilities, or the commercial marketing of research discoveries. It may take the form of fund-raising, appealing to alumni and other donors.

Or-and the most sustainable and potentially lucrative-it may take the form of what has come to be known as cost sharing. The term refers to a shift of at least some of the higher educational cost burden from governments, or taxpayers, to parents and/or students. Cost sharing is thus both a statement of fact-that is, that the costs of higher education are shared among stakeholders-and also a reference to a policy shift of some of these costs from a predominant (sometimes a virtually exclusive) reliance on governments.

Cost sharing is most associated with tuition fees and "user charges," especially for room and board. However, a policy shift in the direction of greater cost sharing can take several forms:

1. *The beginning of tuition (where higher education was formerly free or nearly so):* this would be the case in China in 1997, the United Kingdom in 1998, and Austria in 2001.
2. *The addition of a special tuition-paying track while maintaining free higher education for the regularly admitted, state-supported students:*

such a dual-track tuition-fee scheme preserves the legal and political appearance of free higher education while introducing some new revenue. The preservation of the status quo of "free higher education" is particularly important (and is frequently enshrined in a constitution or a framework law) in many transition economies-such as Russia, most of eastern and central Europe, and other countries that were once part of the former Soviet Union, as well as countries in East Africa with their legacy of African socialism.

3. *A very sharp rise in tuition (where public-sector tuition already exists):* a shift in the direction of greater cost sharing requires that the rise in tuition carried by students and/or parents be greater than the rise in institutional costs generally in order for the government's, or taxpayer's, share to be lessened. This has been the case recently in most of the states in the United States and most of the provinces in Canada.

4. *The imposition of "user charges," or fees, to recover the expenses of what were once governmentally or institutionally provided (and heavily subsidized) residence and dining halls:* this has been happening in most countries, including virtually all the transitional economy countries, and notably and controversially, most of the countries in sub-Saharan Africa, where subsidized living costs at one time absorbed the bulk of higher educational budgets. In the Nordic countries of Sweden, Norway, Finland, and Denmark, where higher education remains "free," the expenses to students are exclusively the costs of student living. Student living costs are very high in these particular countries and are "shared" neither by taxpayers nor (at least officially) by parents. Rather, they are borne mainly or entirely by the students, largely in the form of student loans (costs still shared by the taxpayer in the form of repayment subsidies).

5. *The elimination or reduction of student grants or scholarships:* this strategy is sometimes approached simply by "freezing" grant or loan levels, or holding them constant in the face of general inflation, which then erodes their real value. This began happening to the once generous grants in Britain (which were later abandoned altogether) and has happened to the value of the maintenance grants in most of the transitional countries of the former Soviet Union and eastern and central Europe, as well as in Asia and in many countries in Africa.

6. *An increase in the effective cost recovery on student loans:* several approaches can be taken in this vein. More-effective cost recovery can be accomplished through a reduction of the subsidies on student loans (similar to the diminution in the value of non-repayable grants). It might also be accomplished through an increase in interest rates, a reduction in the length of time that interest is not charged, or through a cut in the numbers of loans for which the repayments, for any number of reasons, are forgiven. The effective cost recovery might also be accomplished through a tightening of collections, or a reduction in the instances of default.
7. *The limitation of capacity in the low or tuition-free public sector together with the official encouragement (and frequently some public subsidization) of a tuition-dependent private higher education sector:* number of countries-notably Japan, the Republic of Korea, the Philippines, Indonesia, Brazil, and other countries in Latin America and East Asia-have avoided much of what would otherwise have been significant governmental expenditure on higher education by keeping the public sector small, elite, and selective. Much of the cost of expanded participation is thus shifted to parents and students through the encouragement of a substantial and growing private higher education sector.

Although cost sharing may take on these different forms, the imposition of, and/or large increases in, tuition fees provides the greatest financial impact. Tuition fees can be both financially significant, ongoing, and designed to regularly increase, thus keeping pace with the inevitably rising per student costs of instruction. However, a rebate may be needed in the form of grants or discounts to preserve accessibility. Also, unlike most forms of faculty entrepreneurship, tuition fees do not divert faculty from the core instructional mission. Many observers also assert that higher tuition has the positive effect of improving the quality of teaching and the relevance of the curriculum, providing another key benefit. Yet, tuition fees are also the most politically charged and ideologically resisted form of cost sharing and have therefore become a symbol of the conflict between people who believe that government must continue to provide higher education free of any charge and those who recognized the great unlikelihood of government coming up with annually increasing revenue and who thus accept the imperative of cost sharing.

Competing and Compelling Public Needs

National, global, political, and ideological contexts play a key role in shaping the trends that determine both the financing of higher education and policy solutions for the resulting austerity. At one end of the spectrum, there are groups who accept the appropriateness of governmental control of virtually all institutionalized means of production (including universities and colleges), as well as governmental allocation of resources, the establishment of prices, and the remuneration of workers. High levels of taxation, governmental regulation, and public employment are acceptable, and the emphasis is placed on the income disparities, economic instability, competition, and commercialism associated with markets and capitalism.

Toward the other end of the continuum are the views associated with the desire to diminish the size of the public sector, including publicly owned and financed higher education. Here, government, including both politicians and civil servants, is considered less productive and often self-serving. In keeping with this mistrust of governmental institutions (including public universities) and governmental employees (as well as faculty and staff of these public universities), groups at this end of the political spectrum tend to be more critical of what they perceive to be governmental waste and more insistent on greater measures of accountability. At the same time, there is greater acceptance of the economic instabilities and disparities in income and wealth that follow capitalism as a necessary price for the dynamism and high productivity of private enterprise.

As in any portrayal of a range, most countries, governments, and polities are somewhere near the center but always feel pressures from the extremes. Universities-especially public, but private universities as well-always operate in a country-specific political and economic context as well as in an historical context and in an increasingly globalized international context. The financial problems as well as the possible solutions and their likelihood of adoption all occur within these larger social and political contexts. Almost everywhere, higher education institutions, systems, and the societies in which they operate are faced with a complex set of problems that turn on the common issues of inexorably rising per student costs, increasing enrolments, expanded roles for higher education, more demands for institutional accountability, limits on governmental taxing capabilities, and lengthy queues of socially and politically compelling competing public needs. There are many difficult choices to make and an unquestionable need to identify and implement workable solutions that make sense for each country's unique social and political context.

Ultimately, the increasing reach of tuition fees and other forms of revenue diversification, as well as the pressures for accountability or institutional autonomy, are mostly attributable to three fundamentally important aspects of higher education around the world today. First, a virtually universal higher educational production function accompanies a trajectory of rising unit costs. Second, the increasing demand for higher education in many contexts exacerbates this rising trajectory of costs, or revenue needs. And third, governmental revenues in most countries are unable (or at least unlikely) to keep up with these rising revenue requirements. These factors are now currently playing out in the midst of a profound global economic crisis, which presents the higher education sector around the world with challenges to meet current needs and plan for future developments. Finding ways to sustain quality provision of higher education, with appropriate access for qualified students at affordable rates for students, families, and other key stakeholders, will require careful planning that attends to both short- and long-term needs. Furthermore, these efforts will likely only succeed insofar as they combine flexibility, innovation, and creative collaboration among relevant constituents, while sharing a common commitment to a vibrant and sustainable higher education sector.

References

Knight, J. 2006. *Higher Education Crossing Borders: A Guide to the Implications of the General Agreement on Trade in Services (GATS) for Cross-border Education.* Vancouver, BC, Commonwealth of Learning.

Levy, D.C. 2006. The private fit in the higher education landscape. J.J.F. Forest and P.G. Altbach (eds.), *International Handbook of Higher Education*, Dordrecht, The Netherlands, Springer. 281-292.

Maurrasse, D.J. 2001. *Beyond the Campus: How Colleges and Universities Form Partnerships with their Communities*. New York, Routledge.

Obasi, I.N. 2006. New private universities in Nigeria. *International Higher Education*, No. 45, pp. 14.

4

Private Higher Education and Privatization

At the time of UNESCO's last global overview of tertiary education, private higher education had already surged globally. This expansion has continued, intensifying and spreading to additional regions and countries. Today, some 30 percent of global higher education enrolment is in the private sector. Additionally, the extent and importance of the growth of this new sector is attracting more attention (though still insufficient) than it was 10 years ago.

Privatization means many things in higher education. While a public university is generally considered to be an institution funded by and responsive to a local, provincial or national government, private institutions do not reflect a consistent model. Private institutions may operate entirely with private assets or partially with public funds; they may be for-profit or nonprofit; they may be accountable to the host government or operate completely outside of local regulation; they may have owners or investors or operate as foundations.

The trend toward privatization also has meaning in the public sector where institutions are being encouraged (if not required) to decrease their dependence on public funds, to be more "entrepreneurial" and competitive, and to demonstrate efficient professional management. Some of these ideas would have seemed ludicrous a few decades ago but are now fundamental to strategic plans and new policy almost everywhere.

Few of the themes of the present UNESCO report can be adequately understood without attention to the private sector of higher education-as most of the growth in higher education worldwide is in the private sector. Private higher education has had a significant impact on the discussions of quality, equity, new learning modes and, perhaps most of all, access. Private higher education is less central to themes of knowledge development, research, and planning, but as governments and international organizations, including UNESCO, increasingly realize the growing role of this sector they are seeking ways to integrate and shape it more.

The growing importance of private institutions and the tendency to privatize the public sector are key international trends. Indeed, the two types of privatization interrelate and affect one another.

Growth: Regional Dimensions

Well into the 20th century, higher education was overwhelmingly public-in regard to enrolment, legal status, government-centered standardized rules, finance, and dominant normative orientations. In fact, higher education had become more public over a long period of time.

Growth from elite to "mass" higher education obviously occurred first in the developed countries and almost always in the public sector, Japan being the striking exception. But in the developing and postcommunist countries, the transformation occurs mostly in the private sector. It is in that part of the world that private growth is most notable. Fewer and fewer countries (Bhutan, Cuba, the Democratic People's Republic of Korea) host no private higher education.

Looking regionally and working in descending order beginning with the regions with the largest private sector, Asia comes first. East Asia has the largest concentration of countries with proportionally larger private sectors. Countries with over 70 percent of enrolments in private higher education include Indonesia, Japan, the Philippines, and the Republic of Korea. Malaysia approaches 50 percent. China and much of Southeast Asia (e.g., Cambodia and Vietnam) remain below 15 percent but are experiencing rapid expansion, although total cohort enrolment rates are still quite low. Thailand and New Zealand are just marginally below 15 percent, Australia around 3 percent. South Asia sees striking private growth, with India above 30 percent and Pakistan not too far behind. Toward western Asia data are spottier but Kazakhstan and Iran are roughly half private.

Latin America has a longer widespread history than Asia of dual-sector development. By the late 1970s Latin America was already approaching 35 percent private enrolment, and today it is closer to 45 percent. Again, there is variation by country, but now few cases are under 20 percent. Countries with majority private sectors include Brazil, Chile, El Salvador, Guatemala, and Peru. Where the private sector has recently lost share, notably in Colombia, the cause is not numerical slippage on the private side but sudden growth on the public side, largely through elevation of institutions into the "higher education" category. Argentina is alone among major countries and systems in maintaining a large public majority.

Compared to Asia, Latin America has had more stable private higher education shares, but the most striking case of stable shares is the United States-hovering between 20 and 25 percent for decades (compared to roughly 50 percent enrolment in the mid-twentieth century). US proportional stagnation, juxtaposed to global growth, leaves the present US private higher education enrolment share below the global share, though obviously US private higher education is the most important in the world-with the largest absolute private enrolment and towering above other systems in its graduate enrolment, research activity, and finance.

In central and eastern Europe Estonia, Georgia, Poland, Latvia, and especially Poland, have passed 20 percent. The jump from an entirely public sector to a substantial private sector in the five-year period following the fall of communism marks the most dramatic concentrated growth seen in any region. Still, some countries in this region have not experienced more than a small-percent increase in private-sector enrolment. At least as importantly, stagnation has characterized the last 10 years, and some countries have actually had declines in private enrolments. There is a demographic challenge, and as cohort numbers fall, many private higher education institutions could shrink or die off.

Notwithstanding its private precursors (including colonial ones), sub-Saharan Africa has come late to modern private higher education but the growth is notable (Mabizela, et al., forthcoming). Breakthroughs began in the 1980s, but it was in the 1990s that there was major and widespread growth. Most countries host private institutions, with Anglophone Africa greatly outpacing Francophone Africa. Kenya, Nigeria, Uganda, and others are among the countries with important private sectors, yet most countries' private share remains comparatively small. Kenya, having ascended to one-fifth private, is a rare African example of slippage, not due to demographics so much as public universities' taking in "private" paying students. Nowhere in Africa is the private sector more than a fourth of total higher education enrolment. Yet the sector is growing and garnering more and more attention.

Western Europe remains the developed region with mostly just marginal private-higher education sectors. Privatization in the last 10 and more years has been more about changes within the public sector. Portugal has been the major exception, once reaching the 30 percent range for private share of total enrolment. Spain has some academically prominent private higher education institutions. The Netherlands (majority private) and Belgium have long been exceptions, too, but their private sectors have operated mostly with government funds and similar sets of rules. Yet even in western Europe there is change. The United Kingdom's sole private university may be joined by nonuniversity institutions, as is already the Norwegian case.

Beginning to register private higher education enrolment is the Middle East (and North Africa). "American universities" have dotted the horizon in Egypt, Jordan, Lebanon, and elsewhere, with Kurdistan joining this group. Israel was one of the first countries in the region to allow the development of a private sector. Turkey hosted private institutions until the 1970s, when they were closed down; this sector is re-emerging anew only recently. Arab governments plan and promote private universities, often through agreements with European and US universities. Astonishing is the private surge across the gamut of political regimes, as shown by Egypt, Oman, Saudi Arabia, and Syria.

Types of Private Higher Education

There has been great growth in private higher education, even considering regional variations. However, private higher education is far from being a homogenous sector. It is important to understand the phenomenon by identifying its major forms. Four categories are elite and semi-elite, identity, demand absorbing, and for-profit, though there is some category overlap. One can tinker with how to place and regard an assortment of cross-border relationships and private/public partnerships. Restricting the partnership label to formal agreements between private and public higher education institutions, we see a tendency for the privates to be colleges, the universities to be public.

Identity Institutions

In much of the world, most of what we can call identity institutions has been religiously based. In fact, as with many non-profit sectors, in education and beyond, the first wave of institutions often have religious foundations. Moreover, religious institutions appear more reliably non-profit than are many other private institutions.

For Latin America, Europe, and later Africa, early private universities were usually Catholic. In the United States, the early colleges, such as Harvard and Columbia, were tied to Protestant denominations.

In addition, identity institutions may be based on gender. Although there were once single-sex institutions for men and women, today there are few remaining for men only and a decreasing number of women's institutions.

Although religion defines a major sector within private higher education, two changes have recently modified the picture. One is the increasing mix of religions, including many with evangelical or Islamic orientations. Where Muslims are a minority in the population, private institutions can offer an attractive option; where they are a majority, religion may find expression in the public sector.

A set of values may make institutions with ethnic or religious orientation more attractive. The values of specific populations or subsectors may clash with the general perception of dominant values at public universities. Where these values stress authority, safety, specific ideas of morality and the like, they make institutions more attractive to conservative groups, in particular parents of daughters. Private enrolments tend to be higher for women than men. In fact, women's colleges are another important subtype. There is a longstanding tradition of women's private higher education in the United States and a similar significantly prominent trend in Asia.

Elite and Semi-Elite

US tradition notwithstanding, the notion of a widespread nexus between private and elite in higher education is highly misleading. It is important for our global analysis to remember that the US case is unique.

The US higher education system is the only one in the world in which private higher education dominates the top tier. Few other systems have any private elite universities. For the two most prominent global rankings of universities, 63 universities make the top hundred in both rankings, and 21 of those are private. However, each of those 21 privates is a US institution.

The two rankings are the *Times Higher Education* Supplement World University Rankings and the Shanghai Jiao Tong Academic Ranking of World Universities. The private non-US institutions beneath the top are mostly European universities with ambiguous private/public status and a couple of Japanese private universities. Relevant, too, in the poor private representation is that the developed world has been overwhelmingly public in higher education (outside Japan and the United States. By the standards used to classify world-ranked elite or "world class" universities the private sector outside the United States hardly registers.

The private presence is much stronger in the semi-elite category. These may be among the leading higher education institutions in their country, as national rankings may show. Below the very top, semi-elite private universities may compete with a set of good but not top-tier public universities. Bangladesh, Pakistan, Poland, Thailand, and Turkey are just a few national examples where this is the case. There is still a legitimate case to be made that much of Latin America has elite private universities that attract best-prepared students over the public universities, at least in many fields and even increasingly doing research and graduate education.

Semi-elite institutions stand between elite and non-elite and thus have above-average selectivity and status. Their salient characteristics appear to include priority on good practical teaching or training and not the kind of research that defines world-class universities (although they may do good applied research). The social-class of students may be quite high, often including accomplished graduates of the secondary system, and also including those capable of paying private tuitions. Some, but not nearly all, semi-elite institutions, are niche institutions concentrated in a given field of study or on a cluster of related fields, especially business. Most semi-elite institutions are explicitly and often successfully job oriented.

Semi-elite institutions are also often economically and politically conservative, Western-oriented, even U.S.-oriented. They seek foreign ties and recognition and often teach courses in English. They favor markets and scoff at dependency on the state. Many are quite entrepreneurial and some have serious academic aspirations. They are very private: their income is almost strictly nonpublic, led by tuition; they pride themselves on tight business-like management, and they aim to serve those pursuing rational self-interest. Given the lack of world-class private higher education (outside the United States), the semi-elite surge is particularly noteworthy, especially as it appears to fit all regions.

Demand-Absorbing Institutions

Notwithstanding the importance of semi-elite growth, the largest increase in private higher education is distinctly non-elite. This is mostly "demand absorbing" as student demand for access to higher education has exceeded the supply of slots available at public and private institutions, even where that supply is also expanding. Contributing to the proliferation of private non-elite institutions has been a lax regulatory environment in many countries. In every country in which private higher education becomes the majority sector (and in many where it becomes a large minority sector), it is this demand-absorbing subsector that has been numerically significant. It tends to be both the largest private subsector and the fastest-growing one.

This private subsector is often comprised of institutions not labeled "university". Furthermore, many private institutions labeled "university" are not. Rather they are technical or vocational institutions, on the definitional borderline of higher education and border between for-profit and nonprofit.

Demand-absorbing private higher education is commonly denounced aggressively. Much of the denunciation is valid but sometimes applicable to low-level public institutions as well. For scholarship and informed policymaking, however, it is crucial to recognize two subcategories of these non-elite private institutions. The larger subcategory is indeed very dubious in academic quality, seriousness, effort, and transparency. Yet, the other non-elite type is serious, responsible, and usually job oriented. This non-elite group has opportunity for both growth and improvement. This type of institution is often well managed and may even show certain traits of some semi-elite institutions. More empirical study of non-elite institutions is needed. In any event, both the serious and dubious demand-absorbing institutions tend to enroll comparatively disadvantaged students.

For-Profit Sector

Most for-profit institutions could be subsumed into the non-elite category. It is common in Africa that private higher education divides into comparatively substantial religious, for-profit, and demand-absorbing subsectors. These subsectors can overlap as with Mozambique's religious and South Africa's for-profits both being demand-absorbing. For-profits are not academically elite institutions, though some may have semi-elite characteristics. Yet many for-profits are exploitative institutions, taking advantage of unmet demand and delivering a poor-quality education.

Legally for-profit institutions constitute a small higher education subsector, but there is notable growth here in all developing regions. Moreover, the for-profits represent the fastest-growing sector within US higher education, already incorporating some 8 to 10 percent of total enrolment, or more than one-third of total private enrolment, though concentrated in programs of just one to two years.

Furthermore, a growing part of the for-profit expansion is taking place internationally and operating across national boundaries. Laureate is the largest international company operating in this area. Most ubiquitous in Latin America, Laureate buys dominant shares of existing universities.

Whitney International and the Apollo Group (owner of the University of Phoenix) also operate abroad. Other for-profits-Kaplan and Corinthian Colleges, for example-find their niche within the United States.

There are other examples of for-profits in addition to large corporate-run universities. A small number of for-profit institutions are family owned and operated. Other types of "for-profit" activity are emerging as universities based in the United States, United Kingdom, Australia, and elsewhere establish profitable cross-border partnerships with a private local partner. Universities that may be public in their home country operate as private enterprises abroad.

The for-profit sector reflects many key characteristics of commercial industry. It charges fees for service (it is tuition-based) and rarely gets any public support. When not family operated, the sector is run mostly on a business model, with power and authority concentrated in boards and chief executives; faculty hold little authority or influence; and students are seen as consumers.

Privatization

Related, but not the same as the rise of private higher education, is the privatization in all sectors of postsecondary education. By privatization, we mean the necessity for institutions and systems to earn income in order to pay for (at least part of) their operation. Privatization can include, as has been discussed in this trend report, higher tuition fees and other charges to students so that a part of the cost of education is shared by students. It can also mean earning funds from consulting, licensing, selling intellectual property of various kinds, university and industry collaboration that produces income, renting university property, and many other sources of income. Privatization has become a necessity in many institutions and systems because of budgetary problems created by massification with simultaneous reductions in public investment and has been legitimized (in part) by the "private-good" arguments for higher education.

Countries such as Australia and China have been explicit in asking universities to earn more of their own operating expenses by generating their own revenue. Others have more indirectly made privatization necessary by inadequately funding the postsecondary sector and forcing institutions to seek alternatives.

Privatization seems to be a significant force in much of the world. Some critics have argued that forcing greater emphasis on revenue-generating activities creates general problems for the traditional roles of higher education, with a negative impact on both teaching and research. Others point to the benefits of academe embracing market forces and opportunities as well as to the need for higher education to pay for more of its costs.

Notwithstanding the salient differences among types of private higher education, some generalizations can be made. It is highly probable that growth will take place in all parts of this sector. Most growth will take place in the developing world but in the developed world as well. Non-elite and functionally for-profit institutions are the fastest growing; semi-elite types are also expanding in number but on a smaller scale. The potential is less clear for other private models. Private higher education is not the same today as it was 10 or 25 years ago, and it is unlikely to remain as it is today into the future. But many basic types and patterns will persist. Further growth in absolute numbers and even share of total higher education enrolments seems a near certainty.

References

Altbach, P.G. Levy D.C. (eds.), 2005 *Private Higher Education: A Global Revolution*, Rotterdam, Sense Publishers. 1-12.

Cao,Y. 2007. *Chinese Private Colleges and the Labor Market*, Ph.D.

Gupta,A., Levy, D.C. and Powar, K.B. 2008. *Private Higher Education: Global Trends and Indian perspectives*. New Delhi, Shipra Publications.

Mabizela, M. 2007. Private surge amid public dominance in provision of higher education in Africa. *Journal of Higher Education in Africa*, Vol. 5, No. 2 & 3, pp. 15-38.

5

Centrality and Crisis of the Academic Profession

The growing tension between enrolment demand, constrained budgets, and greater accountability has resulted in a discouraging environment for the academic profession worldwide. No university can achieve success without well-qualified, committed academic staff. Neither an impressive campus nor an innovative curriculum will produce good results without great professors. Higher education worldwide focuses on the "hardware"-buildings, laboratories, and the like-at the expense of "software"-the people who make any academic institutions successful.

To understand the contemporary academic profession, it is useful to examine the status and working conditions of the academic profession worldwide. The academic profession is aging in many countries. In much of the world, half or more of the professoriate is getting close to retirement. In many countries, too few new PhDs are being produced to replace those leaving the profession, and many new doctorates prefer to work outside of academe. Too few incentives for advanced doctoral study and an uncertain employment market for new PhDs, along with inadequate financial support in many fields, deter enrolment and ensure that many students drop out of doctoral programs. Countries with rapidly growing higher education systems are especially hard hit. Vietnam, for example, requires 12,000 more academics each year to meet expansion goals, and only 10 percent of the academic profession currently hold doctoral degrees. While the profession in the developed countries faces different challenges from those in developing nations, the professoriate faces significant difficulties everywhere.

Like higher education generally and largely as a result of massification, the academic profession has become differentiated and segmented. It is hardly possible to describe the profession as a whole. Academics who teach at research universities typically hold a doctoral degree and have full-time appointments, with some expectation of career advancement. Those employed at other kinds of universities and other postsecondary institutions more frequently do not have the highest academic qualifications, are paid less than their peers at the top of the system, teach more, and in general have less adequate working conditions. There are also vast differences among countries, and according to discipline.

As sociologist Burton Clark noted, academics occupy "small worlds, different worlds". Academic salaries are highest in the wealthier countries and lowest in the developing world. A recent study noted that average salaries are in some cases as much as eight times higher in North America and western Europe than in China and India, and some developing countries have salaries below them. Working conditions, career structures, and access to good laboratories and libraries also vary significantly in different tiers of the academic system within a country and among nations as well.

Global examples of the current state of the academic profession will illustrate contemporary realities. These examples are chosen to highlight significant themes.

Rise of the Part-Time Profession

To be most effective, professors need to be truly engaged in teaching and research. A significant proportion ofi profession members must have full-time academic appointments and devote attention exclusively to academic responsibilities and to the universities and colleges that employ them.

The full-time professoriate is in retreat. Latin America is the homeland of the part time "taxicab" professor, rushing between teaching jobs or between class and another profession. Except for Brazil, and a few smaller universities elsewhere on the continent, in almost all Latin American countries up to 80 percent ofi the professoriate is employed part time. Paid a pittance, they have little commitment to the university or to students. It is not surprising that there are almost no Latin

American universities among the top 500 and little research productivity. In the United States, only half of newly hired academics are full time on the "tenure track"-scholars who can hope for a career in higher education. The rest are part-time "contingent" faculty who are paid poorly for each course and have few benefits. A new class of full-time contract teachers has grown in recent years as a way for universities to ensure flexibility in staffing. Traditional tenure-track academic appointments tend to be most common in the upper-tier colleges and universities, thus increasing inequalities in the academic system as a whole. While most western European academics are full time, part-time and temporary staff are growing in number.

In many countries, universities now employ part-time professors who have full-time appointments at other institutions. Many eastern European countries, China, Vietnam, Uganda, and others are examples of such a higher education sector. Academic salaries are sufficiently low, and the universities expect that faculty will earn extra funds to supplement their own incomes and in some cases to subsidize the university's own budget. At some Chinese universities, professors are expected to practice consulting and other outside work as part of their academic duties. In other cases, universities set up additional degree-granting colleges and ask the faculty to perform extra teaching at those schools, enhancing university revenues and individual salaries at the same time. It is also the case that professors at state universities in much of the world help to staff the burgeoning private higher education sector by "moonlighting."

The decline of a real full-time professoriate is undermining high-quality higher education. If professors cannot devote their full attention not only to teaching and research, working with students outside of the classroom, and participating in the governance of their universities, academic quality will decline. As the British say, "penny wise and pound foolish."

Deteriorating Qualifications

It is possible that up to half of the world's university teachers have only earned a bachelor's degree. No one knows for sure. What we do know is that the academic profession is growing rapidly, and facilities for advanced degree study are not keeping up-nor are salary levels that encourage the "best and brightest" to join the professoriate. In China, the world's largest academic system, only 9 percent of the academic profession has doctorates. Thirty-five percent of Indian academics have doctoral qualifications. In many countries, significant parts of the profession have a bachelor's degree, and some have not even attained that basic degree. In most developing countries, only academic staff at the most prestigious universities hold a doctoral degree-usually under 10 percent of the total. The expansion of graduate (postgraduate) programs has been identified as a top priority worldwide, but expansion has been slow because the demand for basic access is so great. It is the case that qualified academics are not being produced fast enough to meet the demand.

Inadequate Compensation

It is no longer possible to lure the best minds to academe. A significant part of the problem is financial. Even before the current world financial crisis, academic salaries did not keep up with remuneration for highly trained professionals everywhere. Now, with tremendous financial pressures on higher education generally, the situation will no doubt deteriorate further. A recent study of academic salaries in 15 countries shows full-time academic staff can survive on their salaries. However, they do not earn much more than the average salary in their country. Relatively few of the most qualified young people undergo the rigorous education required for jobs in the top universities.

Highly trained individuals frequently flee to higher paying jobs in other professions or, in the case of developing countries, leave for academic or other jobs in Europe or North America. While the "brain drain" is a complex phenomenon, it is clear that the exodus of many of the most experienced academics from, for example, sub-Saharan Africa to South Africa, Europe, and North America has caused severe personnel problems in African universities.

Bureaucratization of the Professoriate

In years past, even if academics were not well paid, they held a good deal of autonomy and control over their teaching and research as well as their time. This situation has changed in many academic systems and institutions.

In terms of accountability and assessment, the professoriate has lost much of its autonomy. Assessment exercises and other accountability measures require a lot of time and effort to complete. The pressure to assess academic productivity of all kinds is substantial, even if much of that work is in fact quite difficult or impossible to accurately measure. Much criticism has been aimed at the British Research Assessment Exercises, which many claim has distorted academic work by overemphasizing certain kinds of academic productivity.

Universities have also become much more bureaucratic as they have grown and become more accountable to external authorities. Accountability is both appropriate and necessary in contemporary academic institutions and systems and is not necessarily inimical to the community of scholars. Often, however, heavy bureaucratic control is deleterious to a sense of academic community and generally to the faculty's traditional involvement in academic governance. The power of the professors, once dominant and sometimes used by them to resist change, has declined in the age of accountability and bureaucracy. The pendulum of authority in higher education has swung from the academics to managers and bureaucrats, with significant impact on the university.

Global Academic Marketplace

Just as students are internationally mobile, so, too, are academics. There are no accurate statistics concerning global flows of academic talent. The numbers are quite large. In general, academics go from developing countries to North America, western Europe, and Australasia. There are also significant flows from sub-Saharan Africa to South Africa, from South Asia to the Middle East and Africa, from Egypt to the wealthier Arab countries, and from the United Kingdom to Canada and the United States. A key motivator in this flow is salary, but other factors such as improved working conditions, and particularly research infrastructures, opportunities for advancement, academic freedom, and others may also be involved.

At one time, this phenomenon was labeled a brain drain, but in the era of relatively easy air travel and the Internet, many internationally mobile scholars keep close contacts with their home countries. These diasporas can play a significant role by keeping in contact with the academic communities in their home countries and sharing research and experience. Yet the fact remains that the global flow of academic talent works to the disadvantage of the developing world. There are some small signs the situation is changing. More Chinese scholars are choosing to return home after sojourns elsewhere, for example. Universities in Singapore, Hong Kong, China, and elsewhere are attracting Western academics with high salaries and favorable working conditions.

The challenges to the academic profession are complex and very much tied to broader criticisms of the professions generally in many countries. Some of the problems are directly linked to mass higher education and the financial and other challenges massification has created. It is not difficult to identify the path to a restored academic profession-and thus successful higher education systems. The academic profession must again become a profession-with appropriate training, compensation, and status. This means that academic programs, to provide master's and doctoral degrees, must be significantly expanded. The rush toward part-time teachers must be ended and, instead, a sufficient cadre of full-time professors with appropriate career ladders appointed. Salaries must be sufficient to attract talented young scholars and to keep them in the profession.

In a differentiated academic system, not all professors will focus on research-typically the gold standard in terms of prestige and status. Most academics mainly teach, and their workloads should reflect this. It would also be impossible to return to the days of unfettered autonomy and little if any evaluation of academic work. Yet, accountability and assessment can be done in ways that are appropriate to academic work rather than punitive exercises.

If there is any good news in this story it is that more professors enjoy what they are doing and feel a loyalty to the profession. The 1992 international Carnegie study of the academic profession found surprisingly high levels of satisfaction, and the 2008 Changing Academic Profession global survey found much the same result. Academics feel a commitment to teaching and research, enjoy the autonomy they have to determine their own work, and like interacting with students and colleagues. Despite their problems, academic life has significant attractions. The challenge is to ensure that the academic profession is again seen by policymakers and the public as central to the success of higher education.

The Student Experience

Students constitute the most central stakeholder group in higher education around the world. Over the last decade, major shifts have occurred in the size, demographic makeup, needs, aspirations, and expectations of the student population across the globe. These developments have exerted significant pressure on individual institutions and entire systems of higher education in many countries. Efforts to respond to new student realities have resulted in a wide range of institutional and systemic adjustments that have changed-and continue to change-the size, shape, and very nature of higher education. These developments, in turn, have affected the student experience of higher education, presenting students worldwide with a new and particular set of challenges and opportunities. Some half-dozen fundamental issues stand out as central to an understanding of the interplay between students and higher education over the last decade. These include:

- Demographic changes
- Diversification of the student body
- Transformation of higher education institutions/systems
- Rising demands for relevance
- Increased calls for cost sharing
- Globalization and internationalization

Demographic Changes

Over the last decade, the world population is estimated to have grown from approximately 5.9 billion to more than 6.7 billion. Today, "more than 1.5 billion people are between the ages of 10 and 25," representing the "largest-ever generation of adolescents". As young people have moved in increasingly large numbers through primary and secondary levels of education, there has been a sustained increase in student enrolment in higher education over the last decade. This has held true in both absolute and relative terms and comes as a result of a variety of demographic and systemic factors, as well as overt policy decisions and national development aspirations. The most recent UNESCO figures estimate that there are some 150.6 million tertiary education students globally. This is roughly a 53 percent increase over UNESCO's 2000 estimate of 98.3 million tertiary students worldwide. The gross enrolment ratio figures for this same time frame reflect upward trends as well. UNESCO data suggest that globally, the gross enrolment ratio for tertiary education has grown by 37 percent over the period from 2000 to 2007, from 19 percent to 26 percent. Most of the most dramatic growth in overall youth numbers over the last decade has occurred in the developing world, while particularly robust increases in higher education enrolment have been seen in regions such as East Asia and the Pacific, central and eastern Europe, and Latin America and the Caribbean.

Common consequences of the rapid and sustained demand for tertiary education in recent years have been the creation of new institutions, the expansion of existing ones, the introduction and extension of distance learning options, and the growth of a private higher education sector to supplement the educational opportunities provided by the public sector. Real benefits have accrued to students in many of these contexts.

Expanded possibilities for higher education enrolment in general, and a sense of choice in terms of institutional size, type, and location are some of the most obvious examples of an improved situation for students in higher education systems that have grown and diversified in the last decade.

At the same time, difficulties and disadvantages have also plagued rapid expansion in many quarters. Growth in systems has often occurred in ad hoc ways, resulting in less-than-optimal deployment of limited resources, short-term solutions to long-term challenges, and uneven benefits for stakeholders.

Quality has also been a central concern in such environments. In some cases, the creation of new institutions has outpaced capacity to monitor and assure quality. In other cases, extremely large, "massified" institutions-grown exponentially to accommodate expanded student numbers-have not been able to maintain traditional standards in a resource-stretched context. The *Global Student Statement to the UNESCO World Conference on Higher Education +10* (2009) specifically highlights the link between access and quality, asserting:

> quality is a distinguishing characteristic that provides a guide for students and higher education institutions. High quality and accessibility should be two sides of the same coin. Accessible higher education that is not high quality is worthless and high quality education that is not widely accessible is meaningless.

Meanwhile, the expansion of student numbers in many countries has presented a major challenge for systems where the tradition has been to provide access to free or highly subsidized tertiary education. In financial terms, this has become an unsustainable model, placing pressure on systems to fundamentally restructure the "social contract" between higher education and society at large. In many cases, emotions-particularly among students-have run extremely high around this subject, creating not insignificant political challenges and social tensions.

The highly divisive, nine-month, student-led strike at the National Autonomous University of Mexico in 1999 offers an important example of a powerful student response to fee increases; it also reflects the real way in which broader political and economic issues can play out in higher education institutions.

While growth and massification of higher education have been the norm in many countries, the situation in the world's more developed countries is quite different, although challenged by demographic changes in its own right. A rapidly aging population in the North forces higher education systems and institutions there to consider new and different student paradigms. These societies have faced fluctuations in traditional-age student numbers and have also begun to respond to the new and unique demands of lifelong learning. The European Union's Lifelong Learning Programme, which has allocated "nearly D7 billion for 2007 to 2013," aims to enable "individuals at all stages of their lives to pursue stimulating learning opportunities across Europe.

Nontraditional learners (particularly older individuals) and international students are coming to play an increasingly important role in the higher education systems of many developed countries. In addition, the growing diversification of societies in North America and much of Europe due to immigration patterns also demands a serious rethinking of pedagogies, curricula, and research agendas. By necessity, these must now take into account a wider range of cultural, racial, linguistic, and overall "identity" factors at play in tertiary institutions.

Diversification of the Student Body

Broadly speaking, evidence suggests that higher education systems around the world are increasingly serving a more diverse group of students. In general, this development is a source of great encouragement and hope for those who see fundamental connections between higher education and positive personal and professional outcomes for individuals, as well as enhanced economic, social, and political developments for nations with a broad base of highly educated workers.

However, traditionally underrepresented groups continue to face serious challenges. Underrepresented groups may be understood to include, among others, ethnic, racial, cultural, and linguistic minorities; "the poor, those living in places far from major urban centres ... people with disabilities, migrants, refugees, those deprived of their freedom"; women and working adults.

In many parts of the world, involvement in higher education by these groups still does not reflect the full scope of their numbers in the broader society. Nor are these students assured equal access to the same kinds of institutions (the most prestigious, for example) as students from the more dominant groups in society, graduating at the same rates, or accruing the same benefits as a result of their tertiary education experiences.

Where progress toward broader social inclusiveness has occurred, diversification of the student body has placed a complex new set of demands on higher education institutions and systems around the world. Central to this discussion is the need to reconsider the fundamental questions of what is taught, when, and how, and what constitutes quality in higher education. There have been widespread calls to incorporate new approaches into teaching and research, as well as new curricula and administrative structures that respond more appropriately and effectively to the unique identities of the new kinds of students pursuing higher education.

Program structure and delivery are deeply implicated in this changing context, as are the perspectives and experience of the faculty responsible for delivering instruction and intellectual guidance, the staff tasked with supporting bureaucratic activities and student services, and the administrators charged with providing institutional leadership.

Institutional transformation-whereby universities evolve to provide meaningful opportunities for many different forms of knowledge and ways of learning-is seen by some as an ideal objective in the face of a diversifying worldwide student population. Indeed, the 2009 *Global Student Statement to the UNESCO World Conference on Higher Education +10* calls unequivocally for "Education for All!", and urges that greater attention be given to the provision of "adequate support measures, specifically designed to adapt to the needs of the individual learner". The political challenges of this kind of commitment are considerable, however. Even in contexts where there may be consensus that greater social inclusiveness in higher education is a positive value, implementation of real changes at institutional and national levels can rub up against deeply held beliefs about "meritocracy, national cohesion, and democracy". As greater numbers of nontraditional students are actively recruited or otherwise find their way into tertiary education around the world, the importance of responding to the unique needs of new kinds of learners will prove to be increasingly central to the higher education enterprise.

Transformation of Higher Education Institutions/Systems

As the tertiary student population has grown in size and complexity in much of the world over the last 10 years, the landscape of higher education institutions has, in many contexts, expanded and evolved in response to the changing student population.

Primary developments in this area have been the dramatic growth in the private higher education sector, the increasing popularity of professionally oriented programs (notably in the fields of business and information and communications technology), and the more widespread provision of higher education opportunities with flexible formats for working adults. Also important have been the trends to establish new universities and/or to modify existing institutions by expanding their size and scope, elevating non-universities to university status, or merging multiple institutions. All of these developments may in some way be seen as responses to increased calls for access and/or perceived needs to better serve a new generation of learners with particular educational needs and aspirations.

The growth in numbers of private higher education institutions, and their increasing share of worldwide tertiary education enrolment, has been a remarkable feature of the last decade. Much of this activity has been fueled by student demand for access in general and for access to certain types of programs and fields of study in particular, accompanied by an inability of the public higher education sector to keep pace with this demand. In some parts of the world, students have become frustrated with failing public institutions that are prone to overcrowding, substandard facilities and services, and political and bureaucratic gridlock (including prolonged strikes and closures). They have therefore turned, in many instances, to private higher education in search of a more stable and viable educational experience.

In other contexts, private higher education has served to fill a void for minority groups seeking a more comfortable or welcoming environment. This has been especially true for female students or those coming from particular religious traditions or ethnic/racial backgrounds in societies where the minority student population has found it difficult to integrate into the mainstream higher education sector. The rise in recent years of religiously affiliated private universities in Nigeria, for example, provides some insight into this trend.

The shifting needs and interests of students have also contributed to an increase in popularity of many professionally oriented programs and institutions. Characterized as a "vocationalization" of higher education in many corners of the world, student enrolment globally in the business, information and communications technology fields, and other similarly "practical" areas of study, have changed the higher education landscape. An explosion in the last decade of master of business administration (MBA) program offerings around the world is a prime example of this trend, with countries like China rapidly introducing Western-style business schools in the last 15 years.

In the case of the MBA surge, students in ever-greater numbers have been seeking a competitive credential that enhances employment opportunities, while institutions have looked for ways to increase tuition income and prestige. In many ways, this has been mutually beneficial for students, institutions, and social stakeholders such as employers. However, there have also been problems associated with such trends. Notable among these is lack of locally relevant teaching materials (such as case studies for Chinese MBA programs), and questionable quality assurance oversight in a context of rapid expansion in order to meet the "market demand" for these specific credentials. In countries with limited resources to apply to the higher education sector, concerns may emerge about the preservation of less-popular programs in fields such as the arts and humanities, where employment outcomes are ostensibly less promising.

Partly as a way to accommodate the increase in number and types of students served (and in some cases as a way to actively attract new learners), some higher education systems have undertaken broadly based efforts to split, merge, or otherwise retool institutions in their systems or add brand new universities to the mix. In many cases, this has occurred in the context of a national reform agenda.

The student-related objectives embedded in such agendas have ranged from providing more and better choices for the student population, to simply keeping up with the growing number of learners or the expanding interests of students in particular fields of study. New institutions may bring with them real opportunity, innovation, and excellence. However, Damtew Teferra notes that "expansion and quality are often in constant counter-play, especially so where resources are in short supply." Overly ambitious or narrowly conceived reform or expansion efforts may sacrifice quality and prevent a clear focus on the achievement of broader objectives, to the ultimate detriment of the student population.

The transformation of higher education systems and institutions over the last decade has represented a notable effort to achieve some convergence of evolving student needs and tertiary education interests and capacity over the last 10 years. Yet, the complexity of issues and factors involved has made for a most-challenging environment and an uneven range of outcomes in this area.

Relevance

In the rapidly changing global economic environment of the last decade, "relevance" has become a key consideration in higher education in many corners of the world. Students have exhibited an increasing tendency to want educational experiences that are directly relevant to their personal and/or professional interests and objectives, particularly as relate to employability. Practically oriented programs and fields of study, as well as pedagogical approaches stressing "real world" applications, have seen an appreciable rise in popularity. At the same time, new demands on higher education have made it increasingly important for the tertiary education sector in many countries to demonstrate its social and economic relevance to the societies served. To this end, many universities have moved to provide the kinds of applied academic and professional programs that are both sought by larger numbers of students and considered fundamentally linked to economic expansion. In other countries, an emerging interest in liberal arts and humanities, as well as interdisciplinary studies, has been noted. Here, the development of more versatile, well-rounded graduates has been a key objective.

Evolving approaches to teaching are also quite important to the discussion of relevance. Key developments here have been the introduction of new program options, such as part-time programs, online study possibilities, and courses that allow students to acquire credit for current or prior professional experience, among others. These innovations seek to more effectively meet the needs of contemporary students, many more of which are balancing work and/or family obligations, returning to schooling after a break of some years, or pursuing lifelong learning interests and goals.

In countries where the focus has long been on rote learning, emphasis has shifted in recent years to developing students' analytical and critical thinking skills, as well as a clearer understanding of how to learn. Along with curriculum and pedagogy, research has also been an important factor in the move toward relevance. In this area, some tertiary institutions and systems have focused more on expanding research capacity and developing entrepreneurial activities as a means to commercialize valuable technologies, and contribute to the advancement of national development agendas.

From the perspective of the student experience of higher education, each of these trends has brought with them a complex set of benefits and drawbacks. The expanded ability to develop key skills and access programs in preferred fields of study is a very positive trend for those students who, a decade before, might have had to settle for enrolment in courses that lead to few real employment options or in which they had limited interest. At the same time, unregulated access to particular fields of study can lead to over-enrolment, which, in turn, can adversely affect the quality of programs and the student experience within them. Clustering of large numbers of students in specific areas can be detrimental to learners seeking individual attention and guidance, stretching already limited resources to accommodate oversized cohorts. After graduation, employment prospects can be scarce for those coming out of overenrolled programs. This is problematic not only for individuals but also for societies facing workforce surpluses in some areas and shortages in others.

Meanwhile, it is true that the rush to expand applied research activities has generated revenue and prestige for some institutions, and provided students with new opportunities to be exposed to cutting-edge research within the context of their studies. The downside of this trend, however, is the potential for a focus on research to undermine teaching activities. This shift may occur if the research function of an institution is privileged in such a way-financial, political, or otherwise-that a sizable proportion of time, talent, and resources is diverted away from the teaching function. There is also the problem of the migration of resources and prestige away from fields of study considered less relevant to personal financial advancement and broader economic development, which are nonetheless very important to the cultural life of a society.

Cost Sharing

In close conjunction with the demographic trends that have brought larger numbers of students into postsecondary education, there has been a corresponding financial strain on higher education around the world. In order to fill the gap between supply-heavily subsidized if not wholly publicly funded in many countries-and growing demand for postsecondary access, many higher education institutions and systems have moved to introduce or raise tuition and student fees. In many parts of the world, this represents a profound change in both policy and practice, with a very direct impact on students and their families. These effects can be seen in both positive and negative lights.

In terms of positive effects, being obligated to pay for some portion of the costs associated with higher education does give individuals a quantifiable stake in the higher education process and outcome. Students (independently or actively encouraged by their fee-paying families) may focus more energetically on the process of moving swiftly and successfully through the higher education experience, decreasing the time to degree, and increasing the overall efficiency of the system.

In contexts where students have tended to languish for years in tuition-free systems-sometimes even earning small salaries in the form of student stipends-the incentives to graduate (particularly in countries of high unemployment) have been limited. Cost sharing in some instances has rendered inertia more uncomfortable and costly, arguably reducing the attractiveness of life as a "career student." The shifting of some of the burdens of cost onto students and their families can also be understood to have empowered these groups to some extent, transforming them into consumers of higher education with a choice, in many more countries, of where to spend their tuition monies.

At the same time, cost sharing also presents important challenges. Most obviously, the imposition or raising of tuition and fees can have a serious exclusionary effect, erecting real barriers to access among students with limited resources. It also has the potential to ghettoize poorer students in particular kinds of institutions or fields of study based solely on socioeconomic, rather than academic, factors.

Meanwhile, although the responsiveness of tertiary institutions to the demands of fee-paying students can yield dynamic and innovative results, there are concerns that these efforts can be shortsighted, ultimately undermining student choices as well as the public good ethos of much higher education around the world. For example, those institutions and/or systems that put a premium on programs able to generate their own revenue through tuition and fees may eliminate programs unable to meet this threshold.

Areas of study with low enrolment numbers, often in more obscure or highly specialized fields, are vulnerable in such contexts. Also difficult to sustain in these circumstances are more expensive areas of study, such as medicine and the sciences, which require costly laboratories and supplies. The scope of students' educational possibilities may be narrowed, which may have a detrimental effect on the long-term vibrancy of a given institution, tertiary system, or broader society. Furthermore, whereas cost sharing can be an empowering force for students in some cases, in others it can cultivate a distinctly utilitarian, consumer-oriented approach to higher education. In this setting, the focus is overwhelmingly on the private-good aspects of the enterprise rather than the more expansive concerns for the development of students as citizens or for the public good.

The move toward increased cost sharing by students and their families represents an extremely important shift in the student experience of higher education around the world over the last decade. The *Global Student Statement to the UNESCO World Conference on Higher Education +10* (2009) urges "a deep investment in the higher education of students globally," and states that "higher education needs to be... a fundamental right for all," regardless of a student's ability to pay. However, fiscal and economic realities the world over make it likely that cost sharing will continue to be an issue of concern for higher education and exert an influence on the student experience in a variety of ways across the globe.

The student experience of tertiary education has been affected by globalization and internationalization, most notably through the expansion of student mobility, the growth in cross-border provision of education, and the emergence of international university rankings and the quality assurance movement. Enormous benefits have accrued to many students as a result of these developments, although the student experience of internationalization and globalization has also been fraught with difficulties and inequities for many.

Opportunities for students to spend all or part of their higher education careers outside of their country of origin or residence have risen dramatically in the last 10 years. Although it has proven to be exceedingly difficult to get reliable data on international student mobility, indications are that the worldwide flow of students has grown appreciably over the last decade. UNESCO estimates that there were some 1.8 million internationally mobile students in 2000, which grew to over 2.7 million in 2007.

Furthermore, the potential for significant growth over the coming decade is quite realistic. At the same time, while it is difficult to assess personal, professional, and academic outcomes in any systematic or large-scale way, a preponderance of anecdotal evidence suggests that the benefits of international study for most students are quite positive-enjoyable, meaningful, and often life changing. Only a small portion of the world's tertiary students experiences these benefits, however.

Given the costs involved in overseas study, most internationally mobile students-with the exception of small numbers benefiting from special funding and scholarship programs-are full fee-paying students coming from privileged socioeconomic backgrounds. They represent select segments of the student population in the home country-Caucasian women in the United States, for example, or male graduate students in much of the developing world, for another. This information suggests an uneven access to international study opportunities exists, which perpetuates other inequalities among students, at both local and global levels.

The arrival of foreign higher education providers in various parts of the world has also been a positive development. These entities have in some cases given students new options for study in contexts where the local supply of tertiary education could not meet demand and also introduced new programs, materials, and pedagogical approaches that bring an informative international dimension to the teaching and learning processes. But in some instances, unscrupulous foreign providers have offered substandard academic services or perpetrated outright fraud, operating as nothing more than "degree mills."

An uncertain quality landscape for students enrolling in unregulated cross-border providers, as well as the potential for foreign providers to impose inappropriate curricula or teaching methodologies, are just some of the ways in which internationalization can harm more than help the student experience. The inability of students to gain recognition at home for degrees earned abroad at high-quality institutions or to gain meaningful employment in the home country after studying overseas or in international institutions operating locally further complicates the experience of higher education's international dimension for the world's students.

Raising public levels of awareness about institutional regulation, accreditation, and levels of quality, as well as credential recognition issues, is extremely important in this context. The UNESCO Portal on Higher Education Institutions is an example of an international effort to provide students, families and other stakeholders with access relevant information in order to make informed decisions.

The emergence of international university rankings and the quality assurance movement also represents a mixed blessing. Students receive obvious benefits in the push to raise the levels of quality and competitiveness. Resources pumped into these efforts have, in many cases, raised the level of academic quality (at least in some areas) and enhanced institutional prestige in others, providing students with better academic experiences and more widely recognized credentials. Students have suffered, however, in contexts in which the effort to obtain certain international league-table standings, or a particular quality assurance agency endorsement, has not been in alignment with real student needs. The failure of institutions or systems to adequately serve local students, by pursuing ambitious (and not always appropriate or realistic) internationally oriented agendas, is yet another example of how internationalization can harm the student experience of higher education.

The evolving global and international dimensions in tertiary education have exerted important effects on higher education systems and institutions around the world, some enormously positive, and others more worrisome. These developments have and will continue to affect the ways in which students experience tertiary education, as globalization continues apace and many aspects of internationalization expand and mature in the coming decade.

Shifts in student numbers, characteristics, needs, and interests have had an enormous impact on higher education around the world over the last 10 years. Student concerns will continue to demand attention in the coming decade as the variables associated with this key stakeholder continue to fluctuate across the globe, exerting a range of direct and indirect influences on the size, scope, quality, and nature of the higher education enterprise worldwide. How best to accommodate and effectively serve an increasingly large and more diverse tertiary student population will be a central consideration for policymakers and institutional leaders moving forward. Effective responses to enrolment growth and diversification will require careful attention to individual, institutional, and systemic needs, as well as local and global contexts.

The student experience in the 21st century will likely be characterized by more years of engagement with education over the course of a lifetime, as well as greater options in terms of what when, and how to study. In most parts of the world, students will increasingly need to finance their studies from personal resources. This may negatively affect the time to degree for many students, but it may also encourage new and different kinds of learning as students combine formal education with work and other activities. Students and their families will require more detailed and comprehensive information on the relative merits of different study options as the higher education sector expands and evolves in many countries and the incidence of cross-border delivery grows. Finding ways to protect students' rights and enhance their roles in governance and decision making will be especially important if higher education is to respond effectively to changing student profiles and needs the world over.

From a global perspective, the student experience of tertiary education appears poised to take on greater complexity than ever before, presenting considerable challenges and opportunities for the higher education sector around the world in the coming years.

Teaching, Learning, and Assessment

University systems have changed profoundly in the last 10 years. Larger and more diverse student populations, a growing interest in professional education and lifelong learning, the privatization of higher education, financial constraints, enhanced attention to quality and accountability, and evolving tendencies for postsecondary institutions and national systems to situate themselves in international and global contexts are just a few of the most important trends of the last decade.

Individually and collectively, these developments have exerted important pressures on the core functions of higher education, including teaching and learning. These changes have had significant impact on how and what students learn and the way that knowledge, skills, learning, and teaching are assessed.

While it is difficult to generalize globally, the mission of the majority of institutions in most countries today is to teach less of the basic disciplines and offer more in the way of professional programs to a wider range of students than in the past. Greater attention is also being paid to students' need to develop skills, knowledge, and attitudes so as to operate effectively in more complex, fluid, and ambiguous environments. Students must be primed to engage in learning activities across many more phases of their lives, and institutions must be prepared to meet the needs of a wide range of nontraditional learners. A profound challenge, inherent in the need to effectively accommodate both teaching and research functions, will engage higher education systems and individual institutions.

Even though these important changes are taking place, relatively little research exists on the status and role of teaching and learning in higher education around the world.

Analysis about assessment is slightly more prevalent due to the education community's heightened awareness of accountability and quality assurance, particularly in Europe and thc United States. Overall, however, teaching, learning, and assessment in the context of global higher education require significantly more research to make better judgments about current trends and their impact on individual countries and institutions.

A recent and far reaching example of shifting teaching, learning, and assessment paradigms can be seen in the Bologna process, which is attempting to achieve real interchangeability between universities across Europe and beyond. The primary objectives of the Bologna process are to bring compatibility and quality assurance across Europe's many and varied higher education systems, while promoting transparency, mobility, employability, and student-centered learning. All of these developments require potentially enormous changes in how academics and institutions understand and approach teaching and assessment. Further, they encapsulate broader global trends to develop a clearer understanding of what constitutes meaningful higher education "inputs" and "outputs." These discussions have generated a great deal of excitement in many quarters but also represent real challenges and concerns for many stakeholders around the world.

Teaching in the Traditional University

Twenty years ago, universities in most parts of the world were much more highly selective than they are today, accepting relatively small percentages of secondary school leavers. A high proportion of the subjects taught included the basic science and arts disciplines. Given that academic reputations were built on research, however, it follows that research, not teaching, was the top priority.

Teaching usually meant lecturing to very bright and highly motivated students. Assessment was usually norm-referenced to determine which students were the most effective at remembering and understanding what they had been taught, and students were graded accordingly. Poor results were attributed to student deficits such as lack of motivation or talent, rarely to poor teaching.

In most university contexts around the world, oversight of teaching was left to departments, which often gave individual teachers a virtually free hand to teach as they liked. Academic appointments and promotions were and still are, for the most part, made on the basis of research output, not teaching proficiency. When recognized, teaching excellence was often showcased through competitive awards to individuals, which only confirmed to many that teaching was a gift possessed by the rare few, not a skill to be cultivated. Among those universities fortunate enough to have teaching development and educational technology centers-mostly outside of the developing world-workshops provided opportunities to improve teaching and assessment but were attended only on a voluntary basis and by more self-motivated teachers. The prevailing conception of teaching emphasized what teachers did, not what students learned.

Until fairly recently, teaching meant "covering" a body of *declarative* knowledge-that is, knowledge that could be "declared" in books or in lectures-while assessment measured how well students received that knowledge based on their ability to regurgitate it on examinations. Less thought was given to *functional* knowledge-that is, knowing how to apply theory to practical situations. In sum, traditional university teaching was knowledge centered rather than student centered. Although under researched in a global context, today an emerging dialogue focuses on the need for more student-centered approaches to teaching, the "inputs," and more meaningful assessments regarding student learning, the "outputs."

Factors Transforming University Teaching

Massification has produced-and continues to do so-an enormous impact on universities today. Student intake is much higher than before, approaching 60 percent of school leavers in many parts of the developed world (and even higher in some countries). The larger student population is also more mature in age and more international, with diverse abilities and motivations. Postsecondary education is thus oriented toward vocational and professional instruction, with a focus on functional knowledge. Given the pressures of massification and the evolving educational outcomes, lecturing about declarative knowledge can no longer be the default teaching method. Several other important developments stand out as key drivers of change in the areas of teaching, learning and assessment.

Teaching and Learning Theory and Outcomes-Based Approaches

Research about student learning and the "scholarship of teaching and learning" in general have provided a philosophy, a technology, and an impetus for universities to design more effective teaching and assessment. Teaching models have evolved from the primitive "blame the student" approach (meaning that a failure to learn is due to the student's lack of talent or effort), to the teacher-centered scenario of acquiring "tricks of the trade" to initiate good teaching, and to the most up-to-date student-learning research that defines good teaching by examining whether students achieve desirable and predefined learning outcomes.

Ideally, this approach involves engaging students actively in the learning process. Theoretical developments that prioritize learning outcomes have led some participants in the higher education community to shift from a teacher-centered input model, to one that is student centered and based on outputs. Good teaching, in other words, would focus less on what *teachers do* and primarily on what *students learn.* This paradigm shift is playing out dynamically in some learning environments but is encountering obstacles in others.

Public Good Versus Private Good Considerations

Shifts in the debate about whether postsecondary education is more a public good or a private good have altered some stakeholder relationships with higher education around the world. This trend reflects a growing sense that the personal benefits of obtaining a degree may be as important as (or even more so than) the societal benefits of an educated population. With increasing numbers of students paying more money for their education (in both cash-strapped public institutions and in the growing private higher education sector), students have higher expectations of the education supplier and the "product" they receive. The complex side effects for education include the fact that universities, if they are to survive in an increasingly competitive "knowledge market," must look at the quality and relevance of their teaching activities in ways they never have before.

Quality Assurance and Institutional Accountability

Governments have in recent years insisted on greater accountability from higher education, which has included new emphasis on quality assurance. Initially, quality assurance meant retrospective managerial assessments that operated irrespective of teaching theory or research findings on what constituted good teaching. In the last 10 years, however, quality assurance agencies have increasingly used a theory-based lens to define effective, or good, teaching and assessment. Example organizations include the Quality

Assurance Agency in Britain, the University Grants Committee in Hong Kong, and the Australian Universities Quality Agency. If used reflectively across the whole institution, quality assurance mechanisms can bolster teaching and learning, rather than simply maintain the status quo. Meanwhile, in some (but certainly not all) cases, demand from students, governments, employers and other stakeholders has forced universities to take leadership responsibility for teaching rather than leaving it to department heads and individual professors.

Excellent reasons, related to education outcomes, support universities having some centralized influence over teaching. Developments in the theory of teaching, and of outcomes-based approaches to student learning in particular, have provided the means by which universities can construct new approaches to teaching and assessment, new resources for teaching and learning, and new outcome standards that ensure high-quality teaching across all departments.

Emerging Curricula and a Shifting Sense of Education's Purpose

In recent years, there has been renewed conversation about the purpose of education, particularly in light of the recognized role higher education plays in developing human resources for a growing global economy. In this process, questions are being raised about the curriculum.

Social leaders and educationalists (particularly outside of the United States) are asking whether a traditional professional focus, which prepared students for work in the industrial economy, is adequate in the evolving and ambiguous knowledge economy. Professional education, sometimes called specialization or vocational education, typically refers to curricula that focus on preparing students for a specific career like law, medicine, business, or engineering.

New conversations are emerging, however, about the value of and potential need for liberal education. Sometimes referred to as general education, liberal education (or liberal learning) emphasizes a broad interdisciplinary curriculum focused on creativity, critical thinking, cultural awareness, problem solving, and communication skills. The knowledge economy is more often requiring a workforce of generalists who are adaptable, know how to learn, and can "manage and assimilate greatly expanded quantities of information". Although not in great numbers, liberal education institutions and programs are starting to appear around the world, where they have previously not existed. In places like Russia and eastern Europe, which have witnessed changing political and economic structures in recent years, as well as in other emerging democracies, liberal education is being considered as a means for developing a critical and participatory citizenry.

Questions about curriculum and higher education's purpose are particularly salient in developing regions where emerging economies require both specialists trained for science and technical professions as well as strong leaders with generalist knowledge who are creative, adaptable, and able to give broad ethical consideration to social advances. It will be important to think carefully about how teaching, learning, and assessment might need to change if liberal education emerges as a trend worldwide.

Competition and Cooperation Between Teaching and Research Functions

Teaching and research are unquestionably two core functions of the academic enterprise around the world. These functions are understood and managed today in various ways across institutions and national systems, presenting complex challenges as well as new opportunities. The traditional prestige associated with research has been amplified in recent years by the focus of highly influential ranking systems and league tables on research activity and output. Money and attention often flow to institutions that excel in research, placing teaching-oriented institutions at a disadvantage for attracting funding and non-financial support.

However, producing a skilled labor force is more than ever a critically important function of higher education. Thus, the teaching function cannot be disregarded in the race to achieve research prestige. Meanwhile, the rising relevance of research in professional graduate education and interdisciplinary fields (which typically focused more exclusively on teaching) is serving as a catalyst for enhanced engagement between research and teaching functions in new and different areas.

These and other developments in higher education have suggested a paradigm shift in university teaching in some countries over the last 10 years, and they are beginning to exert pressure for change on a more global scale. Where evolution in philosophy and approaches to teaching, learning, and assessment have emerged, some notable changes are occurring, particularly among universities that accept institution-wide responsibility for teaching and assessment. These include a focus on outcomes-based approaches to student learning and attention to the complex interplay between curriculum innovation and approaches to teaching, learning, and assessment.

Teaching as an Institutional Responsibility

There is potential momentum building for institutions to assume centralized oversight for teaching-quality practice and development. Although it is too early to call this centralization a trend, it has been most prevalent in North America and Europe, as well as discernible in Australia and in select Asian contexts like Hong Kong. In these settings, many universities have developed policies and procedures that enhance the quality of teaching and assessment across all departments in the institution.

A variety of strategies have been used to advance this agenda. Perhaps the most prominent among these has been the establishment of teaching and learning development centers. Ideally, these centers play an integral role in the university's teaching and learning structure, providing university-wide staff development in line with the institution's approach to teaching, student learning outcomes, and best practices revealed through the scholarship of teaching and learning.

The strength of these facilities depends on whether they are frequented by not only the enthusiastic teachers but by a wide range of faculty and instructors seeking to improve their classroom work. However, because research institutions focus on research rather than teaching, little incentive is provided for instructors to develop their skills or be concerned with teaching quality. For this reason, centers are most effective in improving teaching quality and assessment if endorsed by the central administration or when teaching quality, assessment, and learning outcomes are made an institutional priority. With proper support and institutional culture, teaching and learning centers can provide critical resources for all teaching staff across all departments, assist departments in solving classroom and curriculum challenges, provide programming for new faculty and instructors, and assist with course design and evaluations.

In many contexts, teaching and learning centers are also requested to advise their institutions on questions of policy and operational procedure affecting the quality of teaching and learning across the university. Specific examples include designing student feedback instruments that are sensitive to nontraditional teaching methods and approaches to student learning. This approach can be a critical component to improving learning outcomes, given that most general-purpose feedback questionnaires assume that the lecture/tutorial is the default teaching method.

Teaching and learning centers can also help guide university policy in the area of student assessment, for example, by articulating research-supported rationales for helping institutions move away from norm-referenced to criterion-referenced assessment. This shift is fundamental to outcomes-based teaching and learning but is frequently resisted by traditional academics and administrators who persevere with the belief that grade allocation should follow the bell curve.

In some contexts, teaching and learning centers also play an important role for students. Many centers include tutoring services or learning-skills-development workshops that help students recognize how they learn and encourage students to take responsibility for their own learning in and outside of the classroom.

Technology can play an interesting and essential role in an institution's centralized approach to teaching and outcomes-based handling of student learning. For example, faculty may be required to use e-learning platforms such as BlackBoard or WebCT. This process-painful though it may be for many individuals-typically forces teachers to think more reflectively about course design, delivery, and assessment. It can stimulate creative new ways to engage students and to incorporate highly contemporary materials, while sensitizing faculty to the range of new challenges and possibilities inherent in the application of educational technologies.

On a global scale, however, enhancing teaching and learning by using expensive technology often requires costly equipment and expertise that magnifies the digital divide between developed and developing parts of the world. These opportunities, therefore, are significantly more accessible to more resource-rich higher education sectors and geographic regions.

In short, institution-wide approaches to teaching and assessment, including making teaching a centralized priority and the possibility of curriculum changes (mentioned earlier), are increasingly recognized as able to create more dynamic contexts for enhanced student learning. Already, some tertiary institutions around the world are developing strategies to facilitate such environments. However, to be most effective, a coherent theory of teaching and learning, preferably rooted in notions of outcomes-based student learning, is essential, as this provides a clear framework for making decisions and policies about teaching and learning, from the level of the individual classroom through to the president or rector's office.

Outcomes-based Approaches to Student Learning

Outcomes in higher education are crucial on a variety of levels and for a variety of reasons. Most fundamentally, it is critical for interested stakeholders-students, educators, employers, and governments, among others-to recognize and appreciate the relevant added value from public and private investment in higher education. In many cases, the relative value of what is produced by higher education is assessed in terms of the commercialization of new knowledge and innovative technology, specifically through research. However, also of critical importance is understanding what students take away from the postsecondary experience-what and how well they learn and how the skills and knowledge they acquire serve their individual interests as well as a broader set of societal objectives.

Teaching and learning outcomes can be understood in two ways. One model, sometimes called "outcomes based education," refers to institutional or systemic outcomes defined for the needs of external audiences. Averaged student performances, for example, are designed to meet accreditation requirements and the requests off external stakeholders like employers and policymakers. Many US institutions now collect data and have established performance outcomes. However, there are no connections made between these externally driven managerial concerns and the quality of teaching within institutions.

Therefore, a second and critically important understanding of outcomes is captured by the notion ofi "outcomes-based approaches to student learning," which specifically concerns program and course outcomes and the enhancement of teaching and learning both in and, in some cases, outside the classroom (National Committee ofi Inquiry into Higher. Outcomes in this sense date back to the mid-twentieth century but did not gain traction until the mid-1980s when it became clearer that "If students are to learn desired outcomes in a reasonably effective manner, then the teacher's fundamental task is to get students to engage in learning activities that are likely to result in their achieving those outcomes".

Embedded in this statement is a powerful design for teaching that draws on two important principles:

1. The idea deriving from constructivist psychology that knowledge is not transmitted by a teacher but is constructed by students through their own learning activities
2. Outcomes need to be stated upfront and be aligned with both teaching methods and assessment strategies

When teaching, including course design and curriculum development, is based on student learning and involves identifying pedagogy that will produce stated learning outcomes, it is accordingly called "constructive alignment". This approach represents a crucial shift in teaching, away from declarative knowledge to functional knowledge. By articulating in advance intended learning outcomes, appropriate teaching and learning activities are built, followed by meaningful assessment tasks that directly address the outcomes and the degree to which the teaching and learning activities facilitate or hinder progress against the desired outcomes.

Constructively aligned teaching systematizes what good teachers have always done-stating upfront and making transparent what they intend their students to learn, using teaching that helps the students attain those outcomes, and assessing students in terms of how well they attained the outcomes, while remaining open to learning outcomes that emerge organically during the critical exchange between students and instructors.

It is clear that over the last 10 years, real momentum for change in university approaches to teaching and learning has emerged in at least some parts of the world. The challenges of producing those changes across systems, institutions, and disciplines, however, are significant. The traditional research-based university will still exist, but privatization, massification, and commodification greatly increase the need for prioritizing teaching, learning, and assessment, and for effecting changes that are is anchored in credible scholarship and proven strategies.

Teaching and research always played a central role in the traditional university, although the prestige associated with these functions has been decidedly unequal. Contemporary circumstances are highlighting important teaching/research differences, but there is also a growing sense that much can be gained from strategic focus on both areas, across systems and within institutions and even individual programs. One can argue, though, that there is a real (and very complex) "identity problem" around teaching and research that higher education in most quarters has not yet solved. In very practical terms, policy initiatives that seek to designate universities as either research or teaching institutions, with funds directed accordingly, require careful consideration of the broad range of both short- and long-term implications of such strategies.

In some contexts, although research still remains highly prestigious, teaching is now perceived as the major public purpose and activity of universities. To compete in a global knowledge market, universities have had to prioritize teaching and student learning across the whole university. The pressure to improve teaching fortunately comes at a time when research about teaching and learning-the scholarship of teaching and learning-is increasingly able to provide a framework for guiding institution-wide policies and the decisions of individual teachers. Universities-particularly in Europe, North America, and parts of Australasia-are now better positioned to leverage educational theory as a reflective tool for implementing procedures and policies for teaching and assessment on a university-wide basis, rather than departmentally, as has been typical in the past. In some institutions around the world, course design and assessment methods are increasingly based on intended student-learning outcomes, rather than content transmission from teacher to student. A great deal more research remains to be done, however, particularly in terms of understanding teaching and learning dynamics in a wider range of national and institutional settings. Effectively assessing needs, developing culturally appropriate approaches that maximize positive learning outcomes, and finding ways to provide appropriate materials and resources for the least-privileged higher education institutions and systems the world over is a critically important agenda item for the coming years.

References

Agarwal, P., Said, M.E., Sehoole, M., Sirozi, M. and de Wit, H. 2008. H. de Wit (ed.), *The Dynamics of International Student Circulation in a Global Context*, Rotterdam, Sense Publishers. 223-261

Ben-David, J. and Zloczower,A. 1962. Universities and academic systems in modern societies. *European Journal of Sociology*, Vol. 3, No. 5, pp. 45-84.

Clark, B.R. 1987. *The Academic Life. Small Worlds, Different Worlds*. Princeton, NJ, Carnegie Foundation for the Advancement of Teaching.

Florida, R.L. 2002. *The Rise of the Creative Class: And How It's Transforming Work, Leisure, Community and Everyday Life*. New York, Basic Books.

Kerr, C. 2001. T*he Uses of the University*. Cambridge, MA, Harvard University Press Marton, F., Hounsell, D. and Entwistle, N.J. 1997. *The experience of learning*. Edinburgh, Scottish Academic Press.

6

ICTs and Distance Education

Despite massive advancements in enrolment numbers over the last decade (especially in Africa, Latin America and the Caribbean, the Middle East, and eastern and central Europe), the demand for higher education has exceeded supply in many parts of the world, particularly in developing countries where the gross enrolment ratio is still quite low. The demand for higher education has been fueled by numerous factors. First, the number of primary and secondary students has grown considerably in the last decade, creating a large pool of prospective higher education students in the system. Second, the opportunities and demands of the globalized economy are such that lifelong learning has become much more necessary and common in many parts of the world. Third, the competition for existing and growing numbers of jobs requiring training beyond secondary school is escalating the need for more access to higher education.

Countries the world over have been making considerable efforts to expand the provision of higher education to accommodate the regular-age cohorts, as well as to deal with the rising numbers of nontraditional and lifelong learners. However, expansion based on traditional models of educational provision has peaked in many countries, particularly in contexts of limited public funding, and disconnects between supply and demand are expected to persist. This situation has sparked an interest in finding more versatile and cost-effective ways-new and old-of meeting tertiary education needs.

Distance education has thus emerged as an extremely important option for higher education expansion and delivery in many quarters, particularly in the period since the 1990s, which has witnessed rapid and groundbreaking advancements in information and communications technologies (ICTs). Distance education represents an area of enormous potential for higher education systems around the world struggling to meet the needs of growing and changing student populations, as well as ambitious national development agendas. At the same time, real risks and challenges must be recognized and addressed.

Meanwhile, the advent of many new and innovative technologies in the past decade has had enormous implications for higher education. This is directly related to any discussion of distance education but also extends well beyond that specific realm. To different degrees around the world, ICTs have had an extraordinary impact on everything from teaching and learning; institutional management, administration, and finance; to external relations; library services; research production and dissemination; and student life. At the same time, the "actual effects" of new technologies in recent decades have not always measured up to the "sweeping expectations" that have characterized their arrival on the scene. The ICT revolution has presented a broad and complex set of costs and benefits for higher education, yet there remains a great deal of uncertainty about how these effects may play out over time and across very diverse regions of the world.

Key Terminology and Definitions

A wide range of (often overlapping) terms and definitions are employed in the discussion of distance education and educational technology, particularly with the advent of many new technologies in recent years. Even for experts deeply involved in this topic, it is extremely difficult to get firm a grasp on the varied terminology. Indeed, it has been noted that there are:

> more than 20 terms which describe the employment of the new technologies in education, such as: Internet mediated teaching, technology-enhanced learning, web-based education, online education, computer-mediated communication (CMC), telematics environments, e-learning, virtual classrooms, I-Campus, electronic communication, information and communication technologies (ICT), cyberspace learning environments, computer-driven interactive communication, open and distance learning (ODL), distributed learning, blended courses, electronic course materials,

hybrid courses, digital education, mobile learning, and technology enhanced learning.

Meanwhile, the terms *borderless, cross border, transnational,* and *international* education have become fashionable with the increasingly international reach of distance providers and new educational technologies, which also serves to highlight many interesting complexities that relate to educational delivery across national borders.

One way to simplify this discussion to some degree is to focus on what may arguably be the umbrella terms of e-learning and distance education. These terms are often used interchangeably, but their conflation is not always accurate or appropriate, given that many applications of ICT represent more "technologically clever ways of replicating traditional, face-to-face education models" than they do innovative distance models.

Guri-Rosenblit asserts that e-learning and distance education are decidedly "not the same thing". E-learning "refers to any type of learning using electronic means of any kind (TV, radio, CD-ROM, DVD, mobile phone, personal organizer, Internet, etc.)". Furthermore, e-learning is interpreted as "a relatively new phenomenon" used "for a variety of learning purposes that range from supplementary functions in conventional classrooms to full substitution of the face-to-face meetings by online encounters".

By contrast, distance learning involves any effort that does not require students to assemble in a particular location but instead "reaches out to students wherever they live or wish to study". Distance education can therefore be understood more as a "method of delivery than an educational philosophy," while "distance is not a defining characteristic of e-learning". Meanwhile, the terms "dual" or "mixed-mode" education capture the idea of using face-to-face and ICT instructional tools in conjunction with one another, which is an increasingly common approach taken by many higher education providers.

The speed of innovation and the experimental nature of many applications of technology to the higher education sector add another layer of complexity to the efforts to develop a common language around these activities. This "Tower of Babel Syndrome" shows no immediate signs of being resolved.

Manifestations of ICTs in Higher Education

A wide range of ICT elements have been deployed in higher education over the last decade. Notable applications include databases, e-mail, Web sites, social networking tools (such as chat rooms, bulletin boards, and discussion boards), blogs (which are essentially Web sites featuring ongoing posts of information, ideas, commentaries, and other content, wikis ("a page or collection of Web pages designed to enable anyone who accesses it to contribute or modify content", Real Simple Syndication (known commonly by its acronym RSS, for subscriptions to online content from preferred sources), podcasts, online videos, and instant messaging, among others.

Particularly (but not exclusively) in the world's most developed economies, ICTs are ubiquitous in the higher education sector and constitute a basic part of institutional infrastructure. In the last decade, the presence of these technologies within tertiary education has expanded exponentially, and touched virtually all dimensions of the higher education enterprise. Electronic databases house student, staff, and administrative records, as well as course and library materials.

University Web sites situate institutions both globally and locally, providing a public image that can be accessed from anywhere in the world, at any time, and serving as an informational crossroads for all members of the community interested in engaging with the institution. ICT resources-like e-mail, instant messaging, and online social networking spaces-provide avenues for academic collaboration, joint research, and personal and professional networking.

Computer laboratories give students and staff access to hardware and software for coursework and research. Continuously available wireless networks and remote-access library databases have altered the notions of time and place for work and study on campuses. Networked classrooms, equipped with a range of audio and visual equipment, have expanded the range of materials that may be introduced to students and the methods by which information and ideas can be shared.

The open educational resources (OER) movement (a term adopted at a UNESCO meeting in 2002 was famously initiated in 2001 by the Massachusetts Institute of Technology in the United States with its Open Courseware initiative. Since that time, development and use of OER has picked up significant momentum, making notable inroads onto the agendas of the higher education sectors in less-developed countries. OER provide free access to courses, curricula, and pedagogical approaches not available locally. And finally, various combinations of online and virtual resources have laid a most important foundation for the expansion of the distance-education sector in the last decade.

The extent to which new technologies and digital applications are implemented, however, differs importantly across national and institutional contexts. Unfortunately, in the face of a very real "digital divide" between richer and poorer countries and institutions, the capacity for implementation often appears to be inversely proportional to the perceived need and strong desire for access to these resources.

At the institutional level, for example, elite, resource-rich research universities with ample means to access and support state-of-the-art technologies may choose not to employ technology in ways that dramatically expand access, given their missions to serve small numbers of carefully selected, high-performing students and scholars. At the other end of the spectrum, large distance-teaching institutions around the world are eager to employ ICT to expand access, but are hampered by resource-infrastructure deficiencies.

This analysis plays out at the national level, as well. In many developing countries, new technologies are often considered the key to realizing successful cost-effective strategies for increased access to higher education. Yet, there are enormous costs and difficulties embedded in the reliance on ICT. Hardware, software, technical support, training, and continual upgrades are all expensive. And the effective deployment of new technologies in countries where even reliable access to electricity is uncertain complicates matters even further.

For many of the world's developing countries, some people argue that the more traditional "industrial model of distance education still provides a much cheaper and more feasible possibility [for expanding access to higher education] than trying to adopt the new digital technologies". The reliance on "older broadcast technologies such as radio and television" is perceived as less attractive and innovative by many but may provide better and more effective penetration into relevant communities. The fact that the regions of Africa, the Middle East, and Latin America/Caribbean constitute just 17.2

percent of the world's Internet users highlights the key underlying issue of technology infrastructure and access in the developing world.

ICT Promises and Pitfalls

One of the most notable aspects of the ICT revolution over the last decade is the degree to which excitement about new innovations has failed, in many respects, to meet highly optimistic expectations. It has been suggested that this disconnect between hopes around ICT and what they have proven capable of delivering hinges on several false assumptions that were highly pervasive during the initial ICT "craze" of the 1990s. Key among these erroneous beliefs were that

(1) time and space were globally problematic in higher education;

(2) that the desire to broaden access was essentially universal;

(3) that the advantages of the new technologies coming out were self-evident;

(4) that there was no significant difference between accessing information and constructing knowledge in higher education;

(5) that contemporary students of traditional university age were naturally inclined to like and respond well as learners to emerging ICT; and

(6) that the purveyors of the new technologies could not fail to achieve economies of scale and make profits on their innovative products and services.

Indeed, in each of these areas, the last decade has shown that realities on the ground across the globe have been much more complex and that higher education has been less easily prone to penetration by ICTs than previously imagined-particularly as concerns teaching and learning. Another significant factor explaining uneven degrees of ICT acceptance and usage has to do with "cultural and political differences" between countries. The failures of the University of Phoenix (transplanted from the United States to the United Kingdom) and the Open University (which attempted to bring a British distance learning option to the United States), provide interesting examples of such challenges.

Still, the innovative technologies that have emerged in recent years have had a real impact on tertiary education across the globe, presenting the sector with an enormous range of opportunities along with some significant challenges. The ICT explosion does hold the promise of breaking down barriers of time, space, and privilege; lowering costs; and enabling collaboration and creativity in teaching, learning, and research. Particularly in the world's wealthier countries, there has been great progress in these areas. In other parts of the world, however, the penetration of ICT into higher education has exacerbated the gap between knowledge producing "centers" and knowledge-consuming "peripheries".

The world's poorest countries are increasingly left behind as information production and dissemination moves down technological pathways to which they have limited or no access. Everywhere enormous financial strains have been placed on institutions and systems trying to equip themselves for the Information Age and then keep up with subsequent innovation. It is extremely costly, for example, to train and compensate skilled staff using new technologies; provide access to expensive online journals and databases; and assure the security of electronically stored data. There are also very real financial and moral/ethical challenges embedded in the process of dealing appropriately with the dangerous waste generated by obsolete computer hardware and other components used in e-learning.

Perhaps most fundamental to higher education, in most parts of the world there has been a profound and pervasive disconnect between employing new ICTs and truly leveraging them to enhance quality, particularly in terms of teaching and learning. The Information Age arguably requires the strenuous reinforcement of certain basic skills-including reading and writing-along with more advanced skills, like problem identification, problem solving, and the ability to engage in effective "complex communication" with others. In a "brave new world" of limitless choice and vast amounts of data circulating freely in cyberspace, tertiary-level educators have new kinds of responsibilities. Among these are the need to foster disciplined thinking, "navigate... ethical dilemmas effectively and positively," cope with a sometimes overwhelming array of choices, and encourage creativity and initiative in the learning process.

Meanwhile, research indicates that, even in the face of incredibly powerful and innovative technologies, teachers in both developed and developing countries "remain central to the learning process". To effectively harness the potential of new technologies, however, teaching staff require support, training, and guidance, to learn new skills and determine how best to incorporate technology into teaching strategies that make sense for individual teaching styles and student learning needs.

Distance Education Providers and Approaches

Distance learning has been in existence for generations, but the sector has been transformed significantly over time with the advancement and application of new technologies. Beginning with mail correspondence in the early 20th century, distance education then benefited from the emergence of radio and TV platforms, followed by CD-ROM technology some two decades ago. The distance-learning landscape was then dramatically expanded and transformed by the introduction of the Internet, along with such key applications as e-mail and electronic messaging. ICTs have exponentially boosted the potential of distance education to reach enormous new pools of students. It has also allowed for real growth in numbers and types of providers, curriculum developers, and modes of delivery, as well as innovations in both pedagogical approaches and content.

Today, print and electronic options are both employed around the world, and the delivery of open and distance education is typically understood to fall into two distinct categories-synchronous and asynchronous. Synchronous delivery involves all participants at the same time, while asynchronous delivery implies engagement by the various parties involved at different times.

There is a recognized typology of institutions providing distance education. These include single-mode institutions, dual-mode institutions, consortia, and nontraditional providers. Single-mode institutions focus exclusively on providing distance education, while dual-mode institutions offer a combination of distance education and more traditional face-to-face course and/or program options. Consortia are comprised of two or more institutions working collaboratively to provide distance learning. Finally, nontraditional providers may include entities such as multinational corporations, nongovernmental organizations and development partners, as well as governments. Profit-making affiliates of traditional not-for-profit educational institutions may also be considered a part of this group. The scope of actors involved in distance-education provision was especially extensive at the height of the information-technology bubble in the late 1990s and 2000, when many new actors jumped into the arena. Examples run the gamut from Harvard University (an elite private institutions and arguably the world's most prestigious university) to third-tier institutions such as technical and community colleges; from initiatives sanctioned by regional bodies with very targeted areas of focus, such as access expansion for small states of the Commonwealth, to the UN-sanctioned Global Virtual University, and government-supported entities such as the Syrian Virtual University.

For several decades, the sector has been dominated to a certain extent by large-scale "open" universities. The Indira Gandhi National Open University (IGNOU) in India, for example, describes itself as the largest university in the world, with:

> nearly 2 million students in India and 33 other countries through... twenty-one Schools of Study and a network of 59 regional centers, more than 2300 Learner Support Centers and around 52 overseas centres. The University offers 175 Certificate, Diploma, Degree and Doctoral programs, comprising around 1500 courses...

In Africa, the University of South Africa claims to be the continent's premier distance-learning institution, with a total student body "in excess of 265,000," as well as "excellent infrastructure, cutting-edge technology, innovative learner support systems and a significant regional presence in South and southern Africa". Another example in Africa is the African Virtual University (AVU). Initially launched in Washington, DC in 1997 as a World Bank project, it is now an independent intergovernmental organization, headquartered since 2002 in Kenya. Over the last 10 years, the African Virtual University has acquired the largest network of open, distance, and e-learning institutions in Africa. It works across borders and language groups in Anglophone, Francophone, and Lusophone Africa, present in over 27 countries with more than 50 partner institutions.

Meanwhile, the University of Phoenix in the United States claims to be the largest private university in North America, with more than 100 degree programs at the associate's, bachelor's, master's, and doctoral levels. It boasts nearly 200 locations, largely in the United States, Canada, and Puerto Rico. Founded in 1976, the University of Phoenix is a for-profit corporate entity owned by Apollo Group with enrolments of more than

250,000 students who may choose from exclusively online or campus-based learning options, or a "FlexNext" approach that combines both formats. Megauniversities-"with over 100,000 students and using largely distance learning methods"-are found in a wide variety of countries. China was home to three such institutions as of 2003, including the Shanghai TV University. The Korea National University, the Open University in the United Kingdom, Spain's National Distance Education University, and Turkey's Anadolu University also belong to the megauniversities "club" around the world.

The rationales for engagement in distance-education activities are as varied as the actors themselves. Motivations include revenue generation, broadening and expanding access, improving educational quality, and raising institutional profiles. It is extremely difficult to calculate the numbers of students engaged in distance education worldwide. However, the existence of nearly two-dozen megauniversities, a number of which boast having over one million students, speaks to a quantitatively significant phenomenon.

Distance-Education Opportunities and Benefits

Distance education presents important opportunities for the higher education sector globally and has already provided a range of benefits in different parts of the world over the last decade. The advantages of this nontraditional form of higher education delivery may be most immediate and apparent to those systems that have struggled to meet high demands for access-a common phenomenon across much of the developing world, in particular. In Africa, for example, despite considerable growth in enrolment numbers in the last decade, the gross enrolment ratio there hovers around 5 percent, with considerable disparity by country and subregion. Some countries have been expanding access quite aggressively.

In Ethiopia, for example, more than a dozen universities were established within a short period of time, and the country recently unveiled a plan to build 10 more. However, even with this kind of commitment to expansion, the economic state of many developing countries is such that they are far from capable of growing the traditional higher education system quickly enough to satisfy the rising demand. Thus, in the absence of sufficient local and/or traditional providers-and against a backdrop of increasing demand for higher education, owing to the knowledge-driven global economy-alternative approaches to higher education provision are extremely attractive and in some cases really the only viable option. Expanding access to tertiary education through distance education has therefore never been more crucial, and interest in this area has never been more significant. Indeed, a good number of flagship universities and newly established private institutions are already actively involved in the delivery of distance education in a number of countries. For instance, the University of Ghana, considered a flagship university in Africa, started a distance-education program in 2007, while in Ethiopia a number of newly established colleges are also distance-education providers.

Distance education is also of particular interest to small and more isolated countries, which can be severely limited in their abilities to expand traditional brick-and-mortar institutions. Even if they have sufficient resources, it may not be very cost effective for such systems to invest heavily in this area, particularly in light of the constant need to upgrade facilities and technology.

In addition, the ephemeral nature of knowledge in today's fast-paced global information society means that many developments in key fields-such as economics, finance, the sciences, and technology-are extremely fast paced, while the life span of innovative products is quite short. The demands inherent in building and retooling new programs to keep up with these developments may make it more desirable to access programming via distance-education methods.

Of course, all of this does not mean that well-resourced small countries cannot themselves become major providers of distance education. In 2000, the government of the Indian Ocean island nation of Mauritius proposed a plan for developing the country into a "knowledge hub," with building its capacity to provide distance learning as one of its eight strategic initiatives.

In many countries around the world, the need for continuous learning and ongoing skill upgrades has become increasingly apparent. In countries where nations struggle to cater to the traditional-age cohort of 18-to-24-year-olds, the challenge of providing lifelong learning opportunities for broad swathes of the adult population via traditional delivery modes of delivery is daunting. In many places around the world, distance education can and has already played a growing role in filling this gap. Much of the appeal of distance education today is attributed to its ability to accommodate the needs of a wide variety of learners.

By allowing many different kinds of individuals to access information, materials, and coursework remotely, distance education provides great flexibility and versatility and can draw in an enormous range of individuals who might otherwise be unable to physically attend classes-ranging from students who are fully employed, those located far from educational centers, women who are attempting to balance family and school commitments, and even the incarcerated. ICTs have made learning possible virtually anytime and anywhere and in the world, taking flexibility in higher education program delivery to the highest level.

Risks and Challenges of Distance Education

Despite the wide range of benefits that can be derived from distance education, there are also a number of very real risks and challenges that can accompany this mode of educational delivery. One of the most difficult challenges facing distance education currently relates to quality assurance. As distance education markets expand and the importance and acceptance of the sector in higher education circles rises, the emergence of questionable, even fraudulent, providers is cause for growing concern.

The liberalization of the global economy, which is eliminating business and commercial barriers around the world, has made it increasingly possible- and lucrative-for educational providers to operate across borders. These providers are often not answerable to the jurisdictions of the national regulatory systems of users, nor are they fully controlled in the countries where they operate or from which they hail.

Even in systems where quality-assurance and accreditations agencies function well, they often lack clear mandates on matters of program delivery beyond regional or national borders. In addition, most countries have limited resources and regulatory backing to cope with the emerging issues related to distance education, track fraudulent entities and diploma mills, and take appropriate measures to curb unscrupulous practices and providers.

The widely reported case of fraud and diploma-mill activity by the now defunct Saint Regis University is a prime example of how a bogus operation can leverage the relatively thin oversight of distance education-even in a country like the United States, which boasts a fairly robust tradition of quality assurance and accreditation compliance. The expansion and growth of private distance-education providers has also brought with it new kinds of accrediting institutions, often driven by financial gain. This makes the task of identifying legitimate institutions, programs, and providers even more difficult.

Increasingly, distance-education delivery depends on the newest innovations in ICTs. The fundamental challenge here is that access to ICTs and the Internet varies widely around the world. Teledensity-"a term commonly used to describe the number of telephone lines per some unit of the population" (Harvard University Center for International Development, n.d), which can also shed light on the degree to which a community or nation has access to computers, the Internet, and e-gadgets-is not uniform around the world and is an important indicator of the immense divide between "haves" and "have-nots" across the globe. Even in contexts with relevant technologies and infrastructure, barriers still exist, given that the cost of access for those with fewer resources is considerably higher than for those with the necessary financial means.

The disparity in ICT quality and access is seen not only across regions and national borders, but also across rural and urban settings within the same country. Phone and Internet access, power supply (and reliability), and requisite infrastructure are often more available in the main urban areas. Not coincidentally, the largest student populations in distance education still reside in major cities, creating a notable imbalance in distance- (and higher) education access within countries.

The availability of ICTs does not necessarily translate into access to technology resources for education, of course. Numerous regulatory, administrative, technical, and logistical challenges hamper the use and deployment of such technologies. For instance, many developing countries experience a shortage of technical expertise-and/or resources to support it-that is much needed in such areas as user-end support and in the prevention and of e-malfeasance, such as virus attacks, hacking, and phishing. Furthermore, managing available resources, such as bandwidth, has also become more of a challenge. As distance education becomes increasingly dependent on the Internet such issues will continue to hamper the field.

Another important challenge for distance education, particularly in terms of its international dimensions, relates to language. English has emerged as the dominant language of scholarship, research, business, and diplomacy. As a consequence, English-speaking countries (such as the United States, United Kingdom, Canada, and Australia) have been well positioned to operate in the distance-education arena far beyond their national borders. Tertiary programming, using English-language materials and/or instruction, has effectively infiltrated many parts of the world that have traditionally delivered higher education in languages other than English. This trend of breaking down old patterns of higher education delivery that were long driven by colonial language ties has been rapidly accelerated by the advent of high-tech ICTs.

It is also important to recognize that distance education thrives when it can operate in an economy of scale. Distance education curricula and programs are often designed in standard formats for use by a large and diverse set of learners. To a great extent, these products are developed in and marketed by providers situated in the more developed countries of the North. Curricula, program design, methodological approaches, and content are all affected in this process, and developing countries-which are home to a large and growing percentage of end-users of distance-education programs and materials-have little choice but to accept educational products that often do not adequately address local needs, interests, or values.

Key Considerations for the Future

The continual introduction of innovations in educational technologies and the evolving nature of the distance-education enterprise around the world make it difficult to predict future developments. However, several issues bear thoughtful consideration moving forward, especially in terms of the way that institutions look and behave. For example, some suggest that traditional campuses will likely see a degree of qualitative transformation by existing more "on a digital platform of shared information, materials, and experience" that will allow for improved access and quality. A greater reliance on cooperative arrangements, such as consortia, to leverage resources and share costs inherent in implementing ICTs in higher education, may occur. And more and different kinds of dual-mode universities-employing both ICTs and traditional program delivery methods-may emerge.

It has to date been quite difficult to consolidate findings related to the use and effectiveness of ICTs in teaching and learning, but a critical mass of scholars, practitioners, and policymakers seems ready to push for progress in this area. Extracting meaningful research findings on the effects of technology on teaching andlearning has been hampered by the speed of innovation, which often renders study results obsolete as new technologies replace old ones. However, there is an especially important need in the current environment-with the growing focus on lifelong learning and ongoing professional education and (re)training-to provide real flexibility in teaching and learning within higher education, and research is needed to guide these efforts.

And although ICTs have clearly been an incredibly important tool for academics in their research activities, their effects on teaching have been less clear. Furthermore, it appears quite important for teaching staff to receive support and guidance in terms of implementing technology in their teaching activities. Finding ways to do this that are both contextually appropriate and cost effective, looms large on the horizon.

Additionally, making sense of emerging technologies and the ways that these will effect both distance education and other aspects of the academic enterprise are extremely important agenda items for the future. One key example here is the role that m-learning-that is, applications that can be run on mobile phones and other mobile platforms-may play in the coming years. There are exciting possibilities for the ways in which m-learning may open up access in some of the world's poorest countries, where Internet access is most limited and unreliable.

Research out of the Philippines, and South Africa, is laying the groundwork for more exploration in this area. Meanwhile, so-called "immersive education" offers one window on the next generation of educational technologies, focused on virtual and simulation technologies, 3-D graphics and interactive applications, and gaming approaches. Although immersive education applications are potentially very exciting, special attention will need to be paid to how these very expensive cutting-edge tools can be made accessible to under-resourced countries and institutions.

Finally, strengthening capacity in regard to technology issues and open and distance learning is an extremely important objective in a global context characterized by profound inequity. Notable here are such resources as UNESCO's Open and Distance Learning Knowledge Base, and the 19 UNESCO chairs and four University Twinning and Networking initiatives around the world, all focused on open and distance learning topics. These represent important multilateral efforts that hold the promise of not only moving the international discourse forward in this area, but also sustaining quality research and sound policymaking practices.

ICTs and distance education are different but tightly interconnected aspects of higher education that have come to play an increasingly important role in postsecondary policymaking and practice over the last decade. The need to serve larger and more diverse populations of students, in different ways and over a much longer period of their lives, is exerting tremendous pressures on higher education systems and institutions the world over. Distance education has long been a cost-effective and flexible method for drawing in underserved students.

ICTs and related technologies have vastly expanded the potential to deliver postsecondary education at a distance but have also exacerbated inequalities within and across countries. Meanwhile, quite apart from distance education, innovative educational technologies have transformed many institutions around the world-academically and administratively-while creating new linkages and new chasms between rich and poor countries and higher education systems.

Many of the enthusiastic promises held out by early adopters of ICTs-particularly those that touted the democratizing effects of the new technologies at a global level-have either failed to materialize over the last decade or have only been realized in limited and piecemeal ways. There has been an uneven adoption of (and extraction of benefits from) ICTs in higher education around the world, due in large part to the same kinds of resource inequities that vex many other aspects of the higher education enterprise globally. Contextually based needs assessment, significant capacity building (in human, material, and economic terms), relevant research, and ongoing review and support from key stakeholders will be critically important in most parts of the world if ICTs are to deliver on many of the promises they hold, and distance education is to enable the access and flexibility that is so critically needed in many quarters.

References

Arafeh, S. 2004. *The Implications of Information and Communications Technologies for Distance Education: Looking Toward the Future*, Arlington, VA, SRI International.

Castells, M. and Hall, P.G. 1994. *Technopoles of the world: the making of twenty-firstcentury industrial complexes*. London and New York, Routledge.

McIntosh, C. and Varoglu, Z. 2005. *Perspectives on Distance Education. Lifelong Learning & Distance Higher Education*, Paris, UNESCO and Commonwealth of Learning.

Ramos, A., Trinona, J. and Lambert, D. 2006. Viability of SMS technologies for nonformal distance education. J. Baggaley (ed.), *Information and Communication Technology for Social Development*, Jakarta, Indonesia, ASEAN Foundation.

7

Research and Innovation

Research and innovation (the production of new knowledge) are closely linked with the teaching function within the modern university. Both research and innovation, valuable in their own right, have achieved greater legitimacy in society through the use of new knowledge for economic and social development and the employment of university graduates in strategic positions in the private and public sectors. Research has been and continues to be an extremely important contribution of the university to the larger society.

The three missions of the modern university-teaching, research, and public service-live in constant tension with each other at different levels. Governments have tended to set priorities for different kinds of higher education institutions, often designating "teaching only" and "research only" institutional types. Universities, to the extent that they enjoy autonomy to develop their own plans and programs, must often make hard choices in setting priorities and allocating resources, in cases where they retain multiple missions.

Teaching and research do not necessarily live happily together within the same organization. In many universities professors conduct research while actively teaching classes, although these functions are often dispersed and tend to be poorly integrated. Some units (i.e., disciplinary departments) organize teaching, while others (i.e., laboratories, centers, and institutes) manage research infrastructure, research staff, and projects. Other offices deal with knowledge transfer and relations with the community. Research and research training are an intrinsic part of the education process of graduate students-in particular at the doctoral level-but are seldom incorporated into undergraduate programs. Meanwhile, professional and vocational programs traditionally have made better use of accumulated knowledge and tend to emphasize practical applications of knowledge over research training, although this is changing in both new and old professional fields.

The academic profession, whose ranks are largely nurtured by research-trained professionals, is facing an increasingly differentiated labor market. There is now a tendency toward separate "teaching only" and "research only" positions compared with the traditional "teaching and research" position. "Public service" is often included in academic job descriptions and sometimes influences the way professors allocate their time.

A vast literature deals with these changes all over the world. Most recently mass demand for higher education has driven the expansion of "teaching only" institutions and programs since they require less investment. The trend is toward more differentiation between institutions. Teaching-only private institutions, increasingly with distance education facilities, have expanded access in many countries. In Europe and North America, first-cycle (or short-cycle) instructional programs offered by smaller institutions have absorbed much of the demand at lower cost.

Teaching-only institutions attend to the needs of a highly heterogeneous student body and nurture capacity for specialized functions but also help contain public spending on higher education. With new goals in mind, governments often attempt to reorganize, merge, or tinker in a variety of ways with preexisting institutions, assigning specific functions to each of them. The underlying assumption is that the costs of research, teaching, and service activities can be planned and managed more efficiently at higher levels. This assumption usually meets with considerable resistance from institutions and the academic communities.

At the same time that countries are accommodating mass enrolment at the postsecondary level, demand for graduate degrees is increasing as well. Graduate education, however, traditionally involves at least some research training and tends (traditionally) to be taught by professors engaged in research. This is particularly true in disciplinary master's and doctoral degrees where the next generation of professors and researchers is prepared. But this is also increasingly the case with the growing number of professional master's programs and doctoral programs.

Mass systems cannot ignore the importance of the teaching/research link, but many challenges are emerging. The first issue is finding the correct balance of public/private investment to insure that basic research continues, that research is supported in new fields of study, and that research continues in applied fields. The second issue is to find appropriate strategies for the rational allocation of limited resources. Yet another challenge is to integrate the research function more broadly across the university. Cultivating more research capacity in the developing world is also critically important. Finally, the dramatic expansion of "teaching-only" institutions (whether de facto or by design) distances more and more students from exposure to research.

The Knowledge Economy

An important trend has been the spectacular growth of scientific and technological research that forms the underpinning of the knowledge economy. "Big science" has not always favored university-based research. In the past, governments and industry in many countries have steered research funding to dedicated government institutions. In recent decades, however, basic and applied research have prospered in university laboratories as well as in industry, with isolated research institutes losing ground. New fields of study being developed at universities, such as biotechnology, genomics, nanotechnology, optical technology, and information science promise new research that will offer practical applications for industry. Government support to university-based research has increased in recent years to encourage these projects.

Governments worldwide are the largest supporters of academic science, which increasingly takes place within higher education, but private funding of university-based research has also increased. However, large-scale public investment in laboratories, equipment, and expensive research programs requires an appropriate institutional base and tends to be made selectively. Despite the exponential increase in university-based research in recent years, funding for scientific research has tended to be concentrated in a relatively small number ofi institutions. Additionally, the shift from block-grant funding of public universities that covers teaching and research to competitive funding for project-specific awards, which also provide funds for equipment, laboratories, or libraries, has contributed to the emergence of the modern research university. In the new knowledge economy, the boundaries between academic and applied research have become more blurred, leading university researchers to develop closer and more interdependent relations with industry.

The so-called "triple helix" of university/government/industry linkages has resulted in important organizational changes within the university. In some countries and universities, special offices and positions have materialized and prospered to encourage new "entrepreneurial" thinking and to generate new income streams for the university. Thus, the strengthening ofi the research function is clearly contributing to organizational changes that go with increased research capacity.

Although these changes have supported a stronger research role for the modern university, they have also encouraged further differentiation between institutions-research-intensive versus teaching and research or teaching-only universities-and within them.

System-wide Policy and the University

The notion of system-wide design-with individual institutions becoming embedded in national frameworks and regulated through system rather than local institutional planning-has become a major policy trend worldwide during the last few decades. A top-down approach translates into differentiated funding for teaching and research, varying degrees of autonomy to develop research and teaching programs and to award degrees, and changed rules for faculty recruitment, assessment, and promotion.

A recent examination of the relationship between teaching and research in European university systems found three different patterns (Schimank and Winnes, 2000). The first type includes situational relations, with different segments of the university devoted to teaching and/or research. Still declaring the unity of teaching and research as a guiding principle, faculty are assumed to do both and paid accordingly from government block grants that provide basic funding. Within this system, the pressures of enrolment growth and restricted government funding have inclined faculty to dedicate more time to teaching, with a negative impact upon research. Germany and Italy were primary examples of this kind of approach, but things are starting to change in both countries.

A second pattern reflects differentiation of roles, funding, and institutional focus. Early examples of this dynamic were found in Sweden, the United Kingdom, and Norway, and (more recently) in the Netherlands. In these countries, undergraduate teaching is entrusted to lecturers, while professors and research staff are allowed to concentrate on research, which (by policy or de facto) is primarily conducted among a reduced number of institutions.

Finally, the third type is characterized by a strict differentiation between research and teaching institutions-funded and organized independently of each other. This pattern is evident in France but also in many other parts of the world, particularly the countries of the former Soviet bloc. Traditionally, research played a secondary role in universities in these countries and was mainly related to graduate training of young scientists and scholars.

Latin America reflects slightly different patterns. Research is either conducted at separate institutions, as in the third pattern above, or (more often) is concentrated in a few elite (almost always public) universities. Research activity is often further concentrated within the universities in separate centers remote from the instructional activity that supports first-cycle university and professional degree programs.

At the National Autonomous University of Mexico (UNAM)-the largest producer of PhDs in that country-graduate teaching and research are located within so-called research institutes, physically and administratively separated from the *facultades* where undergraduate and professional training takes place. The Center of Research and Advanced Studies, the second-largest producer of research in Mexico is a separate research and graduate training branch of the National Polytechnic Institute.

The concentration of research at a few institutions, often of the "multiversity" type, is reflected in the large numbers of publications that originate from this small group. For example, one public university is responsible for 37 percent of all research papers in Chile; similarly, one university produces 30 percent of the papers in Mexico; a single university produces 25 percent in Brazil; and just one institution is responsible for 18 percent in Argentina. In Chile, for instance, universities are the main actor in science production, with the five oldest institutions responsible for almost 80 percent of the research carried out in the country.

Allocation Strategies and Hierarchies

Research universities worldwide sit at the top of the higher education hierarchy. They are able to concentrate resources and power and often have an influential role within the education system, thanks to the prestige and influence of their faculty and graduates. Government-funding patterns contribute to the status of these institutions. Governments typically reward, with additional funding, those institutions with a proven record of research output and research management. Most governments concentrate their research investment in relatively few institutions. In many countries-including Germany and France, but also China, Russia, some eastern European countries-these institutions have historically played a leading role in international scientific research.

Most European countries, as well as Japan and Canada, have funded academic research through general-fund block grants, with these funds accounting for 50 percent or more of total government R&D support to the universities. The current trend is to allocate research funding to universities on a competitive basis to make more efficient use of research funds and target problem-oriented or industry-oriented research programs. Between 1981 and 2003, the percentage of research funding through general university funds dropped from 78 percent to 65 percent in the 16 OECD countries for which information is available. Governments have balanced the decrease in research support by encouraging research centers to embark on collaborations with private companies.

Research

The United Kingdom has led the funding reform movement in Europe since the 1980s, linking research assessment with further research funding to concentrate efforts in the most productive departments. Germany, one of the more state-dependent higher education and research systems, is currently attempting to restructure its universities-a largely homogenous segment of public research and teaching institutions-through a much more focused research-funding policy. For the European Union as a whole, the share of higher education expenditure on R&D as a percent of the total R&D

spending has increased consistently over the last few years and is currently larger than in the United States or Japan.

Among the new scientific powerhouses, China's policy since the late 1990s has also focused research support on a small number of universities. Specifically, China has provided special funding packages to build world-class universities. The funding packages from the central government-often with additional subsidies from municipal funds-are administered by the central university administration. Thus, it is a vertically managed, noncompetitive allocation based on high-level decisions about which institutions have the capacity to become research-intensive universities. In the words of Qiang Zha:

> Chinese higher education institutions are being structured in a hierarchical way according to their functions and goals. On the top are the national elite universities that focus on research... They educate the majority of doctoral students, in addition to master's and bachelor students. They are designated as the ''national team'' to move China's innovation capacity to a higher level and play a leading role in performing research activities that are of great importance to national development and security as well as collaborating in international research efforts. The universities at the second rank are oriented to both research and teaching, mainly educating master's and bachelor students, with doctoral students only in a few specific disciplines. The universities at the third rank are those that are fundamentally teaching oriented, training mainly undergraduates. Finally, down at bottom of the hierarchy is a new tier of institutions, the higher vocational college, providing only 2-3 year programs... The last two categories constitute the majority of China's higher education institutions, taking on most of the expansion and increasing their enrolment dramatically, while the enrolment expansion in the elitist universities has only been symbolic.

Many governments have found it difficult to rank institutions in terms of their research capacity as a basis for concentrating support. Block funding for research and teaching, usually justified on the grounds of the indissoluble link between these functions, is strenuously defended by the university professoriate in Europe, Latin America, and elsewhere. Retaining a research mission gives universities special status and privileges, not afforded to teaching-only and vocational schools (such as teacher-training institutions). Still, academic research production and government support remains largely concentrated among a handful of institutions although the "research-university model" is becoming the standard that most universities aspire to.

Trends for Hosting Basic and R&D

The strengthening of academic research worldwide has been a rather striking feature of the overall growth trend in scientific research during the last few decades. Among the rich countries (i.e., members of the OECD) the share of R&D carried out by higher education has increased at the expense of government institutes, and has grown even faster than R&D performed by industry.

Basic research has been identified as a special feature of academic research:

> In 2003, it accounted for about 18% of the gross domestic expenditures on R&D in the OECD area, up from 15% in 1981. The higher education sector represents less than one fifth of all R&D expenditures in the OECD area, but it carries out the bulk of basic research in most OECD countries. In 2003, on average, 54% of an OECD country's basic research was carried out in the higher education sector. And the government and higher education sectors accounted together for 82% of all basic research.

Among OECD countries, the early model of science and technology policy in support of fundamental research included both dedicated institutions with government support-such as the CNRS in France, the Max Planck institutes in Germany, the Consiglio Nazionale delle Richerche in Italy, the Consejo Superior de Investigaciones Científicas in Spain, and Riken in Japan-and university research. More recently, however, branches of former research-only institutes have moved to universities and over time have developed closer links to them.

In the developing world, scientific and technological research after World War II was largely a state-supported enterprise concentrated in separate government research institutes. "Big Science," whether in India, Brazil, or Argentina, or in the socialist countries following the example of the Soviet Union, was typically housed outside of the university, as was most applied research in fields such as agriculture and food production, public health, and industrial technology. This has changed quite radically since the 1990s with the downfall of the Soviet Union and of the Soviet-dominated Eastern European Bloc, although with sharp differences between countries.

> The shares of higher education and non-university academic research in Hungary and Estonia in the 80s and still in the early 1990s reflect the typical "socialist" science system with smaller university sectors and relatively large shares of nonuniversity academic research. In Estonia, the situation was

> extreme-the share of the governmental sectors exceeded that of the university sector. The situation dramatically changed in the course of the following ten years. The relation between the two sectors in Estonia very much resembled that of Finland in 2003. The industry sector was already present in 1993, but remained constant until 2003. The development in Hungary was slow, and reflects minor and less pronounced changes. Nonetheless, the data reflect a trend in the direction of the western model.

China straddles both models-continuing to support and develop independent research institutes while simultaneously investing heavily in university-based research. Public research institutes make (in absolute numbers) the second-largest contribution to international science. Enterprise research contributes only marginally to international publications, but it provides 6 percent of the content found in national publications. Hospitals are important producers of publications domestically, but not internationally.

In Brazil, independent research institutes are still important in terms of research production in applied fields such as public health and agriculture, but disciplinary research production is concentrated primarily in seven public universities. These universities were responsible for 60 percent of the internationally indexed research production coming out of Brazil. A similar pattern is found in Argentina, where the government was reluctant to fund university-based groups before the 1980s but has changed its policy quite dramatically since then.

The growth in university research capacity and output has been well documented. In the 1980s and 1990s, the number of university-based researchers increased about 7 percent a year within the OECD countries, and they produced about 82 percent of the world's scientific articles. The higher education sector devotes 64 percent of its R&D activities to basic research and is the only sector that is mainly devoted to it. Yet, the most distinctive feature of the modern university throughout the world during the last decade is the growing ties to industry for the production of new knowledge.

Since the 1970s the knowledge-production function of universities has become a source of both formal and informal collaboration with industry through contract research, cooperative research, consulting, networking, and increasingly through the mobility of research personnel between academia and industry. In the past, support for science was provided by governments in pursuit of national interests and identified with public enterprise and research institutes. There has been a clear shift, however, with university research more closely linked to private industry in many countries. The notion of a "third stream" of activities, or "third mission" of the university, is actually aligned with research capacity.

University-Industry Linkages

In 1980, only 20 universities in the United States housed their own office for patenting and licensing, but 112 more created them in the following two decades, with university research parks growing rapidly. Between 1980 and 2004, the number of patents issued to US universities increased from about 350 to about 3,300. Research universities, both private and public, now have large permanent bureaucracies to commercialize intellectual property and to turn research into profit centers. Universities in the United States-but not yet in most European countries-have consolidated these functions under high-level authorities within the university, with a technology-transfer office typically at the center of operations.

More recently, these offices have been transformed into technology-transfer complexes that include offices for industrial research, intellectual property, marketing and monitoring technology licensing, commercial development of start-up companies, research parks, business incubators, and venture capital funds. Start-up costs, however, are quite high, thus limiting the number of universities that can bear them. The top 100 research universities, performing some 80 percent of the total research carried out by US higher education, belong to this group. As in much of the world, the concentration of research funds among the top US research universities has remained steady over the last two decades, with only 5 of the top 20 institutions in 1986 not in the top 20 in 2006.

In Europe, government-funding patterns for university research have changed in recent years with a shift toward competitive problem-oriented or industry-oriented public programs. University researchers and research centers are encouraged to embark on collaborations with private companies including incentives to complement their research activities with technology-transfer activities. Still, very little reliable data are available on the phenomenon of university patenting, since most European public universities have lacked the necessary autonomy and administrative skill now routine at many US universities, and have (until recently) tended to resist rather than encourage faculty engagement in patenting activities or linking with industry.

Historically, continental European universities have left intellectual property rights in the hands of faculty and their idustry research partners without university involvement on the order of US and British patterns. In countries such as France and Italy large public laboratories and governmental agencies still dominate the public research system and retain control over intellectual property rights to results of publicly funded research. A recent comparative analysis shows that while in the United States universities and other nonprofit organizations retain almost 70 percent of academic patents filed by domestic inventors, in France and Italy fewer than 10 percent are retained. The "entrepreneurial university" with professional administrators to manage research funding, activity, and output may not be viable in many parts of the world, even when there is a strong research orientation.

Reform and Expansion of Graduate Education

The European model of doctoral training-which has influenced many other countries around the world-was, until recently, based mainly on independent research undertaken by the doctoral candidate with the advice and guidance of one supervisor, closely following the model of a master/apprentice relationship. Historically, only a select number of academically oriented students would pursue this option. The reform and expansion of graduate education, in particular at the doctoral level, has challenged this model. In a growing number of universities and countries the research activity of doctoral candidates is complemented by other forms of training.

A mix of different program designs and structures seems to be common practice in most countries, reflecting the need to increase the number of doctoral candidates and the disciplinary differences to be taken into consideration. Graduate schools modeled after those of US universities are becoming common in many developing countries, although they normally adapt to local institutional cultures and the persistence of long-cycle, professional degree programs in many cases.

Brazil adapted the US university model of a graduate school following the 1968 reforms there. Graduate programs have multiplied since the 1970s and are regularly evaluated, ranked, and financed by CAPES, a government agency in charge of enhancing the quality of the professoriate. The Brazilian system currently awards some 10,000 doctorates and 30,000 master's degrees each year, a 300 percent increase in 10 years. Graduate programs are ranked on the basis of their research productivity and then financed accordingly. Thus, those ranked in the higher categories receive the most fellowship support.

The CAPES evaluation system has led to extraordinary results in terms of the incorporation of research into the university in conjunction with developing graduate-level education. Some limitations apparent in the Brazilian context, however, most likely affect other systems as well. It has been difficult to apply the same basic evaluation criteria for research in science to the social sciences and humanities or applied fields. This highlights the difficulty of dealing with new interdisciplinary areas and taking into account the diversification of the graduate education system.

In the Republic of Korea, the Brain Korea 21 plan of 1998 promoted the concentration of research efforts within the traditional elite universities responsible for doctoral education. Top universities integrate research and graduate education and are measured by their research activity and production of doctorates; most of these top-tier universities have strong undergraduate programs as well.

Through the development of research-based doctoral programs, universities are increasingly involved in cooperation at the doctoral level with other sectors such as industry, independent research organizations, and government. Building strong links between universities with other sectors ultimately supports efforts to increase the transmission of knowledge as an impetus to innovation while retaining the important link between teaching and research. In the new code, the third mission feeds back into a more solid association between teaching and research within doctoral programs.

Research and the Academic Profession

The various changes in the world of academic research in recent years have resulted in markedly different kinds of academic careers. A study of academics affiliated with US university research centers clearly shows major changes in careers paths and productivity within the last couple of decades. "There is now a revolving door between industry and university research jobs". About half of the respondents had held one or more jobs in industry and almost that many began their careers in nonacademic jobs, either in industry or government, including a number who took their first academic job five or more years into their career. Researchers who spend more time in industry and receive more industry funding produce the largest number of patents but tend to have a lower numbers of publications.

In 2006, more than half of recent doctoral holders in science and engineering were employed in academia, but a substantial proportion of them had contract, research-only jobs, with limited terms. "Non-faculty ranks (i.e., full- and part-time adjunct faculty, lecturers, research associates, administrators, and postdocs) increased... 85% in sharp contrast to the 15% rise in the number of full-time faculty".

Research-only temporary appointments are heavily staffed in the United States by international researchers holding temporary visa permits. A recent study of contracted postdoctoral researchers in Australia highlights the insecurity associated with the research-only career and the scarcity of teaching/research positions available upon completion of short-term research fellowships.

It has been reported that since the 1980s there has been a significant increase in the proportion of positions in UK universities offered on a temporary or fixed-term basis, the largest number in research positions. The European Union directives are pursuing the goal of maximizing both flexibility and security in employment. In practice, however, according to some observers security remains a rhetorical gesture:

> Many, but not all, of the positions from which an "early career" researcher may access an academic career will involve at least a period of time on a fixed or temporary contract. In an increasing number of situations, researchers will find themselves negotiating various forms of teaching-intense contracts as graduate teaching assistants, hourly paid lecturers, technicians, or demonstrators, or will negotiate fixed-term teaching fellowships and lectureships. In other situations, particularly, but not exclusively in the sciences, the post will take the form ofi a fixed-term research-intensive position including doctoral scholarships, contract research positions, and research fellowships.

The research function within higher education has evolved in significant ways over the last decade. With a few notable exceptions, research activities traditionally took place outside ofi the university, but this is changing rapidly. Today, research is recognized as an important social role ofi the university, not just in the traditional disciplines and scientific fields, but also in interdisciplinary areas and emerging fields. A worldwide expansion of graduate programs and graduate enrolment has necessitated broader emphasis on research activities.

Research funding and activity are sources of international status and prestige. But research funding tends to be concentrated in elite institutions within countries but further concentrated in wealthier nations. However, a number of developing countries are pushing forward ambitious agendas to improve the amount and quality of their research activities. This is particularly evident in the cases of China, the Republic of Korea, Mexico, Brazil, and Chile.

Research is, to a large extent, dependent on public funding. At the same time, university-industry linkages are becoming more common and more important. These arrangements hold important potential for expanding the possibilities for research funding and capacity development; however, they also introduce not-insignificant dilemmas, particularly in terms of intellectual property rights and the revenue streams that commercialized technologies may generate.

University-industry linkages also provide important career-development options for researchers, who are moving more frequently than ever back and forth between academia and industry. Still, employment opportunities for researchers are not equally promising everywhere. In some contexts, the rapid expansion of the number of researchers has forced many graduates into short-term contract positions with limited career potential.

The increasing importance of-and widespread desire to focus more heavily on-research in many university settings has also highlighted significant variations and tensions relating to the balance of teaching and research responsibilities within institutions. Indeed, the evolving role of research in higher education has brought to the fore fundamental questions about mission, quality, and relevance as these pertain to the multiple stakeholders who look to tertiary education to meet key social and economic needs. In the coming years, a wider variety of institutions as well as national and regional systems of higher education will confront the challenge of finding an appropriate balance between the research imperative and the other critically important functions of tertiary education.

University-Industry Linkages

During the past several decades a significant change has been seen in the way policymakers regard higher education. In contrast to the past-when higher education was a part of social policy-today, it is increasingly regarded as a critical component of national and regional economic policy. The 1980s saw the first wave of change, particularly in the United States, where the Bayh-Dole Act was enacted to facilitate the role of universities in patent-based technology transfer, and various programs were instituted to strengthen university-industry relationships at the federal as well as state levels. Today, many countries have explicit metrics about university engagement with the economy; some, such as England and Scotland, have gone further and established dedicated government-funding streams based on such metrics. Interestingly, the meaning of "desirable engagement" continues to undergo change.

First, the notion of engagement is becoming broader-well beyond the initial focus on intellectual-property (IP) licensing or startups. A recent OECD review concluded that universities could serve a broad range of functions for regional economic development through education, research, as well as culturally related activities. The key policy question no longer consists of a narrow issue on how to make universities work better with industry but a broader one on what they can perform in innovation and economic development, particularly at a local level.

Second, today different universities have varying functions, based on their capabilities and industrial contexts. Research-intensive universities differ from teaching-focused institutions and today regions and nations see inputs from both types as important. Universities in developing countries are quite different from universities in industrialized contexts.

Third, universities are no longer expected to work in isolation; rather, they are perceived to be interactive players who work closely not only with industry but with community and government. They are an integral part of the national or regional innovation systems and a critical component of the evolving triple helix in which universities, government, and industry change their roles through interaction.

What caused this paradigm transformation? Changing global contexts provided powerful impetus. Ongoing globalization has made countries and regions even more aware of their competitiveness. National and regional governments increasingly rely on universities to become an anchor in their national and regional innovation systems, which is critical for their survival as knowledge economies. The paradigm change was in part prompted by the new understanding that scientific discoveries entail significant tacit knowledge. This means that not all scientific information can flow freely out of universities through publications; a certain high value is associated with direct contact with scientists. Geographical proximity matters, as well as face-to-face interactions. Technological innovation is advanced by having a two-way flow of information-not only of science from universities to industry but of technological know-how from industry to universities.

Intellectual-Property Licensing

When they first began to engage in these activities, many universities and governments had inflated expectations about licensing outcomes, particularly concerning revenues. Today a greater realism reveals that not all universities can expect successful licensing, unless they have significant research capacity in areas such as biomedical science, with a critical mass of professionals working in technology transfer offices, a large enough portfolio of patents, and a certain amount of luck at developing a few "blockbuster" patents which make a significant difference in revenue.

In the United States, many universities started licensing activities in the 1980s and 1990s, and the number of new entrants is no longer large. Recent years have also seen mixed signals in terms of performance. The net royalties rose from US$1 billion in 2000 to nearly US$1.6 billion in 2005 (National Science Board, 2008), while the US patents granted increased from 1,550 in 1995 to 3,450 in 2003 but declined to 2,944 in 2005 (though "pipeline" indicators such as numbers of disclosures and patent applications show upward trends). The Europeans, on the other hand, report healthy annual increases in the number of patents granted (24 percent) as well as license income (12 percent) between 2004 and 2007. In Japan, the number of patents owned by universities increased from 2,313 in 2003 to 4,225 in 2007, with licensing revenues rising by over 40 percent during the same period.

There remains significant diversity in the ownership of intellectual property. In the United States, the norm has been for universities to own rights; in Europe, one survey found that a quarter of institutions reported either individual or company ownership of university inventions (Arundel, et al., 2008). In Japan, the situation has been changing rapidly in favor of institutional ownership, and yet a large majority (on the order of 90 percent) of "university-related inventions" were still owned by companies or individual academics.

At universities in developing countries, patenting and licensing have been much less prominent generally, given fewer technologically mature companies and the underdeveloped legal environment to protect intellectual-property rights. However, there are some signs of change, particularly in emerging economies. China has already become one of the major players in patenting with its patent system introduced in 1985 and World Trade Organization membership since 2000. Patenting activities are also increasing rapidly in other emerging economies such as Brazil, Mexico, and India.

Indeed, Chinese universities have engaged in patenting from the beginning. In 1985, over half of all domestic patent applications came from public research institutions and universities (with 50 percent of that share belonging to universities). The proportion dipped in the mid-1990s when there was a general surge of patent applications in China, but it rose to nearly 40 percent in 2005.

Start-ups/Spin-offs

The creation of start-ups/spin-offs was another activity that has been emphasized in many OECD countries since the early days, motivated by the images of successful academic innovations that commercialized key scientific discoveries (particularly in biotechnology) from a handful of US research universities. According to the Association of University Technology Managers (AUTM), 555 start-up companies were created in the United States in 2007, up from 454 in 2000, with a cumulative total of 3,388 companies still operating. In Europe, one survey reported that the number of start-ups increased by 10 percent annually between 2004 and 2007 and that European universities have been more efficiently generating these operations based on funds invested in research than US universities. In Japan, the total number of university start-ups reached 1,773, tripling in six years. However, the simple numbers may not indicate much in terms of true success, as many countries are discovering. As a result, efforts are being undertaken to measure the performance of these companies (e.g., the number of jobs created).

Fewer reports have focused on start-ups in developing countries. Now, emerging accounts on China's experience provide valuable insights. Chinese universities have become active in creating enterprises since the late 1980s, even when they possessed little research capability. Though they are sometimes described as "spin-offs," these entities are significantly different from those in other countries, in that they are owned and managed by universities. Some of these companies have been spectacularly successful, with about 40 university enterprises already listed on stock markets in China and Hong Kong.

However, in contrast to start-ups in OECD countries, these Chinese companies do not tend to entail significant scientific discoveries; rather, the companies function as mechanisms, through which skilled personnel move from universities to the commercial sector. Given very limited technological capabilities of existing firms, creating enterprises was one of the few ways in which universities could contribute to the development of industrial capabilities.

It is not clear how long this practice of university enterprise will continue in China. Both the government and universities appear to be going through a rethinking process, as many enterprises have not been successful and managerial responsibilities are increasingly demanding, especially given more mature market conditions. While Chinese universities may transform the way they deal with their enterprises, particularly with respect to their management relations, without question their universities have been critical in the context of underdeveloped industry by injecting talent through new companies. In that sense, they are similar to that of Japanese universities, in the early phase of Japanese industrial development, where academics were crucial in the adaptation of Western technology.

Industry-Funded Research

The increasingly dominant norm of "open innovation" has led research-oriented companies to work closely with universities. This aspect, together with continued efforts of universities to work with industry, is reflected in the continued upward trend in industry-funded academic research in OECD countries; this share rose from 3 percent around 1980 to 6 percent in the

2000s. Although in individual countries, such as the United States and the United Kingdom, the share has declined since 2000; this was a result of recent increases in government research funding.

Countries with less-well-established research capabilities in universities, such as the Republic of Korea and China, have higher proportions of industry funding, mainly because the government funding of university research stands significantly lower. However, some developing countries, with a very limited industrial base, will be unable to pay for technical advice and research work meant to be conducted by universities.

Consulting

Consulting is a common activity undertaken by many academics worldwide. The operation is usually not visible or easy to monitor, given that many academics undertake such work privately. However, the overall significance has been increasingly acknowledged. For instance, in one survey of R&D managers, 32 percent rated consulting as very important for industrial R&D, as compared with 21 percent for contract research, 18 percent for patents, and 10 percent for licenses. In one survey of Massachusetts Institute of Technology professors, consulting was perceived as the major channel of knowledge transfer, followed by publications, graduates, and collaborative research; patents and licenses were deemed one of the least-important channels

The United Kingdom represents an unusual case in which efforts have been made to track the volume of academic consultancy, based on a strong move among universities to "formalize" private consultancy into institutional contracts. University records indicate that the consultancy volume has more than doubled even in real terms in the last six years (though some of this growth is likely attributable to the encouraging effects of the effort to institutionalize contracts), and today its size is significant at 37 percent of contract-based research incomes.

Role of Graduates

Highly skilled graduates are increasingly recognized as key inputs for successful industrial development in a given locality (Puuka and Marmolejo, 2008). In some cases, such as India and China, the large numbers of inexpensively trained graduates, particularly in science and engineering, has been crucial to meet the growing industrial demand. In Ireland and Finland, professional institutions were created as an alternative to conventional university education, which was seen to be unresponsive to industrial requirements. The institutional responsiveness was particularly essential when new disciplines such as computer science emerged and appeared to give countries a competitive edge, as was clear in the case of Ireland.

There is also some evidence that the development of the software industry was greatly facilitated by the early establishment of computer science as a new discipline in American universities. Universities, thus, not only contributed to key knowledge formation but also organized and delivered education programs to supply updated skills. Indeed, the American universities' ability to create and legitimate computer science as a new field was unparalleled by European or Japanese universities.

Responsive education also matters at advanced degree levels, such as master's and PhDs. In retelling the story of Silicon Valley in the United States, one of its founding fathers, Gordon Moore, cautioned against a simplistic overemphasis of Stanford University's role, yet acknowledged liberally the critical function the university played in responsively providing advanced-degree engineers and scientists in relevant fields.

Cooperative Education and Student Projects

An emerging literature describes specific student participation in work-study programs. The co-op education program at the University of Waterloo in Canada is regarded as innovative in three different ways. First, it helps firms identify appropriate graduates for recruitment. Second, students help firms acquire new skills and knowledge from the university. Third, the cooperative students and programs help "circulate" knowledge across local firms and the university. In problem-based learning activities at Aalborg University, in Denmark, student groups work on specific problems identified in local firms and community and government organizations; the program is reported to have similar benefits to the locality and the university as in the case of the University of Waterloo.

Similar examples exist in developing countries as well. In Bolivia, a majority of academic staff rated student internships as one of the most relevant contributions to industry.

Entrepreneurship Education

Much emphasis has been placed on entrepreneurship education in OECD countries. Today, a wide range of programs, from isolated courses on entrepreneurship to comprehensive practical programs, support the development of entrepreneurs, though the full programs are more difficult for universities to offer given the needed expertise and novelty of entrepreneurship as a field of research.

While not much data exist on the prevalence of different types of entrepreneurship education in universities, one Web-based review of 66 universities in sub-Saharan Africa found that over 80 percent offered some course in entrepreneurship, while four universities had specialized entrepreneurship centers.

The Global Entrepreneurship Monitor, an international group of researchers, has been conducting an annual global survey of entrepreneurship since 1999. As an indication of the growing prominence of entrepreneurship education the agency has introduced entrepreneurship training as a special topic in its 2008 survey. This preliminary analysis indicates generally positive relationships between entrepreneurship training and entrepreneurial attitude, aspirations, and activities.

The findings showed a wide variation in the proportion of 18-to-64 year-olds who received training in colleges and universities, from 1 percent in Turkey or 4 percent in the Republic of Korea, 13 percent in Chile and Peru, 16 percent in Finland, to 20 percent in Colombia. Fuller analysis as well as future survey results will no doubt provide a far better global picture of entrepreneurship education going forward.

Executive Education and Professional Development

Executive education is a critical activity in many business schools in North America (and increasingly elsewhere), and many universities also offer short-term, often tailored education programs for working adults. However, this, like consultancy, is another category of activity that is not usually monitored. Again, the United Kingdom provides an unusual example of surveying this activity annually; surveys find that university incomes from this type of contracted activities are also significant-at 62 about percent of contract research incomes.

Culture-Related Developments

Universities can help to set the social, cultural, and intellectual tone of a locality, as highlighted by a recent OECD review. Cultural events surrounding universities can make the locality more appealing to educated professionals and their employers, which is important given that a creative class of professionals is drawn to cultural and creative contexts. To this end, universities in the northeast of England worked actively to create a cultural quarter in Newcastle city center.

Some universities have also taken their responsibility for community development more seriously. The University of Pennsylvania in the United States embraced community development as part of its strategic mission. This was an unusual move for a globally-competitive research university that happened to be located in an economically-depressed urban neighborhood. This university is today engaged in a wide array of community initiatives ranging from economic development plans in collaboration with local communities, extensive support to local schools, and a variety of "service" programs including student projects and volunteering. In Finland, the Jyvaskyla University of Applied Science works with local stakeholders to bring the long-term unemployed back into working life.

Institutional Development for Boundary Spanning

To develop these capabilities significant institutional development has been initiated to strengthen "boundary-spanning" capacity. These changes include establishing appropriate policies and processes, administrative support units, internal organizational structure, and external intermediary organizations such as science parks.

Establishing Policies and Processes

In many countries, setting up appropriate institutional policies and processes has been the first step toward encouraging boundary-spanning activities by individual academics. Many institutions clarified their rules about external engagement. For instance one of the early steps taken by many UK universities was to introduce a "one-day-a-week" rule for consulting/external activities. In Japan, policies to address conflicts of interest and conflicts of commitment have been considered critical. Streamlining processes for external contracts, with clarification of monetary and other rewards that academic staff can expect, have also been undertaken. Some universities explicitly changed promotion criteria to enhance the prospects for promotion through "third stream activities."

For ensuring the general "responsiveness" of education programs, it may not be enough to have externally active academic staff. While boundary-spanning academics are more likely to be aware of external needs and may even reflect such knowledge in their individual courses, is it essential to have processes in place to ensure timeliness and relevance of program offerings.

Administrative Support

Three types of boundary-spanning roles in research, education, and culture require three different types of administrative support units. For instance, many universities in OECD countries have established technology transfer offices since the 1980s to support research-related functions such as patenting/licensing, contract research, and consulting. These perform important boundary-spanning functions. Even in the United States, where technology transfer offices have a longer history, staff to support these offices is still increasing, growing from 929 in 1998 to 1,926 in 2007, with about half of the staff working on nonlicensing activities.

For education-related functions, administrative support units are less visible, but most universities with special programs, such as cooperative education or student projects, have specific administrative support staff and sometimes even units for arranging such activities.

Similarly, for cultural and community-related functions, specific administrative support is also likely to be essential. Again at the University of Pennsylvania, a unit to support community-service activities was developed, first within a department, but moved to become part of the central administration to provide university-wide support.

Internal Organizational Structure

The traditional academic disciplinary structures are often inappropriate for engagement with the external world, as practical issues are usually interdisciplinary. In the United States, external engagements with government as well as industry were greatly enhanced by the development of "organizational research units"-some of which developed as organizational structures to bring together academics from different disciplines to cope with external research needs. Various experiments have been introduced to co-locate university units with businesses and other stakeholders. Examples of this include the North Carolina Centenary Campus or the Science City Initiative in Newcastle, in the United Kingdom.

External Intermediaries

The interest in science parks and incubation facilities has been growing steadily since the 1980s, first in the United States and Europe, but more recently in developing countries as well. Since Stanford Industrial Park was created in 1951, the number of science parks in the United States has gradually increased, with a more rapid growth in the 1980s and the past decade, leading to over 170 science parks today. The United Kingdom's science parks also evolved in close conjunction with universities, starting with Cambridge and Herriot Watt in the early 1970s. The trend expanded in the 1980s and 1990s, with about 100 existing today. Their record of performance has been mixed at best; however, they continue to be regarded as key instruments for regional economic development. One recent study in the United States shows a significant change in their orientation. Science parks are moving away from recruitment of external R&D organizations toward company incubation and new enterprise development. This includes a greater commitment from universities to promote interactivity, in the form of living and work space that is increasingly used to accommodate both academics and industrialists.

In Asia, different types of science and technology parks emerged, often without formal ties with universities. In China, science parks emerged in the late 1980s as part of national policy to establish special technology zones. Today China has 53 national and nearly 200 state-level science parks, along with 63 university-owned science parks developed since 1990. In India, the government initiative to establish simplified administrative processes, particularly to promote information technology businesses led to the creation of 39 science and technology parks in existence today. These areas are more like industrial parks, however, and are particularly focused on facilitating export-oriented businesses. Nonetheless, the most "successful" examples-such as Zhongguancun in China or Bangalore in India-tend to be characterized by proximity to elite higher education institutions.

There has been a global rise in expectations about the responsibilities of higher education institutions in innovation and economic development. Policymakers define higher education institutions as crucial not only for education but also for scientific research, innovation, and regional economic development. The ongoing global economic crisis is unlikely to change such expectations and indeed may even encourage even stronger expectations in this area.

Future Trends

Change is as inevitable as the passage of time, but line of movement in the modern world seems to be accelerating and presenting higher education more complex challenges with each passing decade. But it is important to keep in mind that, as these old and new challenges are addressed, the worldwide changes around us will continue. Shifting demographics, technological breakthroughs, and the volatility of international political and economic conditions make it unlikely that patterns of the past will easily or reliably predict the future.

The main force shaping higher education during the past half century, and certainly since the last UNESCO world conference in 1998, has been the continuing massification of systems-the expansion of enrolments worldwide. The expansion has continued at a staggering rate-from an estimated enrolment of 51,160,000 tertiary-level students in 1980 to 139,395,000 in 2006. Demand for higher education will continue to grow but will come from separate sectors in different countries. Globally, postsecondary education will continue to expand, but in sharp contrast from the past several decades, much of that growth will be in developing countries, especially in China and India.

On the surface it would appear that the developed countries have, in large part, achieved universal access to higher education. But major variations have turned up in some countries and significant access problems for underserved population sectors. Countries such as Japan, the Republic of Korea, and Finland have achieved universal enrolment ratios approaching 80 percent. In a growing number of countries, mainly in Europe and East Asia, demographic trends reflect a decline in the number of young people who comprise the traditional age cohort enrolling in higher education, but the demand has grown among nontraditional populations. Systems and institutions will need to adjust to these new, and in many ways, unprecedented realities.

Although efforts to address demand have successfully expanded access in many countries, expansion has not resolved persistent social inequities. Furthermore, socioeconomic background and parental education all too often influence the level of education an individual will achieve. The underlying causes of inequalities are pernicious and not easily resolved. Underserved students from lower socioeconomic classes, underrepresented racial, ethnic, and religious minority groups; older students; and the disabled will require new services and infrastructure in order to participate successfully. Modern societies are increasingly concerned with greater access for these population groups.

From Access to Completion

What has changed is our appreciation for the complexity of the issues and the difficult choices that need to be made as we try to address them. Access-improving possibilities for entry to postsecondary education-is one of the most complicated of these issues.

Mass enrolment has opened access to previously excluded population groups. In most countries, gender inequality has been eliminated, and the student population in general largely resembles the gender percentages in the general population. Inequality of access, however, continues to affect other population groups such as lower socioeconomic classes, ethnic and religious minorities, rural populations (particularly in developing countries), and others traditionally underrepresented in postsecondary education.

By the time of the last UNESCO report, access was measured with enrolment totals and gross enrolment ratios. We have come to recognize that enrolment growth must also be considered against completion rates. We have not succeeded in making higher education more inclusive or accessible if high percentages of these new students fail. Policymakers and the general public are beginning to take on this broader view of access. In the age of growing accountability, institutions will be measured by their success at supporting students through to completion, not by simply getting more students through the door. This new perspective implies changes-not only in how academic institutions measure success-but will undoubtedly affect reputations and budgetary allocations as well.

The meaning of "completion" has changed, as well. Traditionally, students collected credits, sat for examinations, and were then awarded degrees and certificates. These were the measures used universally to document academic achievement. Increasingly, universities are being asked to be more accountable for what and how their students learn. Greater emphasis is placed on measuring the "value added" as a result of academic study. What does a student learn and how do you measure it? Answering these questions is not easy, and little consensus exists about how this is best addressed. Concern will rise with the nexus of issues surrounding achievement and learning. Initiatives like the Bologna process will test new measures that will undoubtedly have significant influence on future trends.

Diversification

Mass enrolment has created the need for diversified academic systems-hierarchies of institutions serving different needs and constituencies. Diversified systems-necessary for financial, academic, and vocational reasons-will continue to be central to higher education worldwide. In general, governments will manage the diversification with "steering" mechanisms that will control the scope and nature of academic systems.

The private sector will be an important aspect of diversification. It has been the fastest-growing segment of postsecondary education worldwide and will continue to expand in many countries, simply because public institutions will not be able to keep pace with student demand. In academic systems that are no longer growing, the recently emerged private sector is likely to stabilize and become both a permanent and central option amid the diverse array of postsecondary institutions. While most private institutions will serve a mass clientele, some may emerge as semielite or even as elite research universities. Quality will continue to be a major preoccupation for higher education, in general, but special care will need to be taken to ensure that private higher education, and the for-profit institutions, in particular, maintain appropriate standards and serve society in much the same way that public institutions do. New technologies and new providers have only just begun to diversify opportunities. This trend will most certainly continue.

Privatization and Funding

Public higher education has begun, and will continue, to take on practices and characteristics of private institutions. A combination of influences-neoliberal attitudes, limited public financing, increasing costs, the need to address expanded social expectations, and build better management systems, etc.-will oblige public postsecondary institutions to look for additional sources of income. This will be done through increased sharing of costs with students (tuition and fees) and through income generation from other sources-including research, consulting, and university-industry partnerships. The increased privatization of public institutions will continue to have significant impacts on the nature of these institutions.

Tuition and other fees charged to students will increase and become more ubiquitous worldwide. Countries where public institutions currently charge little or no tuition are likely to increase what students must pay to study. Where tuition is already significant, increases are also likely. The amounts assigned to students will vary according to the economic and political circumstances of each environment and probably will reflect differing social philosophies and ideologies, as well. One of the many challenges ahead will be to ascertain that cost does not become a barrier to access when students have the intellectual capacity to study but not the private financial means.

New Technologies

Information and communications technology has already profoundly affected higher education worldwide. The impact can be seen in the communication of knowledge through e-mail, blogs, wikis, and podcasts; the rapid expansion of distance education, electronic publication of scientific journals and books, and to some extent academic management. The new technologies will continue to affect all aspects of higher education. The next stage of this aspect of the revolution will undoubtedly transform our approach to teaching and learning through distance-education programs and within the walls of traditional universities. However, it will not, as some have predicted, replace either traditional universities or traditional modes of teaching and learning.

Information and communications technology will probably not have the dramatic impact on access for the immediate future that some analysts predicted. Individuals with limited resources in developing nations are as likely to be distant from the necessary infrastructure and equipment as they are from bricks-and-mortar institutions. Initiatives to close the "digital divide" are in the early stages, and this action may no longer be as serious a problem by the next trend report. For the present, the extent to which different countries can integrate new technology varies tremendously.

The Concern for Quality

Quality will continue to be a high priority for higher education. During the last decade quality-assurance schemes for higher education have been implemented almost everywhere. At this next stage, the trend is toward standards that can be referenced internationally. In other words, there is a need to move toward mutual recognition and trust so that national programs for quality assurance will provide international validity. Regional conferences and summits have taken place throughout the world to address this challenge. The Bologna process is guiding Europe toward shared benchmarks and standards that will make it possible to compare qualifications awarded in all participating countries.

The growing international mobility of students and scholars is helping to drive the need for a way to evaluate and compare qualifications earned in different parts of the world. This effort will depend on finding a mechanism for certifying and integrating national quality-assurance schemes on an international level. A number of international organizations are engaged in discussions of how best to achieve this process.

Despite more than a decade of formalizing quality-assurance programs, many elements of measuring and monitoring quality remain problematic. The idea of exactly where quality resides in higher education remains somewhat elusive.

Struggle for the Soul of Higher Education

The traditional societal mission of higher education has been under pressure for the last half century. Universities, traditionally seen as key cultural institutions to be responsible for public enlightenment, are increasingly obliged to respond to the many new pressures described in this report. The "commercialization" of higher education has placed considerable strain on its social mission. The debate concerning the primary mission and priorities of higher education will continue in many parts of the world, with a possible hindering of protecting activities that serve the public good in the face of growing financial constraints and market influence.

Individual countries will be challenged to balance local needs and priorities with standards, practices, and expectations articulated at the international level. Will research focus on local needs or be more inclined to pursue issues more attractive to international journals and funders? How will countries ensure that foreign providers and partners will address local educational needs and priorities?

Professionalization of Higher Education Management and Leadership

As higher education institutions and systems have become larger and more central to society and individuals, there is a growing need for professional management and leadership. Training programs are slowly emerging, as are "think tanks" and policy forums. Academic institutions and systems are beginning to collect data about themselves for use in policymaking and improvement. There is a growing need for complete and accurate regional and international data for analysis as well. The higher education enterprise is simply too large, complex, and central to be managed without data and professionalism.

The unstoppable progress of globalization will oblige higher education institutions of all kinds to prepare an increasingly diverse cohort of students with skills and knowledge that will support their insertion into an increasingly borderless economy. Even the current global financial crisis, which will create problems for higher education in many countries, will not fundamentally alter the landscape. This challenge requires policymakers, administrators, and professors to reconsider the structure of traditional degree programs as well as the pedagogy of the past. "Talk and chalk" is far from adequate as we move further into the 21st century.

Larger enrolments result in more diverse student expectations and needs. Expansion and diversification create a need for new providers. System growth requires additional revenue and new channels for obtaining it. All of this (expansion, diversity, and funding shortages) generates concern for quality. This knotted ball of string will roll forward, with each trend adjusting to the endless tugs at higher education as a global system.

References

D'Antoni, S. 2008. *Open Educational Resources: The Way Forward*, UNESCO, International Institute for Educational Planning, Paris.

Herbst, M. 2007. *Financing Public Universities: The Case of Performance Funding.* Dordrecht, The Netherlands, Springer.

Knight, J. 2006a. *Higher Education Crossing Borders: A Guide to the Implications of the General Agreement on Trade in Services (GATS) for Cross-border Education.* Vancouver, BC, Commonwealth of Learning.

Marton, F., Hounsell, D. and Entwistle, N.J. 1997. *The experience of learning.* Edinburgh, Scottish Academic Press.

Maurrasse, D.J. 2001. *Beyond the Campus: How Colleges and Universities Form Partnerships with their Communities.* New York, Routledge.

McIntosh, C. and Varoglu, Z. 2005. *Perspectives on Distance Education. Lifelong Learning & Distance Higher Education*, Paris, UNESCO and Commonwealth of Learning.

8

Cross-Border Tertiary Education

Higher education has become increasingly international in the past decade as more and more students choose to study abroad, enrol in foreign educational programmes and institutions in their home country, or simply use the Internet to take courses at colleges or universities in other countries. This growth is the result of several different, but not mutually exclusive, driving forces: a desire to promote mutual understanding; the migration of skilled workers in a globalised economy; the desire of the institutions to generate additional revenues; or the need to build a more educated workforce in the home countries, generally as emerging economies.

Cross-border higher education has developed differently across OECD countries and regions. By and large, student mobility has been policy-driven in Europe and demand-driven in the Asia-Pacific region, while North America has mostly been a magnet for foreign students. On the other hand, delivering foreign educational programmes and institutions so that students can study at a foreign college without leaving home has been largely driven by educational institutions themselves. It has been made easier by institutional frameworks which grant substantial autonomy to higher education institutions and by the policies adopted by receiving countries.

But the growth and diversification of cross-border education raises a number of questions for governments and higher education institutions. Is capacity being increased to meet growing demand? Is access being widened? Are costs being lowered for students or governments? Is liberalisation an answer to the growing importance of private provision as well as the rise in the demand for higher education? This chapter outlines the current position and puts forward an agenda for OECD policy makers under the following headings:

- quality and recognition;
- access and equity;
- financing and cost;
- using cross-border higher education to build capacity;
- policy coherence.

Migration of International Students

Students going abroad to study is the major form of cross-border higher education. The number of foreign students in OECD countries has doubled over the past 20 years to 1.6 million. OECD countries receive around 85% of the world's foreign students, but most of them are concentrated in just six countries. In 2001, the United States accounted for 30% of foreign enrolments, the United Kingdom 14%, Germany 13%, France 9%, Australia 7% and Japan 4%. The four leading English-speaking countries alone (the United States, the United Kingdom, Australia and Canada) account for more than half (54%) of all foreign students in the OECD area.

Europe is the largest receiving region among OECD countries with 840 000 foreign students but many of these students are moving from one European country to another. About half (52%) of foreign students in Europe are European. North America receives fewer students in absolute terms (with 520 000 foreign students in the United States, Canada and Mexico), but ranks first in terms of openness to other regions, with Asian students representing almost two-thirds (60%) of all foreign students in North America.

Asia heads the list of regions sending students abroad for higher education, accounting for almost half (43%) of all international tertiary-level students in the OECD area. Europe is a close second, accounting for 35%, followed by Africa (12%), North America (7%), South America (3%) and Oceania (1%). About 57% of all foreign students studying in OECD countries were from outside the OECD area in 2001. Looking at individual countries, China (including Hong Kong) sends the largest number of students abroad, accounting for 10% of all international students in the OECD area, followed by Korea (5%), India (4%), Greece (4%), and Japan (4%). More than two-thirds (70%) of all Asian students abroad study in three English-speaking destinations: the United States, the United Kingdom and Australia. While Asian students mainly use cross-border education to acquire a full degree on a full fee-paying basis, American and European students favour a short two-way mobility, in the case of Europeans mainly on a subsidised fee-paying basis.

Table 1: Foreign students in the OECD area – top OECD receiving and sending countries, 2001.

Number of hosted foreign students		*Number of foreign students abroad*	
United States	475 169	China	124 000
United Kingdom	225 722	Korea	70523
Germany	199 132	India	61179
France	147 402	Greece	55074
Australia	110 789	Japan	55041
Japan	63637	Germany	54489
Canada	40667	France	47587
Spain	39944	Turkey	44204
Belgium	38150	Morocco	43063
Austria	31682	Italy	41485
Italy	29228	Malaysia	32709
Switzerland	27765	United States	30103
Sweden	26304	Canada	29326
Turkey	16656	Indonesia	26615
Netherlands	16589	Spain	26196
Denmark	12547	United Kingdom	25198
Hungary	11242	Hong Kong	23261
New Zealand	11069	Russian Federation	22004
Norway	8834	Singapore	19514
Total OECD	**1580513**		

New Forms of Cross-border Education

In fact, going abroad to study is only one form of cross-border education. An increasing number of students are being offered, and taking advantage of, a new option – taking a degree or other post-secondary course offered by a foreign university without leaving their home country. Programme and institution mobility has grown over the past decade and is likely to meet a growing demand in the future.

Programme mobility is the second most common form of cross-border higher education after student mobility. It involves cross-border distance education, including e-learning, generally supplemented by face-to-face teaching in local partner institutions, but mainly takes the form of traditional face-to-face teaching offered via a partner institution abroad. The relationships between foreign and local institutions are regulated under a variety of arrangements, from development assistance to for-profit arrangements.

Commercial arrangements are becoming prominent in the Asia-Pacific region, mainly through franchises and twinning arrangements. Under a franchise arrangement, a local provider is typically licensed by a foreign institution to offer whole or part of a foreign educational programme (generally leading to a foreign degree) under stipulated contractual conditions. Franchise arrangements do however take many other forms. Under a twinning programme, students are enrolled with a foreign provider and are taught a foreign syllabus; they carry out part of the course in the home country and complete it in the home country of the foreign institution. This form of cross-border education typically involves both student and programme mobility.

Institution mobility is still limited in scale, possibly because it involves more entrepreneurial risk, but it has become an increasingly important feature of cross-border education: it corresponds to foreign direct investment by educational institutions or companies. The typical form of institution mobility is the opening of foreign campuses by universities and of foreign learning centres by educational providers. It may also involve the establishment of a distinctly new rather than affiliated educational institution or the takeover of all or part of a foreign educational institution.

Although such services might not offer students the same cultural and linguistic experiences as foreign study, they involve lower personal costs than studying abroad and can lead to beneficial spillovers in the receiving country's higher education sector. In the degree-granting sector, the growth of for-profit cross-border education through programme and institution mobility is mostly driven by "traditional" public or private not-for-profit educational institutions that increasingly offer private provision.

Australia is a striking example of a country whose provision of cross-border higher education is increasingly carried out in the student's home country through programme and institution mobility: between 1996 and 2001, "offshore" enrolments increased from 24% to 37% of all international students enrolled in Australian institutions. Most of these students attended traditional campuses/courses outside Australia (28% of all international students in 2001), while fewer (9% of all international students) were enrolled offshore in distance education, although this number is growing. More than half of the international students from Singapore and Hong Kong, China studying in an Australian educational institution are enrolled in offshore courses.

Policy Rationales and Approaches to Cross-border Education

Four different, but not mutually exclusive, approaches to cross-border higher education emerge. Three of them – skilled migration, revenue generation, capacity building – have a strong economic drive and have emerged in the 1990s while the fourth, mutual understanding, has a longer history.

The *mutual understanding approach* encompasses political, cultural, academic and development aid goals. It allows and encourages mobility of domestic as well as foreign students and staff through scholarship and academic exchange programmes and supports academic partnerships between educational institutions. This approach does not generally involve any strong push to recruit international students. Examples of countries using this approach so far are Japan, Mexico, Korea, or Spain. The European Union's Socrates-Erasmus programme also corresponds to this approach, involving student and teacher exchanges, networking of faculties and institutions across Europe and joint development of study programmes.

The *skilled migration approach* shares the goals of the mutual understanding approach but gives stronger emphasis to the recruitment of selected international students and aims to attract talented students to work in the host country's knowledge economy, or render its higher education and research sectors more competitive. Scholarship programmes may remain a major policy instrument in this approach but they are supplemented by active promotion of a country's higher education sector abroad, combined with an easing of the relevant visa or immigration regulations. Sometimes, specific services are designed to help international students in their studies and their stay abroad and more teaching takes place in English. This approach can have a variety of targets, such as students from certain areas, post-graduates or research students rather than undergraduates, or students in a specific field. This approach generally results in a rise in the number of international students. Examples of countries having adopted this approach are Germany, Canada, France, the United Kingdom (for EU students) and the United States (for post-graduate students).

The *revenue-generating approach* shares the rationales of the mutual understanding and skilled migration approaches, but offers higher education services on a more or less full-fee basis, without public subsidies. Compared to domestic students, foreign students generate additional income for institutions which are encouraged to become entrepreneurial in the international education market. Under this strategy, governments tend to grant institutions considerable autonomy and seek to secure the reputation of their higher education sector and protect international students, for example through quality assurance arrangements. This may be complemented by an active policy to lower the barriers to cross-border education activities through trade negotiations in educational services under the General Agreement on Trade in Services (GATS) or other agreements. This approach generally results in a significant growth of fee-paying student mobility and in strong involvement in cross-border education through revenue-generating programme and institution mobility. Examples of this approach are Australia, the United Kingdom (for non-EU students), New Zealand, and the United States (for undergraduates).

The *capacity-building approach* encourages cross-border higher education, however delivered, as a relatively quick way to build an emerging country's capacity. Scholarship programmes supporting the outward mobility of domestic civil servants, teachers, academics and students are important policy instruments; so is encouraging foreign institutions, programmes and academic staff to come and operate for-profit ventures, generally under a government regulation which ensures their compatibility with the country's nation- and economy-building agendas.

Twinning arrangements and partnerships with local providers are encouraged (and sometimes compulsory) in order to facilitate knowledge transfers between foreign and local institutions. In the short run, this approach results in large numbers of outgoing students and of foreign revenue-generating educational programmes and institutions. Examples of this approach are mostly found in South-East and North Asia and in the Middle East, *e.g.* Malaysia; Hong Kong, China; China and Singapore.

GATS and Higher Education

Educational services are included in the current negotiations under the General Agreement on Trade in Services (GATS) in the World Trade Organization (WTO). The issue of trade liberalisation in educational services has provoked much public debate, and many countries have so far been very reluctant to engage in trade liberalisation negotiations for education services. The mere possibility that certain types of education might fall within the scope of trade regulations and agreements has fuelled a heated debate on the nature of education, especially in OECD countries where it is mainly provided as a public service on a non-profit basis.

Education stakeholders are mainly concerned that the GATS could undermine public funding and subsidies as well as the governments' ability to regulate quality in higher education. However, the public education sector is in principle not covered by the GATS negotiations and no member country has yet expressed interest in including it. Moreover, the GATS has no discipline that compels WTO members or countries making commitments in education services to abandon the public funding of their higher education system or extend it to foreign institutions or students, unless they decide to make such a commitment. So far, no country has made such a commitment. The setting of quality standards is also outside the scope of trade agreements and of the GATS in particular.

The GATS mandates the development of any necessary disciplines to ensure that measures relating to qualification requirements and procedures, technical standards and licensing requirements do not constitute unnecessary barriers to trade in services. But these disciplines do not exist as yet. The GATS does not provide for, or seek to undertake, recognition of qualifications either. Recognition agreements must however be notified to the WTO so that other interested members can know about them. In short, the possible impact of GATS on domestic education systems will depend on the commitments made by countries, which have been limited and conservative so far.

The growth of cross-border higher education has occurred largely in the absence of GATS commitments, driven by factors other than the GATS. It is thus likely to continue irrespective of the GATS, at least in the short run. Whether a country decides to make GATS commitments on education or not, it will still need to deal with many of the issues and challenges that arise from these developments. Indeed, many of the policies that may be needed to manage the growth of cross-border higher education and trade in educational services are unconnected with, and unaffected by, the GATS (*e.g.* student visa requirements and policies regarding quality assurance, accreditation and recognition of qualifications).

Cross-border higher education represents an important source of export revenue in some OECD countries and is increasingly provided through commercial arrangements. Foreign students incur large expenditures to cover living, education and travel costs. Although there are differing views across countries and regions, education is increasingly seen as a potential commercial stake for the future. Export revenue related to international student mobility amounted to an estimated minimum of US$ 30 billion in 1998, or 3% of global services exports. In Australia and New Zealand, educational services rank, respectively, third and fourth in terms of services exports, and fourteenth and fifteenth in terms of exports as a whole.

Main Policy Challenges

Cross-border higher education raises mainly traditional educational policy issues: quality, access and equity, cost, contribution of education to growth.

Quality and Recognition

Countries providing and receiving cross-border higher education have a common interest in strengthening quality provision (either to protect their learners or to maintain the reputation and attractiveness of their higher education system abroad).

The variety of higher education systems and the lack of transparent information about and readability of those systems worldwide leave room for low quality and even rogue providers (degree mills) and rogue quality assurance and accreditation agencies (accreditation mills) to operate. While national quality assurance and accreditation systems partly resolve quality issues in cross-border student mobility, programme and institution mobility often fall outside their scope. Programme and institution mobility can carry quality risks to a greater or lesser extent, for example depending on its form (franchise, twinning arrangement, e-learning, etc.). While still limited in scale, fraud - that is the selling (or buying) of fake degrees - is increasingly becoming an issue: it lowers the overall perception of the quality of cross-border higher education.

The recognition of international degrees is also important for facilitating periods of study abroad and for allowing students holding foreign degrees to work in their own country or, more generally, in the international labour market.

New developments in cross-border higher education raise crucial policy challenges:

- Learners need to be protected from the risks of misinformation, low-quality provision and qualifications of questionable validity by strong quality assurance and accreditation systems, which cover cross-border and commercial provision and non-traditional delivery modes.
- Qualifications should be understandable internationally and transparent in order to increase their international validity and portability and to ease the work of recognition arrangements and credential evaluators.
- National quality assurance and accreditation agencies need to intensify co-operation at international level in order to increase their mutual understanding.

Access and Equity

Cross-border higher education certainly represents one way of increasing access to higher education. Countries facing a problem of unmet demand for tertiary education on a large scale should thus consider as one solution the facilitation of access for their citizens to the different forms of cross-border educational provision (student mobility, programme mobility, institution mobility).

However, student mobility and foreign education can involve equity issues. The growth of cross-border education could lead to the displacement of domestic students by international students, if it is not carefully monitored by governments and educational institutions. Moreover, student mobility remains primarily self-financed by students and their families; students generally self-finance their participation in cross-border educational programmes operating privately in Asia.

Students from lower economic and educational backgrounds participate less in cross-border student mobility. This is also the case for students from minority backgrounds in the United States. In some cases though, cross-border education can increase the access of minorities to higher education: this is the case for Malaysian students from the Indian and Chinese minorities. Student mobility is gender-neutral in the European Socrates-Erasmus programmes and favourable to female students in the United States (because most outgoing US students study humanities), but favours male students in most Asian sending countries, reflecting a higher participation of male students in higher education in these countries as well as, possibly, a tendency for families to invest more in education for boys than for girls. Although some of the gaps between different population groups may be bridged mechanically as equity in access to tertiary education is achieved in the sending countries, the governments and other education stakeholders of receiving as well as sending countries willing to tackle the equity issue in cross-border higher education could:

- improve financial support for participation in cross-border education through targeted and means-tested grants or student loan schemes;
- improve the provision of information on the benefits and costs of cross-border student mobility to students from lower educational and socio-economic backgrounds.

Financing and Cost

OECD countries adopt two broad strategies of funding regarding incoming international students.

The first strategy is to grant international students indirect subsidies. Indeed, as long as it does not require capacity expansion, teaching international students represents a marginal cost for universities. Moreover, where there is a decline in student numbers in a system or in certain fields, international students allow the reduction of the average cost of higher education (by increasing the teacher-student ratio) and the maintaining of variety in their educational offers. Indirect subsidisation alleviates (but does not totally remove) the funding issue for international students. This strategy implicitly relies on a reciprocity principle between countries/institutions, and especially so in a context of growth of cross-border mobility of students.

The second, newer, strategy often places cross-border higher education in a broader reform agenda of funding and governance of domestic higher education systems. So far, the introduction of this fee policy has preceded rather than followed relatively large enrolments of international students. In addition to most advantages of indirect subsidisation, international students contribute to some extent to the financing of the domestic higher education system. Their full tuition fees help universities to enhance their educational and research capacity. They also give them strong incentives to recruit international students, to become more demand-driven and more entrepreneurial, and possibly to undertake for-profit cross-border activities, such as programme and institution mobility. Governments seeking to encourage their publicly funded higher education institutions to recruit large numbers of international students or undertake cross-border commercial activities should thus:

- provide them with effective incentives, including financial autonomy and the ability to control the use of the private resources generated by those activities;
- put effective guidelines and mechanisms in place to ensure accountability for any cross-border entrepreneurial activities of publicly funded higher education institutions.

Cross-border Higher Education for Capacity Building

Cross-border higher education may be as important economically to importing as to exporting countries and can indeed help emerging economies, and developing and transition countries to build or strengthen their capacity in higher education as well as meet their unmet demand, if any.

As already noted, cross-border education is one way of increasing domestic access to higher education, which ultimately contributes to growth and development. While student and scholar mobility facilitates the building of international networks, which are essential to access up-to-date knowledge, partnerships of local and foreign universities in programme and institution mobility induce spillovers that can help improve the quality of local provision. Finally, commercial provision of cross-border higher education can allow the building of capacity more quickly than with domestic or development assistance resources only, and grants receiving countries more negotiating power to dictate their conditions.

However, developing countries should be aware of some of the risks it also involves:

- Developing countries should ensure that foreign provision meets their needs and quality requirements, and that it leads to actual spillovers.
- Cross-border student mobility might in some cases involve a risk of "brain drain" for the sending country: cross-border education without student mobility might alleviate this risk and create job opportunities at home for the students.
- Trade is not likely to play a major role in countries where there are insufficient funds to pay for unsubsidised (for-profit) education; development assistance in education should thus be encouraged in the least developed countries.

Policy Coherence

Because cross-border educational activities bring into play many actors and policy areas in a country, an effective policy strategy regarding cross-border higher education must take into account this diversity and ensure the highest co-ordination, or compatibility, between several policy agendas such as: quality assurance and recognition policy; development assistance in education; other domestic educational policies; cultural policy; migration and visa policy; trade policy; economic policy.

Cross-Border Education and Development

Education is an essential foundation for personal, social and economic success in a globalised economy. But how can developing countries offer enough education, particularly quality tertiary education, to their citizens to enable them to play a full part in creating and enjoying such success?

Many countries, particularly in the developed world, are competing to attract foreign students, or to establish a presence abroad. But they do not always realise that they could also benefit from their own students and academics going abroad or from hosting foreign educational programmes and institutions.

Mobility of students, academics, educational programmes and institutions in both directions should be considered in every country's strategy for building a better-educated citizenry. This is especially true for the developing world where countries are often unable to meet domestic demand for tertiary education, but it is also true for OECD countries when it comes to improving the quality of higher education.

This "capacity-building" approach to cross-border higher education aims to bridge the gap between supply and demand in developing countries, as well as to build these countries' domestic capacity to provide good quality higher education.

Some South-East Asian countries already encourage students to study abroad as well as take measures to attract foreign providers to offer courses on their soil. Indonesia, Malaysia, Singapore, Hong Kong China, Vietnam and China all encourage foreign academics, programmes and institutions to offer their services in their countries. Malaysia also provides extensive scholarships for postgraduate study or training of teachers, academics and civil servants, mainly in the United Kingdom and Australia. Thailand provides scholarships for students and employees in the public sector.

The idea of education for development tends to focus on the fundamental importance of basic education. But the capacity to succeed in today's global knowledge economy depends at least partly on being able to make a high level of skills available to a large number of citizens.

Higher education plays a crucial role by training a country's workforce in all fields, from teachers equipped to give a good basic education to statisticians and policy analysts monitoring capacity development. Many developing countries do not have enough tertiary education places or staff to meet domestic demand. And in spite of progress in recent decades, many will have to continue to expand their systems if they are to catch up with richer economies (Figure 1).

Cross-border tertiary education can help a country expand its system more rapidly than if it had to rely on domestic resources alone. It can also help improve the quality, variety and relevance of domestic higher education systems – three key elements of effective higher education systems that require a critical mass of high-quality academics. Faculty and post-graduate students can obtain a high-quality education or develop their competencies overseas before returning to the university sector in their home country.

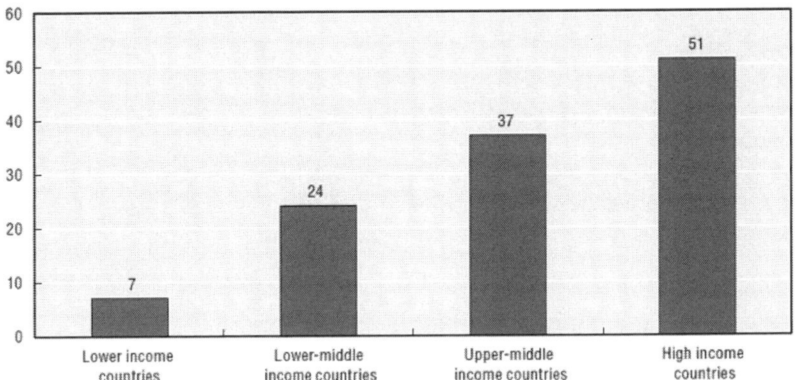

Figure 1. Average Enrolment Rate in Tertiary Education by Countries' Level of Income (2004)

And it is not always necessary for the students to travel. Foreign universities can provide access to their programmes in the students' home country. This links developing countries with cutting-edge knowledge and helps train an effective workforce, while at the same time adding a high-quality faculty to the domestic system.

In all countries, internationalisation allows institutions to compare themselves with their foreign counterparts, through direct competition to attract students and grants, but also, more importantly, through the feedback they get from domestic students going abroad and from international students.

Cross-border tertiary education is not a panacea, however. If the foreign programmes on offer in a developing country are of low quality, for example, or if they are imported as a system totally separate from the domestic education network, they could at best leave the domestic system unimproved and at worst have a negative effect.

There are also potential risks in encouraging students to go abroad to study or to obtain foreign degrees at home. It could lead to a brain drain if the students prefer to stay or go abroad to work, or the education on offer may be irrelevant in the developing country. It could also lead to equity problems if only the wealthiest students are able to afford foreign higher education, at home or abroad.

These challenges have to be addressed with appropriate local strategies or regulatory frameworks for foreign (but also domestic) education provision. These frameworks should consider issues of accreditation, quality assurance, recognition of foreign qualifications, access to public funds for institutions and students, brain drain, etc.

There is some evidence that the oldest form of cross-border education, students going abroad to study, has helped capacity development. In 22 countries, domestic students studying abroad represent over 30% of the country's higher education enrolments. It is also widely recognised that the international mobility of students and scholars allows developing countries to access recent knowledge and research methodologies.

However, there is still little evidence that the newer forms of cross-border tertiary education have directly contributed to capacity development. Some countries have deliberately and consistently invited foreign education providers into their countries, but it is too early to assess the impact of this strategy.

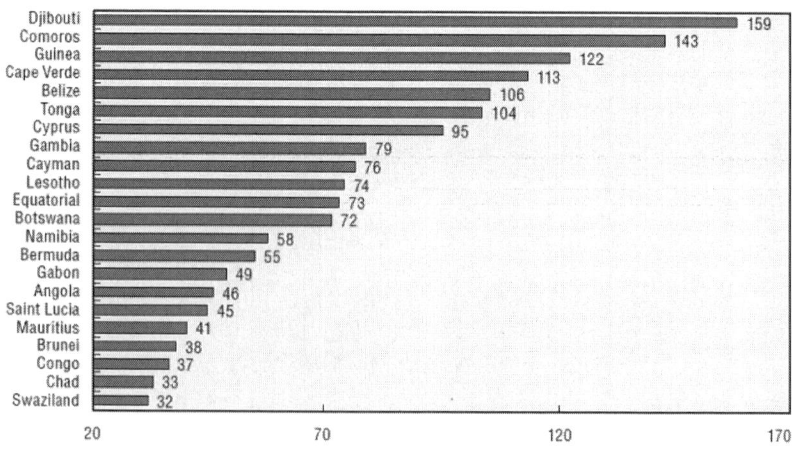

Figure 2. Countries where the Number of Domestic Students abroad Represents Over 30% of the Size of their Domestic Tertiary Education Students, 2004

Malaysia, for example, views cross-border education provision at home as an important and positive component of its capacity development. Foreign providers offered 34% of the 899 bachelor and postgraduate programmes in Malaysia's private education sector in 2006 and the government has encouraged foreign research provision by allowing foreign providers to bid for domestic research funding. Other Asian countries also value foreign educational provision and use it in a strategic way.

In South Africa, however, the impact of foreign provision is far smaller and has experienced some hitches. Its four foreign educational providers, from Australia, the Netherlands and the United Kingdom, enrolled only 0.5% of all tertiary education students in 2000. And in 2003, South Africa's Higher Education Quality Committee did not reaccredit three of the four foreign MBA programmes where 88% of students in foreign programmes were concentrated, while it has banned franchised educational programmes because of quality concerns.

There is thus mixed evidence of the benefits of cross-border education. However, this does not imply that new forms of cross-border education will not have a positive impact in the medium term, or that a marginal effect is not important. It is often because of what happens at the margin that systems evolve. The growth of cross-border education worldwide has for example put quality assurance and the regulation of private provision under new scrutiny, even where the phenomenon is still limited or inexistent. This awareness-raising is definitely a step towards capacity development.

One concern about cross-border education is that it could increase a brain drain from developing countries, rather than increase the circulation of skills between countries. The data on this are incomplete, but do suggest a link. Almost half of the people admitted to Australia in recent years under its skilled migration programme hold an Australian degree, for example. In Canada, it is estimated that between 15% and 20% of foreign students stay on to work there, while in New Zealand, 13% of the foreign students entering

The OECD and UNESCO have developed non-binding guidelines to encourage governments and other stakeholders to respond to the growth of cross-border higher education. The guidelines are designed to help students get easy access to reliable information on higher education offered outside their home country or by foreign providers in their home country. They call on governments and other stakeholders to make qualifications more transparent and to provide greater clarity on procedures for their international recognition.

The guidelines are based on three main principles:

- Mutual trust and respect among countries and recognition of the importance of international collaboration in higher education.
- Recognition of the importance of national authority and the diversity of higher education systems.
- Recognition of the importance of higher education as a means for expressing a country's linguistic and cultural diversity and for nurturing its economic development and social cohesion.

the country between 1998 and 2005 had obtained a residence permit in 2006. In Norway, 18% of the foreign students from outside the European Economic Area (EAA) studying there between 1991 and 2005 stayed on, double the rate of EAA students who have stayed on.

In the United States, the average stay rate for foreign recipients of science and engineering doctorates four to five years after earning their degree rose from 41% to 56% between 1992 and 2001. The figures skyrocketed to 96% per cent for Chinese doctorate recipients from 65% and to 86% per cent for Indians from 72%, but for other countries more students are returning home after completing their studies.

OECD data on stocks of migrants (rather than flows) show that the main sufferers from the brain drain are essentially African and Caribbean countries. More than 70% of Jamaican and Guyanese nationals holding higher diplomas are living and working in an OECD country. On the other hand, despite their high stay rates in the United States after they finish their studies, Indian and Chinese nationals account for less than 3% of the expatriates holding a higher degree in OECD countries.

Of the 113 countries for which information is available, 27 have expatriation rates of their tertiary educated people to the OECD area of over 20%, including nine over 50%. Although holding a degree from a country generally makes it easier to get a residence permit, no consistent pattern can be found between high levels of student mobility and expatriation rates.

There is no common definition of quality in tertiary education, and certainly no common measure of it. But if people want to be educated in one country and work in another, what they are learning needs to be compatible, and credentials earned in one country need to be recognised by another. This in turn means that quality assurance has become increasingly important. Systematic quality assurance practices provide information to governments, students, employers and society about tertiary education institutions and

Specific recommendations include:

- An invitation to governments to establish comprehensive quality assurance and accreditation systems for cross-border higher education, recognising that this involves both sending and receiving countries.
- An invitation to higher education institutions and providers to ensure that the programmes they deliver across borders and in their home country are of comparable quality and that they take into account the cultural and linguistic sensitivities of the receiving country.
- An invitation to student bodies to get involved as active partners at international, national and institutional levels in developing, monitoring and maintaining the quality provision of cross-border higher education.

Progress on implementing these guidelines is currently being monitored.

programmes. Such information increases accountability, transparency, and helps policy makers, institutional leaders, students and employers make informed decisions. To help address this issue, the OECD has developed *Guidelines for quality provision in cross-border higher education.*

There is increasing international agreement on the general principles of quality assurance and convergence on the methods for measuring it. But collecting accurate, timely and appropriate data remains a challenge. Quality assurance requires both financial and human resources and to be meaningful, it must not only provide information, but be linked to both rewards and sanctions. Rewards are needed to provide incentives for good performance and stimulate cultures of quality, and sanctions for poor performance are needed to protect stakeholders.

Many countries have quality assurance systems for their own domestic education networks, but have not even begun to consider how to address the cross-border issue. While policy makers should consider how quality assurance mechanisms can help to serve a regulatory role for local cross-border provision, they should look more broadly at their overall quality assurance system.

Concern about cross-border education sometimes comes from its increasingly commercial nature and its potential imbalance between rich and developing countries. Commercial arrangements are more likely to increase access quickly, as development aid and scholarship programmes typically face budget constraints. Moreover, commercial arrangements to some extent give countries and individuals more bargaining power to get the education they want – provided they have adequate resources to purchase the services. But any private educational provision can raise social inequity if it is not supported by specific scholarship or loan schemes. Should they be only affordable to an elite, commercial cross-border educational programmes would ultimately hinder capacity development.

There is also the risk that as cross-border education becomes an export industry in some donor countries, development assistance for cross-border education will drop for all countries. Certainly, in low-income countries, commercial cross-border education is unlikely to develop unless there is a large enough upper middle class who can afford it. For example, while exports of education services increased in Australia in the 1990s to become its second highest services export item in 2006, amounting to USD 9 billion, its official development assistance to post-secondary education decreased from USD 246 to 4 million between 1995 and 2005. The trends in countries with a revenue-generating approach to the internationalisation of higher education contrast with those in countries with a different strategy: for OECD donor countries overall, aid to post-secondary education more than doubled in current prices over the same period.

If a country chooses to use commercial cross-border education in its capacity development strategy, one option is to enter into international trade agreements, such as the General Agreement on Trade in Services (GATS) of the World Trade Organisation (WTO). By creating a more transparent and predictable legal framework, the GATS can improve the investment climate and help attract foreign investment in higher education.

In light of the regulatory requirements that higher education services entail, concerns have been raised in relation to the potential effects of the GATS on governments' ability to ensure adequate provision of these services. This is intensified by the fact that the GATS is a relatively young Agreement and some of its provisions have yet to be tested in practice.

If GATS commitments have not been made in a particular sector, only limited disciplines apply which do not impinge on governments' ability to regulate the sector. Once specific commitments are made, more significant obligations kick in, the most important of which for higher education relates to treating nationals and foreigners alike (national treatment).

In light of some uncertainties surrounding the scope of the GATS, particularly with respect to the exclusion of services provided under governmental authority, national treatment obligations may lead to unintended consequences. Governments may for instance find themselves required to extend to foreign providers financial and other benefits typically granted to public universities, or face penalties under WTO rules.

Pending a clarification of the scope of the Agreement, Members can schedule appropriate limitations by, for example, making specific commitments to the private sector or excluding publicly-funded institutions. The GATS allows for wide flexibility in this regard. It is thus crucial to carefully examine its provisions and tailor specific commitments to national policy objectives.

The mobility of students and academics has long been part of countries' capacity development strategies. Programme and institution mobility could now also contribute and lead to positive spillovers in tertiary education and their economy.

Whatever development strategy they chose, countries should consider whether cross-border tertiary education should be part of it, and if yes, how.

Cross-border tertiary education can indeed be a helpful capacity development tool. An appropriate regulatory framework in importing countries is important to reap its benefits. Addressing the cross-border challenges and opportunities will typically lead to reconsidering tertiary education policies as a whole and not only foreign provision.

And given its cost to some developing countries, donor countries and agencies should consider helping the poorest countries to do so as part of their development aid strategies.

References

OECD/World Bank. 2007, *Cross-Border Tertiary Education: A Way towards Capacity Development,* OECD, Paris.

OECD. 2006, *The Challenge of Capacity Development: Working towards Good Practice,* DAC Guidelines, OECD, Paris, available for free download at: www.oecd.org/dac/governance/capacitydevelopment

Finn, M.G. 2003, "Stay Rates of Foreign Doctorate Recipients from US Universities, 2001", Oak Ridge Institute for Science and Education, URL: *www.orau.gov/orise/pubs/stayrate03.pdf.*

Larsen, K. and S. Vincent-Lancrin. 2002, *"International Trade in Educational Services: Good or Bad?", Higher Education Management and Policy*, Vol. 14, No. 3, OECD, Paris.

9

Challenges for the Development of Higher Education

Education is a basic need of every society. A better education system can enhance the social, scientific, and technological improvement of a country. The human resource development of a country depends upon the quality of education imparted in country. Higher education caters to the education in the colleges and universities. Allen observed "It is academically consider suitable to present distinctive feature of two stages for the purpose of clarity of concepts and avoiding duplication" Higher education is admittedly a separate stage quite distinct from primary, secondary, elementary, and higher secondary stage.

Higher education is recognized today as a capital investment and is of paramount importance for economic and social development of the country. Institutions of higher education have the primary responsibility for equipping individuals with advanced knowledge and skills required for positions of responsibility in government, business, and other professions.

Quality higher education is a source of great potential for the socio economic and cultural development of the country. Stone, Horejs, & Lomas found "The nation can be transformed into a developed nation within the life time of a single generation." Factors such as the distinctive nature of higher education institutions, international mobility of students, and teachers accessibility of computer based learning pursuit of research and scholarship, globalization of economy, and emerging challenges of the 21st century have a direct impact on the future development of higher education.

The purpose of higher education is not simply to impart knowledge in certain branches of knowledge; it has deeper meaning and objectives. The purpose may be multidimensional and may be termed as personal, social, economical, and cultural. Education and particularly higher education cannot be divorced from its milieu and social context.

Religious, moral, historical, and cultural ethos permeates through the fabric of the educational system of a country. Allen found "In the time of rapid international, political, and economical changes, the universities in South Asia and in developing countries are being transformed. Public expectations about access to higher education direct concern about role that universities can play in innovation and economic development" The applications of principles of market economies to the university systems of all countries have created a new context for higher education.

The people in Pakistan and South Asia are neither deficient in talent nor in moral qualities in comparison to any other nation of the world, but about two centuries of foreign rule and blind imitation of western attitudes and methods, unsuited to the genius and spiritual conditions of its people, have spoiled some of the virtues and have brought a bad name to their intellectual capacities. Hassan observed "Pakistan is unfortunately really backward in education as in certain other spheres of intellectual activities but luckily people are not inherently incompetent or morally incurable." It is however necessary that the diagnosis about maladies should be correct and the measures for curing these maladies should be appropriate in the light of that diagnosis.

Challenges in Higher Education

South Asian countries are facing a critical period in their history, and on that account, everybody concerned with education has a responsibility for knowing what he is trying to do in bring up the next generation and why he is trying to do it. Higher education is faced with very severe challenges in the shape of various economic, social, political, and moral changes, and its future depends on the response made by its people to these challenges.

Commonwealth countries vary widely in terms of their size and level of development. Among the 52 member states, national populations vary from 10,000 in Tuvalu to 1.1 billion in India. While some are developed countries, most are developing countries. The developed countries have massif ed systems of higher education, whereas many of the developing countries have a small but expanding higher education sector. Some of the small states do not have universities of their own and therefore share the facilities of a university, either within or outside their region, for their higher education provision.

Despite this level of diversity, two factors seem to be common among Commonwealth countries: the dominant role of public institutions in higher education development, and English being the language of instruction. The f scal capacity of the state to fund and expand higher education through public institutions has become uncertain in recent years. The use of and reliance on English as the language for academic interactions continues to be encouraged. The latter factor has become even more relevant in the context of globalization, in which the English language enjoys a premium. In the initial years at the end of colonization, the state and public institutions played an important role in economic and educational development. Higher education was publicly funded, and graduates were employed in the public sector. Nowadays, the private sector has become an important player in economic development, in employment generation and in the provision of higher education. The liberalization policies adopted by many governments in the Commonwealth in the context of globalization promoted the role of the market and facilitated the cross-border f ow of goods, services, and factors of production.

The higher education sector not only supported globalization, but also became globalized in the process. The cross-border mobility of institutions, programmes, students, and teachers helped in globalizing higher education. The private sector, cross-border providers, and technology-based modes of delivery changed the landscape of higher education and made it a marketable service across countries. The multiplicity of providers and the proliferation of programmes have brought issues related to the quality of provision, teaching/learning processes and products to the forefront.

It will first discuss the increasing demand for skills in knowledge economies and the need for an expanded higher education sector, before going on to examine trends in the expansion of higher education in Commonwealth countries.

Need for Expanded Higher Education Sector

Globalization, technological changes, the rise of the knowledge economy, and changing skill requirements in the labour market seem to inf uence changes in the landscape of higher education, not just in Commonwealth countries but worldwide. Since the emergence of these phenomena, knowledge-based sectors have become the primary drivers of growth, and the demand for skills and higher education qualif cations is on the rise. The move towards a knowledge economy has been characterized by a change in the pattern of deployment of the labour force and an increase in the knowledge content of products. Knowledge economies have experienced a migration of workers from manufacturing activities to service sector activities, making the latter a dominant sector both in terms of level of employment and income generated. The share of the labour force engaged in service sector occupations doubled or trebled in knowledge economies in the 1990s.

The quantity of knowledge embedded in the goods produced and exported has increased considerably. While the knowledge content has increased, the goods have become, as it were, lighter in weight – in fact, 'weightless' – facilitating their exportation. Knowledge economies engage in knowledge production (R&D) and in the production of knowledge-based goods. Investment in knowledge production is financially rewarding to f rms, increases national income, and helps maintain the potential for growth and national competitiveness for the future. While returns to investments in knowledge-based production may be achieved in the short term, those from investments in research and development (R&D) activities may only be realized in the long term.

Knowledge economies require people with theoretical knowledge to promote research activities, with professional skills to develop production, and with technical skills to produce and support production. These skills correspond to a level of education imparted in universities and institutions of higher education. The International Labour Organization estimated that, in some knowledge economies, nearly 70 per cent of all new jobs require a post-secondary level of education. While the more advanced countries have universalized school education and massif ed, if not universalized, higher education, most of the Commonwealth countries are far from reaching this target. Further, it has become essential that the developing countries expand their higher education sector if they are to catch up with the technological advances of other countries and accelerate their economic growth. In other words, for developing countries, higher education expansion is becoming a prerequisite for progress towards a knowledge economy.

The quantity of skills required has outstripped the capacity of the existing higher education institutions to produce them, even in countries that have the largest networks of higher education institutions. The choice for these countries was either to expand the capacity of their higher education systems to produce these skills domestically, or to import skills from the global market. While the former may be a desirable option in the long run, it would require heavy investment and take some time to build the necessary infrastructure. Thus these countries have preferred a more immediate, ready-made solution and encouraged skill migration, especially from developing countries, leading to a 'global hunt' for talent.

Many developed countries have thus made it easier for highly skilled workers to obtain a visa, with the aim of boosting skill migration. For example, the introduction of the H1B visa in the United States (USA) helped to attract skilled workers, especially from Asia. Nearly 1 million highly skilled workers entered the USA under the H1B visa between 2000 and 2003. The European Union is introducing the Blue Card visa to attract skilled workers from developing countries. Countries such as Australia, New Zealand, and the United Kingdom (UK) have introduced point-based migration policies that give preferential treatment to candidates with higher-level qualif cations.

Even so, it seems that the level of migration has not been suf cient to meet global demands. Further, the quality of the skills possessed by migrants has not always been at the level demanded by the production sectors. This called for a greater output of skilled workers, either domestically or abroad, from institutions with established credibility to assure quality. Attention, therefore, turned to cross-border education, to alternatives such as institutions of higher education in developed countries (student mobility), certif ed institutions/branch campuses in developing countries (institutional mobility), or distance modes of education (programme mobility), which proved to be reliable in ensuring quality.

The cross-border mobility of students was encouraged, especially since it was found that a majority of those who entered OECD countries as students would stay there after their studies. For example, it was found that nearly 90 per cent of Chinese and Indian doctorate students in the USA did not return home after their studies. It is clear from this that, in many developed countries, cross-border education has become fertile ground for recruiting future highly skilled workers. In addition, there were institutions and corporations willing to invest in cross-border institutions or programmes as prof t-making ventures. The private sector and transnational institutions play an important role in this mode of cross-border skill development, which relies more on individual than on state funding. In other words, cross-border education has helped transfer the cost of skill development from the public to the individual domain, and was also a necessary condition for the expansion of market operations in this area.

Higher Education in Commonwealth Countries

Commonwealth member countries are so diverse that it is dif cult to provide a general overall picture of higher education. The Commonwealth includes large and small countries, rich and poor, remote islands and mainland countries. The total population of the 52 countries constituting the Commonwealth amounts to nearly 2 billion – nearly one-third of the world's population. Forty-four of the 52 Commonwealth states are developing countries, while the remainder are economically advanced. Thirty-two of them are small states and 23 have a population of less than 1 million. These factors, which contribute to diversity, greatly inf uence the shaping of higher education systems in the Commonwealth.

Some of the countries are too small to make a university a viable entity. For example, two universities – the University of the South Pacif c (USP), Laucala, Fiji, and the University of the West Indies (UWI), Mona, Jamaica – serve more than half the countries of the Commonwealth. USP is jointly owned by the governments of 12 island countries of the Pacif c region with branch campuses in all of the member countries. The University of the West Indies serves 15 countries in the English-speaking Caribbean region, also with branch campuses in all of its member countries. Many of the 27 countries that are served by these two universities do not dispose of a university on their own territory, although they may have non-university tertiary institutions. Many students from islands and small countries pursue their higher education abroad and are thus included in the enrolment f gures of the universities abroad.

Table 1. GER in higher education in Commonwealth countries

Country	*1985*	*1995*	*2006*	*2008*
Australia	27.7	72.9	73.0	77.0
Bangladesh	5.1	6.0	7.0	7.0
Cameroon	2.2	4.0	7.0	9.0
Canada	69.6	87.8	62.0	–
Cyprus	6.0	17.0	33	43.0
Ghana	1.4	1.4	6.0	6.0
India	6.0	6.6	12.0	13.0
Kenya	1.2	2.0	3.0	4.0
Malawi	0.5	0.6	1.0	–
Malaysia	5.9	11.7	29.0	32.0
Mozambique	0.1	0.4	1.0	–
New Zealand	33.1	59.6	80.0	78.0
Nigeria	3.5	4.0	10.0	–
Pakistan	2.5	3.0	5.0	5.0
Singapore	13.8	33.7	–	–
South Africa	13.25*	18.9	15.0	–
Sri Lanka	3.7	5.1	–	–
Tanzania	0.3	0.5	1.0	1.0
Uganda	0.8	1.7	3.0	4.0
United Kingdom	21.7	58.0	59.0	57.0
Zambia	2.0	3.0	–	–

Note: — = not available; * = 1990

Source: UIS, 2008, for 2006; UIS, 2010, for 2008; otherwise UNESCO, 1998.

At the other end of the scale, the larger countries – such as India, with a population exceeding the billion mark; Pakistan, and Bangladesh, with over 150 million population each; and Nigeria with a population of around 130 million – have several universities. Furthermore, countries such as Australia, Canada, South Africa, and the UK, although smaller than the above-mentioned large countries, also have large numbers of universities. The

Association of Commonwealth Universities (ACU) consists of nearly 500 universities, which is, even so, less than the total number of universities in the Commonwealth.

One of the features of higher education is that it is a sector that is expanding in all regions of the world. Between 1991 and 2006, the number of students enrolled in higher education institutions worldwide more than doubled, from 68 to 143.9 million students. The gross enrolment rate (GER) increased from 13.8 to 25 per cent during this period. However, this expansion of higher education was uneven between regions. For example, the fastest growing region was the East Asia and Pacif c region, home to more than one-third of Commonwealth countries, where the GER more than tripled to 25 per cent. The lowest GER of 5 per cent is in the Africa region, which also constitutes a third of the Commonwealth countries.

This chapter, which provides a detailed discussion on the expansion of higher education in the Commonwealth countries, is restricted to the 21 large states that have universities and higher education institutions and for which information is readily available. It shows the trends in the expansion of higher education over the past two decades in these 21 states.

Trends show that the developed countries of the Commonwealth – such as Australia, Canada, the UK – were not only already more advanced in higher education enrolments, but also further expanded their higher education systems very rapidly between 1985 and 1995. A closer examination of this trend reveals that this expansion was most marked in the early 1990s when enrolment ratios almost doubled. After this rapid expansion in the first decade, enrolment ratios in these countries stabilized or declined in the second decade (1995–2006) and thereafter. The trend was somewhat the reverse in the developing countries of the Commonwealth, with a relative stagnation from 1985 to 1995, followed by an acceleration during the decade 1995–2006, although many of them still continue to have relatively low enrolment ratios. In some of the advanced countries and in South Africa, however, the GER declined during the same period.

On the basis of these trends in the expansion of the system, one can distinguish three categories of countries in the Commonwealth:

1. countries with an extensive higher education system and a stagnating or declining GER in the current decade (e.g. Australia, Canada, South Africa, UK);

2. countries where the GER is rapidly increasing (e.g. Ghana, India, Malaysia, New Zealand, Nigeria, Tanzania, although it is still extremely low in all countries except Malaysia and New Zealand);
3. countries where the GER is low and expansion is relatively slow (e.g. Bangladesh, Kenya, Malawi).

It can be noted that this rapid expansion of higher education in Commonwealth countries first happened in the developed countries, followed by developing countries a decade later. This may be partly due to the fact that the demand for the skills required for the knowledge economy and the pressure to expand higher education were felt first in the developed countries. It was universal formal education in developed countries that exerted pressure on the higher education system to expand. At a later period, these same factors played a similar role in the expansion of the higher education systems in developing countries. It may be equally plausible to argue that, among the developing countries of the Commonwealth, those experiencing globalization have undergone a more rapid expansion of their higher education sector.

The expansion of higher education seems to have been faster in those developing countries of the Commonwealth that have a strong private sector. Many countries introduced laws in the 1990s permitting the operation of private and transnational institutions of higher education, and many such institutions were established during the past decade. It seems that rapid expansion in these countries was dependant on non-state resources, highlighting the association between globalization, markets, and the expansion of higher education, even in developing countries.

Higher Education and Cross-border Mobility

Cross-border mobility is a means of globalizing higher education. Two factors seem to have contributed positively to the process of globalizing higher education in Commonwealth countries. First, the fact that many Commonwealth countries provide instruction in English facilitates the process of enrolling in courses in other countries for many students. Since the English language enjoys a premium on the global labour market, individuals are more than willing to invest in courses of ered in this language. Thus, the language factor is an added advantage in promoting cross-border mobility within Commonwealth countries.

Second, many Commonwealth countries moved away from publicly funded higher education towards market-oriented higher education. Many countries diversified their tertiary education systems and permitted the operation of private-sector establishments and cross-border institutions. With the expansion of the higher education market, private and cross-border providers have become numerous, selling courses and study programmes to foreign students. The deregulation policy measures and the General Agreement on Trade in Services (GATS) helped ensure the continuation of cross-border education in Commonwealth countries.

GATS covers all internationally traded services, including education. Within the education sector, GATS covers f ve education service categories: primary, secondary, higher, adult, and 'other'. Cross-border education under the GATS framework can be delivered through one of four modes :

1. cross-border supply, where services are transmitted across borders (e.g. distance education programmes);
2. consumption abroad, where the consumers (students) cross the border to pursue studies;
3. the commercial presence of the provider, where service suppliers cross borders to deliver the services on-site (e.g. branch campuses or twinning and franchising arrangements); and
4. the presence of individual persons, where an individual crosses borders to provide the service (e.g. staf mobility).

Student Mobility

Student mobility is not a new phenomenon for Commonwealth countries. In fact, for many decades this was the only mode of pursuing higher education in the small states of the Commonwealth. In the absence of universities in small island states, students traditionally sought higher education opportunities abroad. This is true of both the Pacif c and Caribbean regions. The only dif erence may be, perhaps, that in the past study-abroad programmes were funded by the government or external agencies, whereas they are now mostly funded by the individuals themselves.

In fact, the study-abroad programme may work out to be cheaper than establishing universities, which may not be a viable option in many countries. The unit costs of higher or university education are greater in small states since they are unable to establish economies of scale. The study-abroad programmes were mainly supported by external funding. The South Pacif c region is an example of the highest concentration of external funding support for higher education. 'Nowhere else in the world is such a high proportion of post-secondary education carried out by international agencies'. However, it had its disadvantages since higher education budgets in these countries have f uctuated.

The share of education in total budgets grew in many countries due to an increase in aid f ows, especially after the commitment of the donor community at the Jomtien World Conference on Education for All of March 1990. However, external funding was directed mainly towards primary education and, therefore, the 1990s experienced a decline in the share of budgets for higher education in these countries.

There are a few other countries in the Commonwealth that traditionally send a large share of their students abroad for higher studies. This has been the case of Cyprus, which, even after founding its own university in 1992, continued to send nearly 50 per cent of its higher education students abroad. Similarly, Singapore and Malaysia used to send nearly one-f fth of their tertiary education students abroad. However, the motivation encouraging these students to pursue their tertiary education abroad was more the quality of the education of ered in the English language than increasing access or opportunities for higher education. Further, the students from these countries were mainly supported either by national governments or individual funding rather than external funding.

In 2006, the number of students seeking cross-border education globally amounted to nearly 2.9 million, creating a market worth US$40–50 billion. In 2005 alone, the USA earned US$14.1 billion from cross-border education; the UK earned US$6.1 billion; and Australia US$5.6 billion.

There is competition among countries and higher education institutions to attract foreign students. The most prevalent pattern of cross-border student f ow is from developing towards developed countries. The USA attracts the single largest share of foreign students (20 per cent), followed by the UK (13 per cent), Germany (8 per cent), France (8 per cent), Australia (7 per cent), and Japan (4 per cent). Asian countries top the list of sending countries with a share of 45.3 per cent of students, followed by Europe (23 per cent),

Africa (9.9 per cent), North America (3.5 per cent), and South America (5 per cent).

There are some Commonwealth countries among the important global players in cross-border higher education. Countries such as Australia, Canada, New Zealand, South Africa, and the UK hosted a total of 0.74 million foreign students in 2008, accounting for nearly a quarter (24.8 per cent) of the global f ow of international students. One can see that the number of students hosted by these countries increased substantially during the decade ending in 2006. It rose by nearly 1.6 times in the UK, 2.2 times in Australia and Canada, and more than 4 times in South Africa. The biggest increase of nearly 8 times took place in New Zealand. This shows that Commonwealth countries are becoming a favourite destination for international students, although the number of international students declined in Canada and New Zealand between 2006 and 2008.

Table 2. Major host countries in the Commonwealth

Country	*Number of foreign students hosted (000s)*		
	1996	*2006*	*2008*
Australia	92.3	207.3	230.6
Canada	35.4*	75.5	68.5
New Zealand	5.6	40.8	31.6
South Africa	12.6*	53.7	64.0
United Kingdom	197.2**	330.1	341.8
TOTAL	343.1	707.4	736.5

Notes: * = 1994; ** = 1995

Most students seeking admission to universities or higher education institutions in the above-mentioned countries are from other Commonwealth countries. It provides information regarding the sending countries. The number of students sent by the developed countries, with the exception of Australia, increased moderately and was less than the increase in the number of students hosted by them, as can be seen by comparing. The number of students sent abroad increased nearly twofold in most of the developing countries. In some instances, such as Bangladesh, the increase was threefold, and fourfold in the case of Nigeria. While the biggest increase of nearly 3.5 times was experienced by India, Malaysia experienced a decline in the number of students travelling abroad, and in Singapore the increase was moderate. The decline of students going abroad from Malaysia may be partly due to the presence of a number of branch campuses of foreign universities operating in that country.

In 1959, during the first meeting of Commonwealth ministers in Oxford, a Commonwealth Shared Scholarship Scheme was introduced to support cross-border higher education studies in Commonwealth countries. This scheme provided an opportunity for students from other Commonwealth countries to study in the UK, and for British nationals to study in another Commonwealth country.

Table 3. Students sent abroad from Commonwealth countries

Sending country	***Number of students sent (000s)***		
	1996	***2006***	***2008***
Australia	5.4	9.8	9.9
Bangladesh	5.8	18.6	15.3
Cameroon	8.8	15.9	17.5
Canada	29.6	43.2	44.9
Cyprus	8.9	19.1	23.8
Ghana	4.1	8.1	7.2
India	40.4	139.5	170.3
Kenya	5.9	13.9	12.6
Malawi	0.8	1.7	1.9
Malaysia	49.4	45.2	47.4
Mozambique	1.5	2.8	2.4
New Zealand	6.0	7.4	4.2
Nigeria	6.3	21.7	25.0
Pakistan	10.8	23.7	26.6
Singapore	18.1	20.3	18.6
South Africa	3.6	6.6	5.5
Sri Lanka	5.1	11.3	13.9
Tanzania	2.5	4.2	4.1
Uganda	1.6	2.6	2.7
United Kingdom	25.5	26.9	22.0
Zambia	1.5	3.7	4.3
TOTAL	241.6	446.2	480.1

Nowadays, the possibilities for fellowships are declining, and cross-border higher education is increasingly funded by households. With the financing burden shifting from public to private sources, the cost factors are becoming important considerations for students when choosing a country for cross-border study.

The level of fees levied from students of higher education varies among countries in the Commonwealth. Some countries do not levy tuition fees for any students; some countries levy the same level of fees for domestic and foreign students; and some countries levy high fees for foreign students and low fees for domestic students. The major host countries of the Commonwealth (Australia, Canada, New Zealand, and the UK) all levy varying levels of tuition fees. One of the reasons for an increase in the f ow of students to Australia and New Zealand in the 1990s may be due to the low level of tuition fees and low cost of living compared to the UK.

Institutional and Programme Mobility

Another aspect of cross-border education is institutional mobility. Institutional mobility takes place mainly through branch campuses, franchising, or twinning arrangements. While branch campuses are more visible, franchising and twinning arrangements can be less visible, even when quantitatively they constitute larger segments of institutional mobility. The most important players in the context of institutional mobility in the Commonwealth are Australia and the UK. Malaysia is a good example of a host country for institutions since branch campuses can be found there of Nottingham University (UK), Monash University and Curtin University.

India has several foreign institutions in operation, mainly from the UK and the USA. A study of 131 foreign-af liated institutions in India showed that 59 partnered with universities in the UK and 66 partnered with universities in the USA. High-level delegations are visiting India to establish branch campuses or collaborations with Indian institutions. Professor Rick Trainor, President of Universities UK (which represents the heads of all UK universities), led a delegation of British Vice-Chancellors to India to discuss institutional collaborations, and student and teacher mobility between premier institutions in India and the UK.

Private higher education institutions of er an easy entry point for foreign providers. In fact, in many countries transnational providers operate through private institutions. Many of them of er market-friendly courses to cater to private business enterprises – foreign or domestic. Courses in business administration, computer science, accounting, marketing, economics, and communication are very common in such institutions. Collaboration with foreign universities and institutions helps the local private universities to obtain academic credibility and to raise their reputation for quality, which consequently allows them to charge higher fees.

Some private universities in Asia attract foreign students from neighbouring countries. For example, the North South University of Bangladesh enrols students from India, Nepal, Pakistan, Sri Lanka, and other countries. Similarly, the branch campuses of foreign universities located in Malaysia attract foreign students. This is also the case of transnational providers operating in Singapore and South Africa, for example.

Some small island states of the Commonwealth that do not have a university of their own have branch campuses of some (although few) foreign universities or institutions. Other modes of cross-border education are also common in small states; the availability of computer facilities gives access to study programmes and resource materials through distance and Internet education, which are increasingly replacing overseas study, enabling students to pursue higher education programmes in foreign universities without leaving their home country. Thus, the combination of expanding connectivity and the growing reservoir of open education eliminates the disadvantages faced by the small states.

Technological advances have allowed the expansion of programme mobility, and this concerns not only the small states of the Commonwealth. Due to its low cost and the fact that it reduces migration and brain drain, many countries worldwide are increasingly implementing this mode of educational expansion. Any institution wishing to introduce distance education can now use a range of open-source learning management systems or software platforms that support e-learning. Indeed, some of the large states in the Commonwealth have some of the largest distance-learning programmes and virtual universities in the world. Some of the national open universities enrol a large number of students from abroad; the Indira Gandhi National Open University in Delhi, for example, enrols almost 11,000 foreign students.

Some Malaysian universities franchise their programmes to local private colleges. This enables those who were unable to access public universities to study in a private university and obtain a university degree.

Demand for Quality-assurance Mechanisms

In the past, most Commonwealth countries relied on public universities for the provision of higher education. Public universities traditionally had an established mechanism for the control of academic quality. At times, these were influenced, if not controlled, by the state. The quality-control mechanisms focused mainly on the input factors, such as: student selection and admission, staf qualif cations, financial allocations, scores in examinations, etc. Nowadays, the approach to quality assessment is changing as other actors enter the scene. The state is no longer the sole provider of higher education in most countries. The existence of a multiplicity of providers – public, private and cross-border – and modes raises the issue of comparability and the quality of the higher education imparted.

What makes the assessment of quality in the present context dif erent is also its change in focus from the traditional quality-control mechanisms. Quality assurance in the present context focuses not only on input factors but also on the teaching/learning process – an area relatively untouched by traditional procedures – as well as on outcomes, in place of the traditional focus on inputs and the regularity of assessment against the traditional ad hoc approach.

Nowadays, most of the large states in the Commonwealth have set up accreditation agencies to ensure quality in higher education. They are mostly national in character. Accreditation is a process by which an agency – external, public, or private – evaluates the quality of a higher education institution or its programmes in order to formally recognize its ability to meet pre-determined standards and criteria.

External quality assurance (EQA) is very often based on minimum standards, although there are instances where it is based on high-level quality. At the minimum level, standards focus on input factors related to student admissions, staf qualif cations, facilities, and funding. The process factors considered are management and research activities. The focus of EQA is to determine to what extent the institution or programme conforms to the prescribed standards. In a sense, it gives formal certif cation to an institute or programme indicating that it has met the minimum expected standards.

Higher education in many countries is diversif ed in terms of both institutions and programmes. The non-university sector is also expanding its share in enrolment. Although EQA systems can address both the university and non-university sectors, very often they focus only on universities. This is primarily due to the fact that universities enjoy an almost total autonomy in introducing study programmes, while the non-university sector is more under the control of the public authorities or is managed by the private sector. In many countries, accreditation mechanisms are in place to grant private universities a license to operate. In some Commonwealth countries, this licensing process is a three-stage process consisting of provisional registration, full registration, and accreditation. It is alleged that in some countries, EQA operates more as a regulating mechanism of private and transnational providers.

It seems that the globalization of higher education also calls for the globalization of quality assurance and accreditation services. There are accreditation agencies located in one country that cover institutions in other countries. The Council for Higher Education Accreditation (CHEA) in the USA is one example. Recent developments in the area indicate that there is a growing trend towards developing regulatory frameworks for quality assurance at the regional and international levels, in addition to such frameworks at the national levels. The regional regulations in the area of quality control mechanisms focus on the Code of Good Practice in the Provision of Transnational Education, which was established by the Council of Europe in cooperation with UNESCO and adopted at the Lisbon Convention. The code protects students from fraudulent degrees and qualif cations, and prevents the national authorities from devising too strict regulations for transnational education. UNESCO and OECD have developed a set of guidelines for quality provision in cross-border higher education. The other guidelines produced jointly by UNESCO and the Commonwealth of Learning provide a more detailed description of the modalities, especially for countries entering GATS negotiations.

Many countries have invested in setting up accreditation agencies. However, the simple creation of these agencies may not be suf cient to ensure quality. There is a need to make sure that they function autonomously and ef ectively, covering all public, private, and trans-border institutions engaged in higher education. Since the non-university tertiary education sector is expanding, it is important to extend the purview of EQA to all such institutions.

Challenges Facing Higher Education Development

There are broadly three categories of Commonwealth countries with regard to higher education: (1) advanced countries with massif ed higher education systems, (2) developing countries with less-developed but quickly expanding systems of higher education, and (3) small states without a university of their own. The need to expand opportunities may be equally important to the latter two categories, and ensuring the quality of higher education may be a common interest of all countries in all categories.

The first challenge facing developing countries and small states is how to expand the higher education system. It is becoming increasingly clear that expansion of higher education through public institutions has its limitations, given the f scal capacity of the state. The option then is to expand higher education relying on non-state resources. This implies: (1) privatizing public institutions of higher education, (2) promoting private higher education, (3) encouraging cross-border providers, and (4) expanding opportunities for distance learning – the promotion of e-learning.

The privatization of public institutions implies the adoption of market principles in the operation of public institutions of higher education. Cost-recovery methods are examples of this strategy. Many countries in Africa have adopted the pattern of a dual-track system, where one group of students is supported by the state and receives subsidized education, while another group pays for its education. This has been a successful strategy to expand higher education through public institutions in many countries. In fact, in many cases the number of students sponsored by the government increased marginally, while the number of fee-paying students increased substantially. In universities such as Makerere in Uganda, nearly 80 per cent of the students in the public university are private (fee paying). The challenge is how to introduce cost-recovery methods, since experience shows that such ef orts are resisted in many instances.

Private higher education has become a common phenomenon in many countries. The actual number of such institutions sometimes surpasses the number of public institutions, although, in terms of enrolment, public institutions still account for the largest share and accommodate the majority of students. However, it is important to note that the share of the private sector in enrolment is increasing in many countries, reaching nearly one-third of the total enrolment.

There are dif erent types of transnational providers. Some are private institutions in the host and sending countries; some consist of a public institution in the sending country and a private institution in the host country; and some operate in collaboration with domestic institutions of higher education, especially private institutions.

Both private and cross-border institutions levy fees from students. The amount of fees depends on the type of institution. There are two types of private and cross-border institutions – for-profit and not-for-profit institutions. It is important to avoid the commercialization of higher education by these institutions, and there is a need to regulate the opening and operation of private and cross-border institutions. The challenge lies in developing mechanisms to regulate these institutions.

The open and distance-learning systems have widened the scope for expanding higher education. Technological advances and their availability have provided opportunities for people to follow programmes of study and courses at their own pace. This is a particularly important mode for expanding higher education in small states. Higher education through this mode is less expensive than the face-to-face mode. The major challenge will be to ensure the availability of the technology to people who would like to pursue higher education through this mode.

All of these modes of expanding higher education anticipate a transfer of the financial burden to individuals and households. However, this does not mean that the state will cease to fund higher education; it will continue to do so as far as possible. However, the opportunities to pursue higher education will not be limited by the f scal capacity of the state and its willingness to fund students.

There is a need to introduce student-support systems as part of the cost-recovery or private-sector operations. Student loans will be of ered to students to help cover their fees and living expenses. The student-loan schemes introduced in many countries in the 1970s were not a success. However, the new initiatives in student loans seem to be working. Unlike in the past, when loans were given by the government, these loans are more often of ered by banks and other commercial organizations. The challenge is not to distribute loans to students, but to keep track of them and recover them when the students have f nished their studies. In some developing countries, the cost of recovering loans exceeds the amount recovered, and the government has almost abandoned the idea of recovering them altogether.

It is important to ensure equity while the higher education system expands. Cost-recovery measures are not equity-friendly. There is a need to ensure that the interests of those from economically poorer backgrounds and socially disadvantaged groups are protected. Public financial intervention targeting students from these groups may be necessary to maintain equity in the system.

An equally important area is ensuring the quality of the higher education imparted. There is a need for regulation to ensure quality at all stages. This is more essential in the context of the proliferation of institutions and programmes, especially through private and transnational providers. Permission to own and operate a private or cross-border institution needs to be granted after the minimum facilities and conditions are guaranteed. There are instances of fraud in the operation of transnational providers. Some cross-border providers are found to be of dubious quality, with bogus institutions and fake degrees. Some such institutions automatically increase their fees every year. However, some national authorities stipulate the regulations on fees, and prohibit cross-border or private providers from raising tuition fees without their prior approval.

Nowadays, many countries involved in cross-border higher education insist that foreign institutions must already be accredited in their country of origin before they are granted permission to operate in the host country. Further, most countries which agree to cross-border education demand that the establishment of a foreign institution systematically follow the procedures for seeking permission from the concerned ministry (very often the ministry of education) before the campus is opened in the host country.

Finally, the state may not be able to provide funding support to expand higher education. However, this does not imply that state intervention is not necessary. There is a need to separate state intervention from financing issues. Government intervention is needed more to develop policy, provide a framework for action, and ensure equity and quality rather than to finance educational development. Government intervention is needed more to regulate the system than to control and finance higher education development.

References

Bashir, S. 2007. *Trends in international trade in higher education: Implications and options for developing countries*. Washington, DC: World Bank.

Bray, M.; Packer, S. 1993. *Education in small states: Concepts, challenges and strategies*. Oxford, UK: Pergamon Press.

Crocombe, R.; Crocombe, M.T. 1994. *Post-secondary education in the South Pacifi c*. London: Commonwealth Secretariat.

Daniel, J. 2006. *The reality of cross-border delivery in higher education: Challenge, myth and opportunity*.

Hallak, J.; Poisson, M. 2007. *Corrupt schools, corrupt universities: What can be done?* Paris: IIEP-UNESCO.

International Labour Offi ce (ILO). 2004. *Promoting employment: Policies, skills, enterprises*. Geneva, Switzerland: ILO.

Institute of International Education (IIE). 2007. *Atlas of student mobility*. New York, NY: IIE.

10

Internationalisation of Higher Education in Europe

Over the past 25 years, the international dimension of higher education in Europe has become more central on the agenda of European and national governments, institutions of higher education and their representative bodies, student organisations and accreditation agencies.

Stimulated in the 1980's by European programmes for cooperation and exchange in education and research, internationali-sation over these years has moved from a reactive to a pro-active strategic issue, from added value to mainstream, and also has seen its focus, scope and content evolve substantially. Increasing competition in higher education and the commercialisation and cross-border delivery of higher education, have challenged the value traditionally attached to cooperation: exchanges and partnerships. At the same time, the internationalisation of the curriculum and the teaching and learning process (also referred to as 'internationalisation at home') has become as relevant as the traditional focus on mobility (both degree mobility and mobility as part of your home degree). Internationalisation has become an indicator for quality in higher education, and at the same time there is more debate about the quality of internationalisation itself.

The international dimension and the position of higher education in the global arena are given greater emphasis in international, national and institutional documents and mission statements than ever before. Altbach,

Reisberg and Rumbley in their report to the UNESCO World Conference on Higher Education note that

> "Universities have always been affected by international trends and to a certain degree operated within a broader international community of academic institutions, scholars, and research. Yet, 21st century realities have magnifed the importance of the global context. The rise of English as the dominant language of scientifc communication is unprecedented since Latin dominated the academy in medieval Europe. Information and communications technologies have created a universal means of instantaneous contact and simplifed scientifc communication. At the same time, these changes have helped to concentrate ownership of publishers, databases, and other key resources in the hands of the strongest universities and some multinational companies, located almost exclusively in the developed world."

It would be too easy, however, to assume that everything has changed over the past ten years with regard to the internationalisation of higher education, and that this change in Europe is primarily from a more cooperative model to a more competitive model. As Van der Wende writes:

> "Not surprisingly most continental European countries pursue a cooperative approach to internationalisation, which in terms of international learning and experience is more compatible with the traditional values of academia."

In a benchmarking exercise on the internationalisation strategies of fve European universities, De Wit encountered clear differentiations.

> "Striking is the difference between the approaches to internationalisation of three Northern European universities and two Southern European universities with respect to co-operation and competition. Where the two Southern European universities have a traditional cooperative approach, one Northern university has a strong competitive approach and the two Scandinavian universities are moving into the directions of such an approach, although all three mix it with co-operative activities, in particular in the framework of their involvement in the European programmes. These approaches give a more balanced picture to the idea of shifting paradigms for internationalisation from co-operative to competitive, as presented in current debate and study of the international dimension of higher education in Europe."

This was confrmed in a second benchmarking exercise, which nvolved three other European and four Latin American universities.

In other words, the changing landscape of internationalisation is not developing in similar ways in higher education throughout Europe and the world as a whole. There are different accents and approaches. Internationalisation strategies are fltered and contextualised by the specifc internal context of the university, by the type of university, and how they are embedded nationally. For Norway, Frolich comes to the conclusion that *"Internationalisation in higher education institutions (...) is a case of a match between the inherently international character of academic activities and external demands and changing environments."*

But in a comparative study on internationalisation strategies in Europe, Frolich and Vega observe also that *"the internationalisation of higher education is a complex, multidimensional and often fragmented process. The factors that foster or impede internationalisation activities developed at an institutional level cannot be viewed only in the national and international context. There are infuences deeply rooted in the normative and cultural insights, such as history and culture; academic disciplines and subjects; the higher education institution's profles and individual initiatives; national policies; regulatory frameworks; finance; European challenges and opportunities; and globalisation."*

Internationalisation strategies are shaped at the programme level by the different relationship these programmes have to the market and society.

An internationalisation strategy can be substantially different for a teacher training programme than for a school of dentistry or a business school.

And as a result of the Bologna Process more and more internationalisation strategies may be different by level: PhD, master and bachelor. Joris states with reference to developing a list of measures or indicators for quality assessment of internationalisation for Flemish institutions of higher education that different institutions make different policy choices, are differently organized, are of different types and work in different contexts.

The growing importance of internationalisation in higher education on the one hand and the diversity in rationales, approaches and strategies of institutions and programmes on the other hand, call for an assessment of the quality of inter-nationalisation at the programme and the institutional level and the realisation a system of certifcations as to defne the progress and status of the internationalisation at the programme and institutional level.

The rationale for a system of certifcates for internationalisa-tion is described by a Flemish Working Group, which observed that too much already has been said about the why of interna-tionalisation of Flemish higher education but too little about the how and about the quality indicators to be used. According to them important questions about visibility, transparency, focus and demonstrated quality still are not answered, and that is why they look for instruments to do so.

Deardorff, Pysarchik and Yun state: *"with globalisation driving the demand for global-ready graduates, it becomes crucial for administrators to assess these outcomes of interna-tionalisation to determine exactly what our students are learning through these efforts and how effective our programmes are in achieving the stated learning outcomes."*

The following topics will be addressed in this chapter. What do we mean with internationalisation, in particular in the context of increasing globalisation of our societies and the development of a global knowledge economy? What rationales for and approaches of internationalisation of higher education can be identifed? What experience already exists with assessment and benchmarking of quality assurance of internationalisa-tion? What lessons can be learned from these experiences, and what are important aspects to keep in mind when implementing such a label?

Rationales and Approaches to Internationalisation

The changing dynamics in internationalisation of higher education refect themselves both in the meaning of internationalisation and globalisation, its rationales and the approaches to internationalisation by the different stakeholders.

What do we mean by the internationalisation of higher education? First of all, we have to recognize, that there have always been many different terms used in connection to internationalisation of higher education. In literature and in practice of internationalisation of higher education, it is still quite common to use terms which only address a small part of internationalisation and/or emphasize a specifc rationale for internationalisation. Most of the terms used are either curriculum related:

international studies, global studies, multicultural education, intercultural education, peace education, etc., or mobility related: study abroad, education abroad, academic mobility, etc.

Over the past ten years one can note a whole new group of terms emerging which were not actively present before in the debate about internationalisation of higher education. These are much more related to the cross-border delivery of education and are a consequence of the impact of globalisation of society on higher education: borderless education, education across borders, global education, offshore education and nternational trade of educational services.

In 2002, De Wit stated that *"as the international dimension of higher education gains more attention and recognition, people tend to use it in the way that best suits their purpose."* This is even more the case now in view of this further proliferation of activities and terms.

The most commonly used defnition of what we mean by internationalisation at the institutional level is the one by Jane Knight from 1994 : *"a process of integrating an international and cultural dimension into the teaching, research and service functions of the institution."*

Since she developed this defnition in the early nineties, internationalisation of higher education has evolved. *"Internationalisation is changing the world of higher education, and globalization is changing the world of internationalisation,"* as Knight puts it. The debate about globalisation and internationalisation and the recent, rapid evolution of cross-border activities in higher education have strengthened the tendency to explain and defne internationalisation of higher education in connection to a specifc rationale or purpose. In the past 'international education' was the most frequently used term synonymous to internationalisation of education, more recently 'globalisation' has come more commonly used as a term related to or even synonym of internationalisation.

Scott observes that both internationalisation and globalisation are complex phenomena with many strands, and concludes that *"the distinction between internationalisa-tion and globalisation, although suggestive, cannot be regarded as categorical. They overlap, and are intertwined, in all kinds of ways."*

Teichler notes that *"globalisation initially seemed to be defned as the totality of substantial changes in the context and inner life of higher education, related to growing interrelationships between different parts of the world whereby national borders are blurred or even seem to vanish."* But according to him, in recent years the term 'globalisation' is substituted for internationalisation in the public debate on higher education, resulting at the same time in a shift of meanings: *"the term tends to be used for any supra-regional phenomenon related top higher education ( ) and/or anything on a global scale related to higher education characterised by market and competition."*

Altbach, Reisberg and Rumbley state that *"Globalization, a key reality in the 21st century, has already profoundly infuenced higher education.(...) We defne globalization as the reality shaped by an increasingly integrated world economy, new information and communications technology, the emergence of an international knowledge network, the role of the English language, and other forces beyond the control of academic institutions(...). Internationalisation is defned as the variety of policies and programs that universities and governments implement to respond to globalization."*

Knight acknowledges the need for constant updating of the meaning of internationalisation of higher education, as *"the international dimension of higher education has been steadily increasing in importance, scope, and complexity."* As new realities and challenges of the current environment she mentions globalisation and the emergence of the knowledge economy, regionalisation, information and communication technologies, new providers, alternate funding sources, borderless issues, lifelong learning, and the growth in the numbers and diversity of actors.

Therefore, a new defnition is proposed by Knight, which acknowledges both levels and the need to address the relationship and integrity between them: *"the process of integrating an international, intercultural or global dimension into the purpose, functions or delivery of post-secondary education."* She also states that you can see now basically two components evolving in the internationalisation of higher education. One is *internationalisation at home* - activities that help students to develop international understanding and intercultural skills.

So it is much more curriculum-oriented: preparing your students to be active in a much more globalised world. Activities under this at home dimension are: curriculum and programmes, teaching and learning processes, extra-curricular activities, liaison with local cultural/ethnic groups, and research and scholarly activities. And the second movement is that of *internationalisation abroad,* including all forms of education across borders: mobility of students and faculty and mobility of projects, programs and providers. These components have not to be seen as mutual exclusive but are ntertwined in the policies and programmes.

Rationales for Internationalisation

When we talk about internationalisation, it is important to distinguish the question of why we are internationalising higher education, from what we mean by internationalisation. Many documents, policy papers and books refer to internationalisation, but do not defne the why. And in much literature meanings and rationales are confused, in the sense that often a rationale for internationalisation is presented as a defnition of internationalisation.

Literature identifes four broad categories of rationales for internationalisation: Political rationales, economic rationales, social and cultural rationales and academic rationales.

Political rationales such as foreign policy, national security technical assistance, peace and mutual understanding, national and regional identity, have been very important, in particular after the Second World War, and in the Cold War period, when they were very dominant in the internationalisation of higher education. After 9/11/2001 national security has regained importance.

The second group, economic rationales, including growth and competitiveness, national educational demand, labour market, financial incentives, have come more to the forefront in present-day globalization of our economies.

The third group of rationales are the social and cultural rationales. The cultural rationale has to do much more with the role that universities and their research and teaching can play in creating an intercultural understanding and an inter-cultural competence for the students and for the faculty and in their research. And the social rationale has to do with the fact that the individual, the student, and the academic, by being in an international environment, become less provincial. As mentioned before, there is concern that the role of universities in social and cultural cohesion is under pressure these days.

The last group are the academic rationales: developing an international and intercultural dimension in your research, teaching and services, extension of the academic horizon, institution building, profle and status, the improvement of the quality, and international academic standards. Among these, profle and status, as expressed in the growing importance of international rankings, seem to become more dominant.

It is clear that there are different rationales for the interna-tionalisation of higher education. These are not mutually exclusive, may be different in importance by country and region, and can change in dominance over time. In the present time, the economic rationales are considered to be more dominant than the other three, and in connection to these, academic rationales such as strategic alliances, status and profle are also becoming more dominant.

Knight speaks of emerging rationales at the national level such as human resource development, strategic alliances, income generation/ commercial trade, nation building, and social/cultural development and mutual understanding; and at the institutional level: international branding and profle, quality enhancement/international standards, income generation, student and staff development, strategic alliances and knowledge production.

Several authors like Teichler mention a growing emphasis on marketisation, competition and management. Reinalda and Kulesza note that *"since the end of the last century, a shift in higher education has taken place from the public to the private domain, parallel to an increase in international trade in education services (...) These developments enhance the signifcance of the education market as an international institution, but also contribute to changing the structure of that market. In doing so, an increase in worldwide competition is being revealed."*

Nimes and Hellsten observe that internationalisation of higher education tends to have been too much identifed in the past with positive opportunities: *"Under internationalisa-tion, the world is our oyster, or perhaps, our garden, in which sow the seeds from the fruits of our academic labours: powerful knowledges, proven (best) practices, and established systems of scholarship, administration and inquiry."* They look "*to trouble such unproblematized notions and to provide more critical readings and explorations of the process.*" They call for "*review, renewal and critical insight into current practices of internationalisation.*"

All these authors have a strong inclination to call for more attention to social cohesion and to the public role of higher education as an alternative force to the growing emphasis on competition, markets and entrepreneurialism in higher education.

Brandenburg and De Wit in a provocative essay 'The end of Internationalisation' state that there is a tendency to *see "internationalization as "good" and globalization as "evil". Internationalization is claimed to be the last stand for humanistic ideas against the world of pure economic benefits allegedly represented by the term globalization. Alas, this constructed antagonism between internationalisation and globalization ignores the fact that activities that are more related to the concept of globalization (higher education as a tradable commodity) are increasingly executed under the fag of internationalisation"*

Changing Approaches

In the course of history can identify different institutional approaches to internationalisation : the activity approach which describes internationalisation in terms of categories or types of activity; the rationale approach which defnes internationalisation in terms of its purposes or ntended outcomes; the competency approach which describes internationalisation in terms of developing new skills, attitudes, and knowledge in students, faculty, and staff; and the process approach which frames internationalisation as a process that integrates an international dimension or perspective into the major functions of the institution.

The frst three approaches, in particular the activity approach, are most common to internationalisation. Given the growing mportance of internationalisation in higher education one would have assumed that this would result in a development into a more process approach to internationalisation.

This appeared true for the situation in Europe, where one could observe in the late nineties a trend towards main-streaming internationalisation, as well as initiatives in the United States of America to promote internationalisation of the campus by organisations like the American Council on Education and by NAFSA.

Also, competencies became more important factors in the discussion on internationalisation, with the increased focus on the internationalisation of the curriculum and teaching and learning process, *i.e.* the internationalisation at home movement. Rationale approaches, with economic and political rationales driving internationalisation at the (inter)national and the institutional level, can also be identifed.

Rationales are different over time and by country/region, they are not mutually exclusive, and they lead to different approaches and policies. Currently, changes are taking place at a rapid pace in different parts of the world and rationales become more and more interconnected.

The changing landscape of international higher education as a consequence of the globalisation of our societies and economies is manifest in many ways: increasing competition for international students and academics, growth of cross-border delivery of programmes and emergence of international for proft providers in higher education, the changing position of countries like India and China in the world economy and in the higher education arena. They are all realities and their impact cannot be ignored.

In Europe but also elsewhere, in national and institutional strategies and approaches to internationalisation, mobility -either as part of the home degree or for a full degree abroad -has been dominant until the end of the century. In the United Kingdom this has been the case for full degree incoming mobility, in other countries like Greece and Turkey for outgoing degree mobility, and in other European countries for mobility as part of the home degree: exchanges and participation in European programmes, in particular Socrates/Erasmus. In the Communiqué of the Conference of European Ministers Responsible for Higher Education, Leuven on the Bologna Process, there is an ongoing strong emphasis on the importance of mobility: *"in 2020, at least 20% of those graduating in the European Higher Education Area should have had a study or training abroad."*

In the past decade though a gradual shift can be observed where mobility becomes more one of the instruments and elements of internationalisation. Under the impetus of the 'internationalisation at home movement' the attention has become more focused on the internationalisation of the curriculum and the teaching and learning process: how can we prepare our students – being national or foreign – for a future career and life in an increasingly interconnected knowledge economy and society. Mobility is in that approach no longer an objective in itself but one of the ways how to reach this; and international becomes more interconnected with intercultural, where crossing borders is no longer an absolute must but only a plus to get an international and intercultural experience.

That experience can also be reached by an international/inter-cultural classroom setting, in an international company or organisation and/or an intercultural social environment (for instance a internationally/ culturally diverse neighbourhood). Brandenburg and de Wit phrase it as follows: "*Gradually, the why and what have been taken over by the how and instruments of internationalization have become the main objective: more exchange, more degree mobility, and more recruitment.*"

In this context also the recent initiative by the American Council on Education to bridge the current divide between internationalisation and multicultural education is important. While they are distinct, Christa Olson wrote that "*one should not be subsumed into the other (...) the two areas have much they can substantively contribute to each other. Indeed, neither area is complete without consideration of what the other brings to bear in terms of understanding and living effectively with difference.*"

Assessment of Internationalisation Strategies

In 1999, the OECD published a book edited by Jane Knight and Hans de Wit with the title *Quality and Internationalisation in Higher Education*, where an instrument and guidelines were provided for assessing internationalisation strategies based on a number of pilot reviews in institutions in different parts of the world. Two issues were considered at that time relevant: the question of the added value that internationalisation contributes to higher education, and the quality of the inter-nationalisation strategies itself.

The international ranking of higher education institutions is a widely debated example of how measurement has started to infu-ence our profession in a way that differs from the past. The call for accountability by students, faculty, deans, the management of higher education institutions and national governments, as well as the call for quality assurance, is an important issue on the agenda of higher education, in general, and this includes the internationalisation process, programmes and projects. Accreditation, ranking, certifca-tion, auditing, and benchmarking have become key items on the international higher education agenda.

Some important questions that are relevant in addressing the issue of assessment of internationalisation are:

- How do we measure what we do?
- What do we measure?
- What indicators do we use for assessment?
- Do we assess processes or activities?
- Do we carry out assessments with a view to improving the quality of our own process and activities or do we assess the contribution made by internationalisation to the improvement of the overall quality of higher education?
- Do we use a quantitative and/or a qualitative approach to measurement?
- Which instruments do we use, *ex post* or *ex ante* measurements, indicators, benchmarking, best practices, quality review, accreditation, certifcation, audits or rankings?
- Are we focussing on inputs, outputs and/or outcomes?

Several initiatives to develop tools and instruments for measuring internationalisation have been taken in different countries over the past years, following the 'Internationalisation.

Outside of Europe

1. The Association of Commonwealth Universities (ACU) ran The ACU University Management Benchmarking Programme for the frst time in 1996, primarily, but not exclusively, for Commonwealth universities. Both in 1998 and 2008, internationalisation has been one of the themes of ACU's benchmarking exercise. The ACU Benchmarking Programme helps to identify areas for change and assists in setting targets for improvement and identifying techniques for managing change. The Programme focuses on the effectiveness of university-wide processes

and policies rather than narrow departmental functions. It enables members to learn from each other's experience of diffculties and successes across international boundaries.

2. Another initiative is the project set up by the American Council on Education, known as "Internationalizing the Campus".
3. The Association of International Educators NAFSA has a project entitled "Accessing Best Practices in Internationalisation" (ABPI). NAFSA has published an annual report entitled *Internationalizing the Campus: Profles of Success at Colleges and Universities* since 2003. Each year, this publication profles colleges and universities, highlighting best practices in various aspects of internationalisation.
4. The Forum on Education Abroad published *A Guide to Outcomes Assessment in Education Abroad* in 2007 edited by Mell C. Bolen.
5. Also in Japan, the discussion on assessing the internationalisation of Japanese universities is under way, as part of national initiatives to enhance the internationalisation of Japanese higher education. See, for instance, Furushiro, N. (Project Leader) Developing Evaluation Criteria to Assess the Internationalisation of Universities.
6. The Forum Euro-LatinoAmericano di Torino has established a Universities Benchmarking Club, to support each university's continued efforts towards improvement through systematic comparisons of various key aspects among participating universities. It includes internationalisation of human resources as one theme, and is considering to expand to other internationalisation themes as well. The Columbus Programme has established a web-based benchmarking instrument in connection with this project, focussing among other son the internationalisation of the curriculum and implementation of internationalisation strategies.

Inside Europe

In Europe, the following ones can be identifed:

7. The European Centre for Strategic Management of Universities (ESMU), together with CHE and UNESCO/CEPES and the Universidade de Aveiro, has started a European Benchmarking Initiative in Higher Education, sponsored by the European Commission,

which also includes inter-nationalisation. ESMU has been carrying out a benchmarking exercise for its member institutions, based on ACU's model, since 1999. In 2005, internationalisation was one of the themes.

8. The Spanish Agencia Nacional de Evaluación de la Calidad y Acreditación (ANECA) conducted a pilot project in 2005-2006 with the aim of assessing the international relations of universities which involved fve Spanish universities. Based on this pilot project, the European Foundation for Quality Management (EFQM) recently gave the quality mark "Committed to Excellence" to Universidad Pontifcia de Comillas in Madrid for its international relations.
9. The Centre for Higher Education Development (CHE) in cooperation with a group of German institutions of higher education developed a list of indicators, "*How to measure internationality and internationalisation of higher education institutions! Indicators and key figures.*"
10. The Netherlands Organisation for International Cooperation in Higher Education (Nuffc) in collaboration with a group of Dutch institutions, developed an instrument, MINT (Mapping Internationalisation) to help institutions and their programmes to assess their internationalisa-tion. It is defned as an instrument to reach the intended internationalisation objectives; a way to profle and identify the own institution; and an instrument to support audits, and a method to make benchmarking with other institutions and programmes more easy..
11. Flemish institutions of higher education are developing indicators to assess the quality of institutional strategies for internationalisation. (Michaël Joris, 2008)
12. There is the Bologna Process Stocktaking exercise, which includes indicators for the degree system, quality assurance and recognition.
13. And very recently the project Indicators for Measuring and Profling Internationalisation (IMPI), based on the CHE project, MINT, and the ESMU project, which starts in October 2009 with EU-funding and includes the following partners: CHE, Nuffc, Campus France, SIU, ACA and Perspektywy. Associate partners are DAAD, VLHORA, 15 individual universities and up to 15 individual HEIs from the Coimbra group.

The IMPI-project is at present the most relevant activity in line with this chapter. The rationale for and content of the project is described as follows: *"Bologna and Lisbon call for increased competitiveness and globalisation in higher education is developing rapidly, but so far no European-wide approach has been made to measure internationalisation. Transparency and accountability in internationalisation are not in place yet. To this end, a set of indicators will be developed with relevance to all European HEIs. It provides options for comparison on the one hand but also offers opportunities for HEIs to choose their individual profle of internationalisation. Such a set of indicators will be co-developed by national and supranational entities together with a broad set of individual HEIs as well as the Coimbra Group and the DAAD as associate partners to ensure both relevance and acceptance in the community. The project aims at providing HEIs with insight into their performance and means for improvement. The goal is to increase the OVERALL performance of European HEIs in inter-nationalisation. The milestones of the project will be a set of key indicators, a toolbox for HEIs to profle their internationalisation as well as a number of dissemination instruments (workshops, symposium, website) which will bring together stakeholders from different levels to discuss the results and start implementation.*

A two-step benchmarking initiative will ensure that the practicability of the suggestions will be tested. The establishment of some kind of association of HEIs focusing on the advancement of accountability and transparency in internationalisation is envisioned. The project will lead to a considerable improvement in accountability and transparency of internationalisation and through new tools an improvement process on internationality will fnally help to enhance the competitiveness of European HEIS."

In addition to these instruments, there are also developed several *Codes of Practice* for internationalisation.

14. The 'Code of Practice for Educational Institutions and Overseas Students' by the United Kingdom Council for Overseas Student Affairs (UKCOSA) in the mid-1980s
15. The 'Code of Ethical Practice in International Education' by the Canadian Bureau for International Education (CBIE) of 1996

16. The 'Principles for Transnational Education' of the Global Alliance for Transnational Education (GATE) of 1997.
17. The 'Code of Ethical Practice in the Provision of Education to International Students' by Australian Universities of the Australian Vice-Chancellors Committee (AVCC) of 1998.

The last four are taken from Knight (2008, 52-56), who also mentions the ISO 9000 Set of Standards and their possible use for quality assessment of internationalisation and makes reference to the Guidelines for Quality Cross-border Provision of UNESCO/OECD of 2005. (ibid, 127).

There are probably more interesting examples to be found and, although they all seem to have some common bases (in particular the IQR guidelines of the OECD's Programme on Institutional Management of Higher Education, there are also striking differences based on national contexts and institutional cultures.

All of them measure inputs and/or outputs, and not outcomes. According to Hudzik and Stohl, outcomes are *"usually most closely associated with measuring goal achievement and the missions of institutions (...) and are the really important measures."* However, the German indicators project state that only input and output indicators are developed, as outcomes would have required large-scale, in-depth surveys of samples, which was beyond the scope of the project. The Dutch MINT tool also stays clear of outcomes. Deardorff, Pysarchik and Yun, however, state that the assessment of outcomes is possible and that workable frameworks are available.

Instruments dealing with Intercultural Competences are more oriented to outcomes and several tools exist, primarily in the USA, such as Intercultural Development Inventory (IDI); Cross-Cultural Adaptability Inventory (CCAI); Intercultural Confict Styles Inventory; Languages Strategies Survey; Strategies Inventory for Culture Learning; Beliefs Events, Values Inventory (BEVI); Global Perspectives Inventory (GPI); Assessment of Intercultural Competence; and many more.

Quality assurance in general terms refers to the policies, attitudes, actions, and procedures necessary to ensure that quality is being maintained and enhanced.. Woodhouse identifes four different approaches: general accreditation, specialised or profession accreditation, audit or review, and quality assessment. Most of the instruments described above fall in the category of audits and reviews and focus on 'How good are you at achieving your stated objectives'.

Benchmarking is another instrument that is used in assessing the quality of internationalisation. In the list of instruments presented above, several are using benchmarking. Comparison and identifcation of best practices are two additional elements that form key aspects of benchmarking exercises, and the exercise itself is also focused on improvement. Also for benchmarking one needs a list of measures or indicators.

Knight concludes from the Internationalisation Quality Review Process, and this can be extended to the other instruments as well, *"that institutions need a way to monitor internationalisation and collect information on an ongoing basis. Institutions often spend too much time describing in very vague terms the status of the internationalisation. More precise, relevant measures of explicit objectives and targets will help provide the information necessary to analyze strengths and areas of improvements. With the information collected from the tracking measures, institutions can proceed to the more important step of analyzing how to maintain areas of strength, improve areas of weakness, and ensure that inter-nationalisation goals and objectives are met. This is, in turn a precursor to analyzing the results and outcomes of interna-tionalisation endeavors."*

Knight uses the term 'tracking measure' as opposed to 'performance measure' or 'indicator' as it expresses progress rather than output. Both quantitative and qualitative measures should be used. To identify these measures, she states, is a challenge. *"They need to be relevant, clear, reliable, consistent, accessible, and easy to use.(...) Institutions need to be vigilant about their choice (...) Such measures need to be pertinent to the desired objective and limited to the most relevant (...) (and they) need to stand the test of time, as they should be used over a period to get a true picture of progress toward reaching the objective and whether there is any improvement."*

On the use of the terms 'performance indicators' or 'indicators' in the context of internationalisation, Knight observes that there is not a lot of work on them as there is also no consensus on their use yet and that given their quantitative approach and the high level of diversity within institutions they *"operate best at the program level within individual institutions. It has been suggested that the higher the level of their aggregation, the less useful quality indicators become."*

As principle guidelines, the 'Internationalisation Quality Review Process' has learned that the following are crucial:

- Focused on two aspects: progress (measured by quantitative and qualitative measures) and quality (measured by opinion of those who do the assessment)
- Measured according to the objectives and targets set by the institution
- Focused on both organisational and programme strategies
- More oriented to evaluating the process than the outcomes or impact
- Pointed to where improvement is desirable and necessary
- Accepting that there is no ideal or optimal measurement profle
- Focused on how the different elements work together in an integrated and strategic manner
- Need to take place on a regular basis and over a period of time as to reinforce the process.

One can add to that list also that the quality review of interna-tionalisation requires a commitment and involvement at all levels: leadership, faculty, students and administrative staff.

Brandenburg et all make in the context of assessment an interesting distinction between internationalisation (a process with a focus on improvement) and internationality (a description of the present state of internationalisation).

Last but not least, the diversity of the context is most relevant. As mentioned before, there are different types of institutions; different disciplines within one institution; different levels of education; and different institutional, local, national and regional cultures and environments. Instruments for assessment have to recognise this differences and to be able to contextualise the internationalisation process. The key questions of assessment of internationalisation are: why are you doing it, how do you do it, and what do you want to reach with it, and these questions have to be placed in their specifc context.

Lists of Measures or Indicators

This has to be taken into account when a list of measures or indicators is developed. As Joris states, on the one hand the material must be suffciently relevant to design an instrument that can be used for all kind of different purposes, on the other hand it has to serve as a self-assessment instrument to make results visible and measurable, and to serve as benchmarks and allow benchmarking.

He observes that the notion of context is important, as one has to be aware that one should not compare things that are different. The value of an indicator and how relevant the indicator is must be defned by the context in which one uses the ndicator. It is because of those reasons, most instruments, following the example of the 'Internationalisation Quality Review Process', use the term 'Guidelines' or 'Outline', from where the institution or the programme can select those measures which are relevant in their context.

Most instruments refer to a list of categories, for instance the one used by the ACE:

1. Articulated commitment
2. Academic offerings
3. Organisational infrastructure
4. External funding
5. Institutional investment in faculty
6. International students and student programs.

NAFSA uses criteria:

1. The campus has been widely internationalized across schools, divisions, departments and disciplines.
2. There is evidence of genuine administrative or even board-level support for internationalisation.
3. The campus-wide internationalisation has had demonstrative results for the students.
4. The institution's mission or planning documents contain an explicit or implicit statement regarding nternational education

5. The institution's commitment to internationalisation is refected in the curriculum
6. The campus-wide internationalisation has had demonstrative results within the faculty
7. There is an international dimension in off-campus programs and outreach
8. There is internationalisation in research and/or faculty exchange
9. The institution supports education abroad as well as its international faculty, scholars and students.

Nuffc uses the term 'dimensions':

1. Internationalisation objectives
2. Internationalisation activities
3. Facilities
4. Embededness in the organisation

CHE uses the term indicators and gives the following list: Overall aspects

- Input
- Management in general
- Professors
- Young researchers
- Administrative staff/non-academic staff
- Resources
- International networking

Academic research

- Input
- Professors
- International networking in research
- Resources
- International research projects
- Output
- Research fndings

- Young researchers

Teaching and studies

- Input
- Lecturers
- Students (Bachelor/Master handled separately
- Service and administration
- International networks for teaching and studies
- Resources
- Study programmes/Curricula
- Output
- Graduates (Bachelor/Master/doctoral candidates to be
- handled separately
- International reputation

Joris makes reference to Mestenhauser's seven domains:

1. Specialised academic disciplines such as International Relations, Area Studies
2. Foreign language teaching
3. Academic disciplines which (must) have inherent international componentens, such as social and political sciences, journalism, economics, pedagogy, psychology, communications, management, anthropology
4. Courses which are international oriented in other disciplines which are primarily focused on the labour market
5. Exchange of students, teachers and other staff
6. The administration around internationalisation such as management of bilateral contracts and agreements, recruitment of international students, etc.
7. Policy development around internationalisation, governance.

He also makes reference to Elinboe's six characteristics of internationalisation practices:

1. Internationalisation in and of policy

2. Involvement of staff in international activities
3. International curriculum
4. International study opportunities for students
5. Integration of international students and staff
6. International co-curricular units and activities.

The guidelines of the Internationalisation Quality Review Process, also described as the Outline for the Self-Assessment Process, include the following categories:

- Context
- Internationalisation strategies and policies
- Organizational and support services
- Academic programmes and students
- Study abroad and student exchange programmes
- Research and scholarly collaboration
- Contracts and services
- Conclusions.

If you take a close look at them, the overarching conclusion is that these lists include more or less the same categories,. What they also have in common is that they are more directed to the assessment of institutional strategies than to programmes.

This is also the case with the recent publication *'Internation-alisation and Quality Assurance'*, edited by Adinda van Gaalen which addresses as central question "how can we assure the quality of internationalisation of an institution."

As rationale they all have primarily what is cited above for the IMPI project: *"The project aims at providing HEIs with insight into their performance and means for improvement."*

Towards a European Programme for Internationalisation

From the present overview, some issues come clearly to the forefront:

- There appears a need for quality assessment of interna-tionalisation strategies in higher education

- Around the world, in particular in the USA and Europe, several instruments have been developed over the past 15 years to assess that quality
- They use more or less the same programmatic and organizational categories for assessment
- They are focusing on input and output assessment
- They are mainly taking place at the institutional level
- They address the state of the art and/or the process for improvement
- With preference some form of benchmarking as to create comparison and best practice is appreciated.

At the same time, one can observe that:

- Institutions are reluctant to ongoing assessment of internationalisation strategies, as this is a time consuming process
- In the present world of branding and ranking, an instrument without some kind of certifcation is not considered a high priority
- Assessment of institutional strategies denies the diversity of strategies for disciplines and programmes and the different levels within them
- Increasingly, institutions and programmes distinguish between a minimum requirement of internationalisation, applicable to all students and all programmes, and a maximum requirement, applicable to programmes and students with a high international and intercultural focus
- Internationalisation is becoming more mainstream in het higher education agenda, as in the present global knowledge economy internationalisation is strongly linked to innovation, interdisciplinarity and interculturality, and
- Increasingly a link has to be made to learning outcomes for students.

The use of different assessment levels in order to indicate the state of internationalisation (what has been achieved so far) and to provide incentives for improvement (where is it heading to or what is attainable) The certifcation is available at least at the level of the programme or a combination of programmes (bachelor and/or master; schools/faculties) The assessment procedure is not focused on a specifc activity but is comprehensive towards internationalisation (the why, how and what of internationalisation) It should focus on how internationalisation contributes to the overall quality by focusing on qualitative indicators (vision, content, provisional elements and outcomes) while using quantitative indicators (e.g. staff mobility figures) as supporting elements It should be with preference a regional (European) or international certifcate, as the purpose is to position it in a comparative international context The assessment should be done by a team which combines expertise on the subject, on quality assurance and on internationalisation, and should include international expertise and the student perspective Given the global knowledge economy and the diverse society we live in, both intercultural and international competencies should be addressed As much as possible, the assessment should be combined with existing assessment of the programme, as to avoid extra workload and costs.

Based on these observations, it appears advisable to develop a system of certifcation of internationalisation at the programme level. This certifcation should be able to distinguish programmes for the quality of their internationalisation. The following characteristics should be taken into consideration:

— The use of different assessment levels in order to indicate the state of internationalisation (what has been achieved so far) and to provide incentives for improvement (where is it heading to or what is attainable)

— The certification is available at least at the level of the programme or a combination of programmes (bachelor and/or master; schools/faculties)

— The assessment procedure is not focused on a specific activity but is comprehensive towards internationalisation (the why, how and what of internationalisation)

— It should focus on how internationalisation contributes to the overall quality by focusing on qualitative indicators (vision, content, provisional elements and outcomes) while using quantitative indicators (e.g. staff mobility figures) as supporting elements

— It should be with preference a regional (European) or international certificate, as the purpose is to position it in a comparative international context

— The assessment should be done by a team which combines expertise on the subject, on quality assurance and on internationalisation, and should include international expertise and the student perspective

— Given the global knowledge economy and the diverse society we live in, both intercultural and international competencies should be addressed

— As much as possible, the assessment should be combined with existing assessment of the programme, as to avoid extra workload and costs.

References

Chen, D.A.C.; Dahlman, D.J. 2004. *Knowledge and development: A cross-section approach.* Washington, DC: World Bank. (World Bank policy research working paper, No.°3366.)

American Council on Education. 2003. *Internationalizing the Campus. A User's Guide.* ACE, Washington.

AVCC. 1998. *Code of Ethical Practice in the Provision of Education to International Students.* Australian Universities of the Australian Vice-Chancellors Committee.

Knight, Jane. 2008. *Higher Education in Turmoil. The Changing World of Internationalisation.* Rotterdam, the Netherlands: Sense Publishers.

UNESCO. 2009. World Conference on Higher Education: The New Dynamics of Higher Education and Research For Societal Change and Development, 5 8 July 2009. COMMUNIQUE (8 July 2009), Paris.

Van der Wende, Marijk C. 2001. Internationalisation Policies: About New Trends and Contrasting Paradigms.*Higher Education Policy* 14 (3): 249-259.

11

Comprehensive Internationalization

At numerous institutions, both in the United States and abroad, there has been a decades-long interest in and commitment to international programming involving a range of activities such as attracting and engaging international students and scholars, expanding study abroad and student and faculty cross-border exchanges, building cross-border research collaborations, expanding language learning and area and regional studies, and engaging international development.

Higher education internationalization is not a new concept. The movement of students, scholars, and ideas across national boundaries was a prominent feature of twelfth and thirteenth century Europe; communities of international scholars formed as a result at several prominent universities (Wildavsky 2010, 17–18). Such mobility significantly ebbed after the ffteenth century (albeit with pockets of resurgence) until the latter half of the twentieth century.

During the last several decades, powerful new factors have reinvigorated the international dimensions of higher education and the cross-border flow of students, scholars, and ideas as well as global growth in higher education. Altbach and colleagues report a 53 percent increase between 2000 and 2007 in overall global higher education enrollments. Alan Ruby, notes that it is fairly "accepted wisdom" that from a 2000 base there will be a 150 percent increase in higher education seats globally to 250 million by 2025, mostly in the "developing world" and a more than doubling of student mobility from the current three to more than seven million annually by the same time, if not earlier. In just one year from 2007 to 2008 the Organisation for Economic Cooperation and Development reports that global mobility grew nearly 11 percent. The globalization of commerce, social forces, idea exchange, and growth in student mobility drive further significant internationalization of education.

A core reality that distinguishes current discussion and action from that of the past is the scale and scope of what internationalization encompasses—the breadth of clientele served, the outcomes intended, and a reshaping of institutional ethos. There is a growing sense that internationalization is an institutional imperative, not just a desirable possibility.

The business of universities is ideas: the creation of ideas through research and the dissemination of ideas through education and application. Increasingly, the business of universities is as much across as it is within borders, and not just in the free fow of ideas but in the global fow of students and scholars who generate them.

There are fewer workable restrictions on the global circulation of ideas than in almost any other area of trade. With the increasing flow of students and scholars worldwide, it becomes easier to talk about the free trade of minds. With easier travel and the internet providing near instantaneous access to hundreds of millions of idea generators throughout the world, more and more minds flow across borders physically and virtually—with the mode of transportation chosen sometimes having little practical impact on outcomes. "Comprehensive internationalization" is a recognition of these realities.

Internationalization: Outcome and Means

Internationalization applied to higher education has many possible operational meanings. These vary in scale and scope depending on purpose, institutional missions, institutional starting point, the programmatic frame of reference and clientele groups. This is true now and it is likely to be so in the future.

The ultimate purpose behind internationalization is better connection of institutions to a changing local and global environment and providing more relevant service to society and clientele under these changing realities. Internationalization can be a means to prepare graduates for life and work in a global market of products, services, and ideas. But besides producing world-conscious graduates and citizenry capable of broad and efective civic engagement, internationalization can seek to harness institutional research energies for a wide set of purposes including security at home and abroad and economic, social, and cultural development in an increasingly borderless and interdependent world. And, it can enhance research capacity and institutional recognition in the global knowledge society. Internationalization connects institutions to the global marketplace of ideas, brains, and discovery. In short, it is not an end but a means to many ends.

> The instrumental value of internationalization was recognized in the American Council on Education (ACE) 2005 publication, Internationalization in U.S. Higher Education. ACE noted that, "high quality education must prepare students to live and work in a world characterized by growing multicul-turalism and diminishing borders. Higher education institutions across the country are rising to this challenge [through]...internationalization strategies...."

Sheila Biddle, writing in 2002 for the American Council of Learned Societies observed that, "most universities pursue a variety of routes to internationalization, depending on what the initiative is designed to accomplish." So, not only is internationalization a means rather than an end, but the ends may vary from institution to institution and the particular approach to internationalization chosen is dependent on the ends being pursued by any specifc institution.

Varying Starting Points and Foci

Some institutions start from scratch with little or no institutional experience in international engagement. For others the starting point and program focus is associated mainly with student mobility (study abroad and international students on campus). At others, thinking and action might focus on internationalizing the on-campus liberal arts or general education components of the curriculum, and this may broaden to integrating such content into all majors including the professions. At some institutions, particularly those emphasizing graduate education and research, the focus may include building and supporting deep expertise in languages and area and regional studies, as well as cross-border research and applications. Engagement abroad for development in other countries is a large component of some institutions' internationalization. Still others may place emphasis on global partnerships, joint degrees, branch campuses, and long-term development partnerships with NGOs abroad.

Currently only a few institutions integrate all of the above into a systemic commitment to comprehensive internationalization. Tey usually have wide, deep, and long-standing frames of reference and a commitment to internationalize the institution itself across all of its instructional, research, and service missions. These institutions may have an even broader frame of reference—thinking about the globalization of higher education and the institution's place within a global higher education system.

Differentiating Labels and Meanings

A significant difculty in discussing internationalization stems from the many terms used (and often used interchangeably when they are not) to label the concept—for example, "internationalization of higher education," "campus internationalization," "globalization of higher education," "comprehensive internationalization," "internationalization of curriculum and learning," to name a few. There are some important diferences signaled by the various labels used loosely in connection with the concept of internationalization. Some might be seen as ends, others as means or elements to reach an end, and they vary in scope. Matters are further complicated by the fact that some of the words and labels have been used for decades, but over time changing environmental circumstances have caused a metamorphosis of their meanings. Among the more common of the labels used in a contemporary context are the following, and even though they have a defnite relationship to one another, they are not interchangeable concepts.

Campus Internationalization. "Campus" references a place, a "thing," a geographic entity with infrastructure that houses classrooms and research laboratories and an overall environment that supports living, learning, and discovery. Campus internationalization is that component of internationalization that focuses on getting the parts "at home" aligned in the service of internationalization of higher education. In doing so, thinking and action tend to focus on issues such as on-campus courses and curriculum, the role of international students and scholars in the campus environment, institutional policies and services in support of internationalization, and the campus intellectual environment for connecting globally.

International Mobility. The movement of students and faculty across borders for periods of learning and discovery is by its nature the primary experience and active-learning component of internationalization. It moves learning and discovery not only of campus, but across borders to diferent cultures, value systems, and ways of thinking, working, and living. It is usual to think of student mobility, but of equal importance is faculty and staf mobility. Mobile students without mobile faculty and staf creates dissonance in the attempt to internationalize. Unless faculty and staf are mobile, connections to what happens abroad to students and what happens to them on campus will be weak.

Globalization of Higher Education has several meanings. It can and does refer to the massive growth underway in global higher education capacity, particularly in countries outside of Europe, North America, and the Antipodes. It also refers to the growing fow of students and faculty globally and the formation of cross-border inter-institutional collaborations and partnerships.

The development of a global higher education system is recognition of a paradigm shift underway in that higher education institutions are not only a local, regional, or national resource but also are global resources—globally connected. This shift is aided by the appearance of global ranking schemes, the search for common standards, and the creation of multilateral policies that break down impediments to the fow of faculty, students, collaborative education (e.g., joint degrees), and joint research.

Modern and constantly evolving information technology has made borders nearly meaningless to the exchange of knowledge, ideas, and perspective and for social networking. The use of technology in higher education has the capacity to make the world a virtual campus and blurs the notion of a campus as being in a particular place and an institution as being only in a particular geographic location. In these ways, the globalization of higher education provides a non-campus-based frame of reference or context for internationalization.

The globalization of higher education and the emergence of world ranking schemes for institutions are changing the unit of analysis from domestic to global frames of reference. Growth worldwide in collaborations among institutions and expansion of mobility highways for faculty and students are becoming a stable feature of internationalized higher education.

With these changes comes recognition that to be a higher education institution of distinction in the twenty-fisrt century requires systematic institutional attention to internationalization— and for some institutional engagement abroad

Concept of Comprehensive Internationalization

Comprehensive internationalization is a commitment, con-frmed through action, to infuse international and comparative perspectives throughout the teaching, research, and service missions of higher education. It shapes institutional ethos and values and touches the entire higher education enterprise. It is essential that it be embraced by institutional leadership, governance, faculty, students, and all academic service and support units. It is an institutional imperative, not just a desirable possibility.

Comprehensive internationalization not only impacts all of campus life but the institution's external frames of reference, partnerships, and relations. The global reconfiguration of economies, systems of trade, research, and communication, and the impact of global forces on local life, dramatically expand the need for comprehensive internationalization and the motivations and purposes driving it.

The conceptual and operational tent for internationalization has to be large if it is to accommodate all of its possible dimensions. Comprehensive internationalization (CI) is a big-tent label for doing this. It can be the organizing paradigm for the institution as a whole, or one used by academic departments or professional programs at their level of operation. ACE views comprehensive internationalization as internationalization that is pervasive throughout the institution, afecting a broad spectrum of people, policies, and programs, and which leads to deeper and potentially more challenging change.

CI is not a call for all institutions of higher education, or all of their academic units and programs, to engage in all ways of internation-alizing— an impossibility for any individual institution. There is no uniform path toward CI. Varying missions and starting points will produce uniquely tailored responses to the challenges and opportunities of internationalization and globalization. The annual NAFSA Senator Paul Simon Awards for Campus Internationalization are testimony to the broad array of approaches and the genius of diversity displayed by the award-winning institutions.

Nevertheless, there are common features to a commitment to CI. The 2008 NAFSA Task Force on Internationalization deliberately chose to defne the concept as having broad and pervasive meaning.

> "Internationalization is the conscious efort to integrate and infuse international, intercultural, and global dimensions into the ethos and outcomes of postsecondary education. To be fully successful, it must involve active and responsible engagement of the academic community in global networks and partnerships."

CI, efectively implemented, impacts the entirety of campus life and learning and fundamentally shapes the institution's external frames of reference, partnerships, and relations. It will seek to instill international, global, and comparative dimensions not only in the classroom but also in feld and experiential learning. It will encourage the introduction of such perspective into the paradigms of faculty research, graduate research programs, institutional research priorities, and outreach engagement.

The specifc policies and programs that institutions put into place to make CI real are important instruments that will vary across campuses, as will the details of goals and intended outcomes. But it is outcomes that give CI its value.

Ultimately, comprehensive internationalization changes the institution from mainly a local, regional, or national asset to a global one with significant bidirectional and multiple cross-border exchanges. It is a false dichotomy that higher education institutions must either think locally or globally; both are realities for the vast majority of today's institutions although they may have diferent positions on a continuum of local-global orientation.

As recognized by the NAFSA Task Force, "Internationalization can ultimately leverage the collective assets of the higher education sector to create a new generation of global citizens capable of advancing social, and economic development for all." It is a complex process that can permeate every aspect of higher education:

- faculty development,
- curriculum design and delivery,
- instructional design,

- student diversity and faculty diversity,
- research and scholarship,
- training and education for outside clientele,
- development assistance,
- student support services and academic support services,
- resource development,
- financial management,
- risk management,
- institutional competitiveness and positioning,
- and civic engagement.

This list is not comprehensive, but sufficient to underscore the internal and external scope of impact and influence implied by a commitment to CI.

Track Record

The report card for U.S. higher education to achieve the breadth, depth, and pervasiveness of CI is at best mixed. ACE's 2008 Mapping Internationalization of U.S. Campuses concluded that U.S. institutions have made progress, but it is neither complete nor even. The report states, "Many institutions do not see internationalization as integral to their identity or strategy…Few institutions have an internationalization strategy…a gap exists between institutional rhetoric and reality."Earlier ACE findings, although based on data now more than fve-years old, also point to a disconnect between student beliefs and attitudes and what institutions provide and what students actually do. The gaps between aspiration and performance are highlighted in ACE's 2005 report, programmatic components of internationalization. CI ofers a paradigm for a holistic institutional commitment to pervasive international engagement. But, it remains more aspirational than real on the vast majority of U.S. campuses. Building the big tent of CI at U.S. institutions will deepen the engagement of U.S. higher education in the expanding global fow of ideas, minds, and talent.

A Sample of Student Attitudes and Beliefs

- Only 27 percent of students agreed that learning about other countries, cultures, and global issues was useful but not necessary.

- Approximately 85 percent of students believe it is important to know about international issues and events to compete successfully in the job market.
- Nearly 90 percent believe it important to know and understand other cultures and customs to compete successfully in the job market.
- Nearly 60 percent say that all undergraduates should be required to study a foreign language.
- Over 70 percent say that all undergraduates should be required to study abroad.
- Nearly 75 percent say that all undergraduates should be required to take internationally focused courses.
- Nearly 90 percent agree that the presence of international students enriches learning.
- Two-thirds of students believe it is the responsibility of all faculty to help them become aware of other countries, cultures and global issues.

A Sample of Performance Indicators

- Nearly 60 percent of students report never or rarely learning about internationally focused events from faculty, from advisers, in class, or through public announcements.
- Nearly half report that faculty never or rarely bring international reading material into the classroom.
- A little less than half report that they never or rarely bring their international experiences into the classroom.
- Only about a quarter of students report that faculty frequently or always related course material to larger global issues; a third say they never or rarely do.
- Nearly 70 percent of students report that international students and scholars never or rarely give presentations in their courses.
- A third of students say that they have taken no international courses in a year.
- About 14 percent of students surveyed had studied abroad.

Contemporary Rationales for Internationalization

Centuries ago the primary reason for the movement of scholars across borders was enrichment of ideas in the emerging universities of Europe. These universities were innovative cosmopolitan centers that sought to plumb a world of sources and scholars. Today, the rationale for the movement of scholars, students, and for the "re-internationalization" of higher education is more complex worldwide.

Hans de Wit has observed about the evolution of the Western university since the Middle Ages that, "Education came to serve the administrative and economic interests of the nation-states and became an essential aspect of the development of national identity. The scholar [went] from a wanderer to a citizen." However, deWit goes on to say that in the latter half of the twentieth century, "we notice a stronger emphasis from the nation-states and their international bodies on international cooperation and exchange."

Higher education is again drawn into a global network of knowledge and the search for new ideas and applications. Yet, higher education institutions remain important resources for localities and nations. While the search for universal knowledge dominated the raison d'être of the university in medieval times, local and nation-state needs and identities dominated the orientation of higher education since the 1600s. Now both orientations are with us and they are connected.

Two-tier System or Continuum

Higher education faces a dual challenge: the necessity to be globally engaged while remaining usefully connected locally. Although this is probably true for almost all kinds of higher education institutions, some wonder whether the globalization of higher education will actually lead to a two-tier global higher education system with a "top" tier being a relatively few research institutions defning themselves globally to their core, and a second tier composed of the vast majority of the rest being primarily locally/regionally defned.

While some manifestations of top-tier global higher education clubs are already forming, the more useful conceptualization may not be a dichotomy but a continuum. That is, institutions of varying kinds positioned along a global-local spectrum of international engagement. However, it seems unlikely, given the powerful realities of globalization, that purely local orientations can work for almost any institution.

Zero-sum or Synergy

As many do, one could see the local and the global as being in a zero-sum game. Some believe, for example: every classroom seat taken by an international student is one less available to a local student; cross-border collaborative research quickens the loss of our intellectual property and the loss to interests abroad of the advantage of being fisrt with new discoveries; solving problems abroad takes time, energy, and resources away from solving problems at home.

The alternative to the tension of a zero-sum scenario is synergy. For some, this may be a more difcult proposition to buy into as they may find it hard to believe that the sum can be greater than its individual parts—happy talk, with little substance. But it is the reality of globalization and the core of the rationale for CI.

The world knowing more about us than we about them creates an unlevel playing feld in economic and geopolitical terms; internationalization of learning and curriculum is part of the solution. A growing list of problems that beset us (and their solutions) comes from outside our borders and from global forces that play out in the local context—examples abound: communicable disease, the environment, the global economy, markets and dislocations. Research and problem solving that tap into the global fow of discovery and applications provide a net gain in understanding and solving problems as well as achievement of new gains. Increasingly, higher education cannot be an engine of local economic development unless it is on the cutting edge of global knowledge and discovery.

Internationalizing higher education requires lowering boundaries to the international trade of ideas and people (students and faculty) and an opening of access to national higher education systems for a global population. Inevitably, open or free trade will produce advantages and dislocations, the latter sometimes being more readily evident than the former. Free trade advocates will point to many cases and data about advantages and net gains; those dislocated make their own powerful alternative arguments and "free trade" becomes a tough sell. The idea of "us" versus "them" and concerns about who benefts remain powerful. Marginson cuts to the quick of the matter when he notes, "as the national policy maker sees it, 'These public-knowledge goods are all very well, but what's in it for us? Why should we pay for everyone's free beneft?'"

It seems inescapable, though, that contemporary manifestations of internationalizing higher education do come down to the reality of lowering higher education trade barriers with the essential companion rationale of accessing the best ideas and talent for a wide array of purposes. The growing movement of people and ideas across borders in the interest of competitive advantage is a matter of who is willing and able to pay. With global economic and social development, especially in expanding economies such as China and India, many more are both willing and able to pay; the hording of talent and ideas may fatten across international borders but concentrate in top-tier institutions.

Categorizing Motivations

Jane Knight and Hans de Wit believe that four categories of rationales have emerged to provide the contemporary set of motivations for internationalization of higher education.

- academic—global (universal) search for truth and knowledge
- socio-cultural—cross-cultural knowledge and understanding
- political—maintain and expand infuence
- economic—improving local/ national competitiveness in the global economy and marketplace.

Although de Wit does not say so, it is possible to think of these four categories both as ends in themselves and as means to other ends. For example, knowledge for its own sake such as acquiring in-depth understanding of another culture or society for reasons of personal curiosity, or knowledge that provides a basis for new applications to solve problems in other societies. For example, in-depth knowledge of the culture, can provide a basis for winning acceptance of new methods to control disease.

The motivations for CI are complex and outcomes are not always easily predictable, as pointed out by de Wit. International exposure can challenge or confirm beliefs and feelings about own place; international engagement may not increase just the local and national competitiveness but also the stature and strength of the higher education institution itself.

From Irrelevance to Imperative

Many have characterized U.S. higher education as a latecomer to contemporary internationalization, with the implication that other higher education systems (e.g., European) were much earlier adherents and practitioners. Whether such a temporal comparison is fair or not, the more important point is that globalization has imposed an urgency throughout the world regarding internationalizing higher education. Although the U.S. research university, the current envy of the world, had its origins in the German university model of the late nineteenth and early twentieth centuries, there has been a certain inward-looking character to U.S. higher education that, whether deliberately or not, paralleled a historical inward orientation of the American psyche overall.

For a variety of reasons the isolationist tendencies of U.S. society came under serious challenge after World War II, and a succession of events have yielded a shifting set of motivations for the international engagement of many U.S.-based institutions, including colleges and universities. Yet, for some, the challenge of internationalization remains unreal. At a national higher education conference a few years ago, a keynote speaker reported that a senior and respected faculty member of his institution had asked, "Why would we send our students to study abroad; surely, there is nothing they can learn there beyond what we ofer here."

American Isolationist Tendencies

Nearly since inception, a powerful inward looking current has driven the U.S. social, political, cultural, and educational frames of reference. Independence from England and George Washington's advice to avoid entangling alliances engendered a long trail of isolationist politics. Even John L. O'Sullivan's doctrine of manifest destiny (to project the U.S. system and ideals fisrt westward across the continent and in the late nineteenth and early twentieth centuries outward beyond North American borders) are refections of an inwardness— projecting internal U.S. methods, strengths, and values outward. Assimilation of diverse immigrant populations into the U.S. culture through the great melting pot, while giving a nod to the contributions of other cultures, had assimilation as its end goal. The ferce individualism of the American ideology, glorifed in Jeferson's yeoman farmer, and a companion disdain for the powers of government reinforced a national frame of reference for self-reliance and "going it alone."

America felt comfortable and safe in the Western Hemisphere with separation from the old worlds that immigrants sought to escape. In the Western Hemisphere there was little threat from north or south, particularly after promulgation of the Monroe Doctrine, and ocean barriers protect both east and west.

The United States was big enough to be self-reliant, and powerful enough to enforce it. The prominent roles played by the United States in World Wars I and II, and particularly in the aftermath of World War II, seemed to confirm the concept of American "exceptionalism." Americans saw themselves as "the best" and took pride in the belief that everyone else really yearned to follow the American example (many did, again almost from America's inception).

The post-World War II period provided renewed attention to elements of a vigorous manifest destiny—projecting inward strengths outward. As a geopolitical strategy, a simplistic isolationism was discredited; the atomic bomb and missiles made oceans irrelevant; John Foster Dulles' "domino efect" portrayed a steady march of threat toward the United States if unchecked. National defense required military presence and engagement abroad. However, it was the spread of U.S. democratic ideals, culture, and values abroad that was seen by many as the best supplement to military presence to provide the more enduring basis for making the world safe.

Americans took comfort in the belief, and not without reason, that the national purposes were basically honorable, its values defensible, and that "doing good" was the objective. The U.S. Information Agency was created to project American ideals and methods; the U.S. Agency for International Development moved tens of billions of U.S. dollars abroad to assist economic, social, and political development because development was the enemy of unrest and instability.

However, development programs were not only intended to "do good" but defned assistance as also showing people the presumably superior American way of doing it. Development was the projection of assistance, not partnership. In moving away from isolationism as a dominant geopolitical philosophy, the United States retained a conviction of being best and took comfort in inwardly derived strengths. Engagement abroad was not a two-way exchange. The United States would teach but was less interested in learning.

An Inward-Looking Education System

For much of U.S. history until the latter half of the twentieth century, what was taught in K–12 classrooms was similarly inwardly focused. European history was ofered, a refection in part of dominant immigrant origins, but by comparison scant attention typically was paid to Asia, Africa, and Latin American history and culture. Geography courses focused attention on the United States, sometimes Europe, and maybe a bit about Africa, Asia, and Latin America. Students had to work hard to find adequate coursework about the world outside the United States.

It is not that international, comparative, or world content was entirely missing from curricula, but rather it was the paucity of what typically was available in most educational systems. Of equal and perhaps more importance, such knowledge was seen neither as a core subject for the masses like reading, writing, and arithmetic, nor an important component to creating an educated citizenry or workforce. Such knowledge was nice, a conversation piece, sometimes exotic, but rarely if ever considered broadly necessary. The omissions were system wide, from K–16 and beyond, because even in most colleges and universities such course-work was difcult to find outside of history and the humanities, and a few social science disciplines in sufcient quantity and frequency.

In the K–12 system in particular, one of the main goals was homogenization, socialization, and assimilation of the immigrants into the mainstream English-speaking culture. Not only was it thought unnecessary to teach other languages, but the native speakers were discouraged from using their fisrt language.

However, in the last third of the twentieth century a significant change was afoot in K–12 curricula, making instruction and learning more inclusive and outward looking. Similar changes in content in college and university curricula, study abroad, and building faculty expertise were also well underway. These eforts predated conscious recognition of globalization, but globalization added the accelerant to a massive rethinking of the role of internationalization in education.

A Change in the Wind

In the last part of the 1950s and early 60s, disquiet arose about America's place in the world. The popular book of the late 1950s, The Ugly American, suggested that not all was necessarily right about U.S. objectives, methods, or worldview. Sputnik shook the United States to the core during the same period. Some Americans began to question their view of the nation's preeminence among nations, asking themselves, "Could it be that we aren't alone, the best, and are losing 'fisrt place'?"

The National Defense Education Act (NDEA), passed in the aftermath of Sputnik, gave major thrust to developing science, technology, engineering, and mathematics (the so-called STEM disciplines). Developing national expertise about the outside world in the form of "area" and language study was also funded by the act. NDEA was ground breaking as a large-scale efort by the national government to systematically develop a portion of the nation's higher education capacity, even though education is a function constitutionally reserved to the states. Title VI of the NDEA, emphasizing the development of area and language expertise, was unprecedented in its potential scope and focus for building outward-looking, campus-based capacities. The Ful-bright-Hayes program (enacted about a year later) ofered support for dissertation and faculty research abroad, adding a mobility dimension to the Title VI programs.

A focus of Title VI was on developing expertise, and not necessarily on developing an educational system for massifcation of international knowledge and learning. As Biddle points out, a signif-cant motivation for passage of the legislation was national defense—not to make us become more outward looking and broadly knowledgeable as a nation. Becoming more expertly aware of the world outside was a means to the end, not the end.

Even so, Title VI unquestionably delivered the catalyst for higher education to more seriously bring the world into the classroom and onto the campus; it gave a boost to language study, including the less commonly taught languages, and it supported graduate work and faculty engagement abroad. It, along with international development opportunities funded by entities such as USAID, began to build a cadre of internationally experienced and engaged faculty on many campuses.

At the same time, a new generation of college students sought and was given other ways to engage the world. Many joined the Peace Corps; many more began to study abroad. Many of these students are now a part of the senior but graying leadership in international programming both inside and outside of U. S. colleges and universities. The vast majority was then and still remains deeply committed to engaging the world outside collaboratively.

Beginning in the 1960s and 1970s, and through a variety of eforts and changing attitudes, the process of educating students to the world outside and building faculty expertise and engagement abroad began in some earnest partly as a result of Title VI funding but also because of the awakening interest within higher education. The development of an "internationalization ethos" was nascent but underway. Still, it was seen largely as focused on the few who were interested, rather than being an integral part of education and learning for all.

Globalization's Challenge

By the 1980s and 1990s, if not signif-cantly before, many in higher education were becoming acutely aware of the unlevel playing feld created by an inward focus and inattention to looking and learning abroad. The world was undergoing massive change, not simply in the form of new nations (such as the former Soviet republics) and national confederations (such as the European Union) but in the emergence of a new world paradigm dubbed "globalization."

Distinguishing between the terms "international relations" and "globalization" was an initial confusion. Eventually, the former came to mean relations between and among sovereign nations while "globalization" was defned as the rise of factors and forces that transcend borders and sovereign states.

Globalization alters and weakens political and economic boundaries, and intensifes the cross-border fow of nearly everything—but especially knowledge, ideas, and learning. Even though global forces are mediated through the local context, they in turn shape local cultures and economies. Those local entities that remain largely unable to act efectively within the globalizing currents are disadvan-taged as never before.

Michael Paige draws a further useful distinction between globalization and internationalization.

"Whereas globalization is about the world order, internationalization is about organizations and institutions, such as universities.

Internationalization means creating an environment that is international in character—in teaching, research, and outreach.

Paige quotes Jane Knight who sees, "internationalization at the national sector, and institutional levels…as the process of integrating an international, intercultural, or global dimension into the purpose, functions, or delivery of postsecond-ary education." Knight holds that, "internationalization of higher education is one of the ways a country responds to the impact of globalization…." This position further reinforces that internationalization is a means to ends and not an end itself. It is precisely a proliferation of ends (goals or objectives) that characterize the widening of contemporary motivations to internationalize. Tey now easily include (in no particular order):

- expanding cross-cultural knowledge and understanding given the increased frequency and necessity of cross-cultural contacts and relations
- strengthening a higher education institution's stature and value added in teaching and research in a global system of higher education
- enhancing national and global security
- improving labor force and local economic competitiveness in a global marketplace
- enhancing knowledge, skills, attributes, and careers for graduates to be efective citizens and workforce members.

The movement toward globalization has numerous implications for both the depth and breadth of higher education's commitment to internationalization, particularly the rationale for it. The reasons for looking outward and becoming outwardly knowledgeable have proliferated both in terms of places of interest and breadth of challenge and opportunity.

Globalization is aided and legitimized by the emergence of nearly instant global communication and information sharing. Easier travel, labor migration, the global spread of research capacity, globalization of scholarship, and the growth of the global higher education system reinforce an expansive multilateral trade in ideas.

Manifestations of a global higher education system include, but are not limited to, rapidly expanding exchanges of students and faculty, the emergence of global institutional ranking schemes, dual and joint cross-border degree programs, international higher education consortia, cross-border collaborative research and projects, and rapid growth of global higher education capacity.

Competition and Collaboration

Higher education globalization has both competitive and collaborative dimensions to it. As the demand for higher education expands globally, capacity is not keeping pace, and competition for the best faculty, students, and administrators is intensifying across borders. Competition is spreading globally to produce envelope-pushing research, which enhances institutional reputations and simultaneously feeds the growing needs of a knowledge-based society.

The stakes for collaboration are strengthening, too. It is impossible for every institution to be best in everything. All good ideas are not invented "here," wherever "here" happens to be. Cross-border collaborations can produce win/wins for partners. But to accomplish these collaborations, faculty need international perspective and opportunity, internationalized campus environments, and policies and administrative structures that support cross-border collaborative research and problem solving.

While the end of the Cold War may have removed a somewhat singular security-related focus for supporting language acquisition and area studies, the concomitant fragmentation of power in some countries and regions made other challenges more visible (e.g., civil wars, religious and ethnic conficts, intensifcation of identity politics, migration, and refugees). In this environment, language and area studies take on new importance and greater diversity.

From the comparatively understandable bipolar geopolitical environment of the Cold War era, a new multilateral environment has rapidly emerged, expanding the multitude of languages and cultures of critical relevance. Languages and cultural milieus that seemed irrelevant in an earlier era because societies were only loosely connected to the bipolar realities of orthodox constructs of international relations, or encased and suppressed by powerful regimes, now take on new salience. In turn, this has expanded the concept of national security to be inclusive of a wider range of challenges, such as economic competitiveness and national position in the world.

Globalization has been at least as much a phenomenon of economics as of politics. As corporations, large and small, engage in business activity abroad, their needs for language skills, cross-cultural awareness, and knowledge of opportunities abroad diversify and intensify. Tis, then, challenges many of higher education's traditional international priorities, which either have been directed internally toward the interests of a small number of students and faculty, or abroad by some institutions toward assistance in developing the capacities of other nations.

Although a commitment to CI presents challenges in terms of capacity, cost, and institutional change, not committing to it would accelerate the consequences of the unlevel playing feld. The need to efectively participate within a global reconfiguration of markets, systems of trade, research and discovery, communications, and quality of life dramatically expands the rationale for internationalization.

Comprehensive Internationalization and Institutional Realities

The manner by which higher education institutions make CI operational will necessarily difer to match varying institutional mission, values, and goals. However, to be fully integrated into the fabric and ethos of an institution, CI must closely align to, and be seen as enriching, core institutional missions. All organizations allocate resources to ft their strategic organizational priorities. If CI is not seen as integral to institutional strategic goals and priorities, it will be marginalized.

Arguably, all higher education institutions engage to some degree and manner in the three core missions of instruction, research, and outreach engagement. However, the relative attention and priority given to these varies across types of institutions.

Institutions with significant commitments to both undergraduate and graduate programs engage all three core missions and some look for ways to integrate them. Some institutions give special status and priority to graduate education and research; liberal arts institutions focus on undergraduate instruction and learning; community colleges provide the fisrt two years of undergraduate education as well as specialized programs, degrees, and certifcates preparing students for particular job skills. Institutions vary in their commitments to community engagement and problem solving, but increasingly most do to some degree—some both at home and abroad. As institutions vary greatly in size, so will the complexity of international programs' organizational structures that facilitate CI.

Scope and Organization of Comprehensive Internationalization

A set of framing issues or questions can help set the stage for defning the parameters for CI and for what is possible for a particular institution. Individuals can consider these, but they also form an agenda for discussion among those exploring internationalization as a group in their institutions.

Strategic Considerations at the Institutional Level

Designing an institutional strategy for CI requires fisrt exploring a set of key questions.

1. What are the intellectual drivers and motivations for CI?

Ultimately, the currency of the higher education realm is defned in terms of intellectual objectives and outcomes related to discovery and learning. What do advocates of CI expect as outcomes? What do they promise or imply as benefts of CI?

Identifying motivations for CI and accompanying expectations are vital parameter setters and contribute both to building a convincing rationale for allocating fnite resources and for accountability. At any institution CI will be validated by expectations and accomplishments in student learning, research, strengthening key institutional curricula or research thrusts, enhancing institutional capacity, reputation, and revenue, and service to clientele and stakeholders. The motivations to internationalize can and often do relate to all of these.

Motivations carry expectations and either implicit or explicit goals that provide the basis for accountability. The more complex the motivations are, the more challenging will be expectations and standards of accountability. Resolving questions about motivations and expectations up-front is a critical "framing issue."

2. How well is CI linked to institutional missions?

CI must link inwardly to institutional missions and outwardly to institutional clientele, just as any institutional initiative must. To strengthen prospects for success, comprehensive internationalization needs to be infused throughout institutional missions and ethos. Such a limited view of internationalization is simply incompatible with the fundamental ethos of any institution of higher learning.

3. Who are CI's clients?

This question is fundamental to tailoring any efective CI strategy. Is CI for only some students, or all; a few faculty, or most; alumni and lifelong learners; external clientele (e.g., business, government, etc.)? What is the "geography" of clientele: close to campus, the state, or national or international?

Upon graduation most students today will have to interact efectively with colleagues and organizations abroad; many will work abroad, some in multiple locations. The vast majority of graduates will work in multicultural teams in the United States, many such teams will include team members from around the world, and some teams will be linked electronically to far-fung locations. Being a workforce-ready graduate has increasingly global and knowledge-society meanings and demands. The Organization for Economic Cooperation and Development (OECD) opines that existing educational systems are insufciently equipped to meet this challenge, and they will need to expand access, funding, and innovation.

Community and outreach clientele are also similarly afected. As businesses large and small engage global markets, their need for access to country and regional knowledge and expertise expands. As diverse and expanding immigrant populations join communities across the United States, knowledge of the cultures from which these new residents come becomes important for schools, the legal system, health providers, employers, and social services, to name only a few. Just as universal access to international, global, and comparative knowledge is important for traditional student groups, so does it become important for community and lifelong-learner clientele.

A comprehensive approach to internationalization will deliver globally informed content into the vast majority of courses, curricula, and majors. Integration of comparative and global perspectives into research and scholarship of faculty is equally important if the benefts of cross-cultural and comparative understanding are to be fully extended through outreach to citizens, businesses, and public officials.

Institutions fulfll obligations to their locale by playing a role in internationalizing home communities, becoming bridges between organizations abroad and at home; and facilitating exchanges of students, interns, personnel, and research to meet community needs. The idea of internationalizing community service is front and center. There is potential reciprocity in that the diversity of cultures and languages represented in U.S. communities can be a source of talent and experience for helping to internationalize the on-campus environment.

For a CI institution, outreach and problem solving are engaged at home and abroad, recognizing that problems and their solutions are increasingly

borderless and multilateral. By inference, the relevance of international, comparative, and global learning and perspective applies not only to all students and faculty/staf, but to external clientele as well.

4. What is the scope of institutional leadership and strength of its commitment to CI?

Commitment to internationalization must be broadly based, not driven by a few personalities. Without organizational support, birth and sustain-ability are doubtful. If development of CI at an institution is driven by a few powerful and infuential personalities, the question of whether CI can survive them must be raised. If CI is driven by administrative leaders, a commitment from key faculty will be needed to provide the intellectual content and to shape the curriculum and pedagogies to accommodate it. The longer term staying power of support and drive for CI depends in part on whether internationalization has the character of being the "favor of the month," or whether there are deep intellectual drivers for it. A deep intellectual recognition is that globalization is a paradigm shift that inexorably will reshape twenty-fisrt century higher education knowledge creation and knowledge dissemination. This kind of underpinning speaks in favor of the long-term success of CI on any campus.

Moving from Strategy to Programming

Additional issues arise when moving the concerns cited above to thinking about programs and future actions to implement CI.

1. How programmatically encompassing will CI be?

CI can be seen as inclusive of all or some of the following: study abroad, international students and scholars, on-campus curriculum, languages, world-region and thematic global expertise, cross-border research/ scholarship/ service, global problem solving and international development activity, "globalizing" institutional ethos, and building global connections and partnerships.

The greater the number of programmatic dimensions and the wider the reach to various populations, the more comprehensive the efort becomes by defnition. In turn, the greater the opportunity will be to fundamentally reshape institutional ethos, knowledge creation, and knowledge dissemination paradigms.

2. Which countries and regions?

As a result of globalization and the permeability of boundaries, the number of regions and countries of economic, geopolitical, and cultural interest have multiplied. Acquiring the necessary knowledge and expertise for a global array of languages and cultures and the diversity of clientele will be a significant challenge for most, if not all, institutions.

Some countries and regions already draw considerable attention because of their burgeoning economies and growing position in the global marketplace; they are signif-cant suppliers of labor or raw materials, or a source of products. Some others generate interest negatively— by being a nexus of instability, unrest, and radicalism that can serve as a base for projecting mass violence around the world. And in other cases, interest is created by cultural appeal or because their higher education systems and research and development capacities ofer us both challenge and opportunity in the world of ideas and technology. Unquestionably, some nations or regions will have more than one of these compelling characteristics.

The great challenge, of course, is that it is impossible for any single institution to be a source of knowledge and expertise covering the entire global waterfront. Institutions will not only have to set priorities but also pay more systematic attention to developing consortia of expertise to help cover the waterfront.

3. Which academic disciplines and professions?

While humanities, languages, and social and behavioral sciences remain core elements in international education, professional disciplines take on renewed importance not only because of the globalization of markets, but the globalization of problems and solutions in almost all areas. Additionally, problems now easily jump boundaries and require knowledge from professional and applied programs such medicine, business, agriculture, environmental science and policy, education, and telecommunications, to name a few. Professional programs certainly contribute to a more contemporary understanding of comprehensive internationalization, but they need to become more globally engaged and aware to be efective in dealing with specifc cross-border challenges such as, tainted food products, invasions of nonnative plants and animals, unsafe toys, and the like.

Indeed, all disciplines and professions today are better informed by global perspective, shaped by it, and capable of contributing globally. Josef Mestenhauser (1998), an early and highly respected leader and theorist in international education, saw "an advanced level of internationalization…involv[ing] not only internationalizing key courses but also identifying the international dimensions of every single discipline."

People and Processes to Support Internationalization

Strategy and implementation plans need people and processes to support and sustain them. Key questions to consider include:

1. Who will be responsible and assessed for contributions to CI?

Institutions need to consider which units will be responsible for and assessed on contributions to CI. Only some academic units, or all? Are institutional service units expected to be involved and supportive? And will institutional leadership (presidents, provosts, deans, and directors of major academic and service units) hold units and people accountable for contributions? The wider the net of responsibility, the more involved and comprehensive institutional discussions will become about the nature of commitments to CI.

There are three types of units important to comprehensive internationalization.

Academic units. The role of these units is obvious for the substantive and intellectual contributions essential to internationalization. Without connection to academic departments and their faculty and the substance of ideas and learning, internationalization risks becoming a vacuous process. For example, study abroad without learning objectives and structured learning connected to the curriculum and refected in intellectual outcomes risks being little more than tourism for credit.

Specialty international programming support units. These units play critical roles in connecting the campus beyond national borders. The most obvious and important examples are the "mobility" ofces (examples include ofces of study abroad, international students and scholars, etc.). Area and thematic study centers and internationally focused research centers help identify and facilitate research and learning opportunities abroad for faculty and students. Language departments are both academic units and support units. English as a second language (ESL) programs are critical bridging units for international students and scholars. The potential list is long.

General university service units. Although sometimes ignored, these ofces and programs are in strategic positions on campus to either help or hinder (by omission or commission) facilitating and supporting CI.

Campus-based general service units have multiplied over the last few decades in response to the growing complexity of regulation and because of appreciation for a wider range of academic support services needed for successful student learning and to support the increasingly complex research enterprise. The importance of these service units relates not only to successful student learning and expanding research and outreach missions generally, but to successful CI as well.

2. Will key sectors support it?

Key questions to ask when building support for CI across the campus include:

- What roles must academic governance play?
- Will key university support units assist with academic and nonacademic student needs?
- Will faculty be on board?
- Will accreditation bodies approve; will they impose unworkable conditions?
- Must any other outside entities approve (e.g., government funding authorities)?

But perhaps the most important opening question is whether there is a fertile climate of awareness and real openness to internationalization. Although it is hard to imagine in the twenty-fisrt century a lack of awareness of globalization and its impact on higher education, the entire enterprise may well turn on whether there will be a dedication to action and the institutional staying power for CI. Ultimately, there must be sufcient commitment across the entire institution to follow-through and move from rhetoric to action.

3. How is leadership and support organized for CI?

The more "comprehensive" the CI vision, the more complex its support infrastructure is likely to be. Who will give organizational leadership and drive to visioning, building, and nurturing CI, and what must the support infrastructure be?

The answers to these questions require reference to traditional campus patterns of organization. For example, is there precedence on campus for central ofces to provide campus-wide leadership in key areas (e.g., for graduate programs or information technology), and do these provide sufcient precedence for establishing a central leadership and coordination model for internationalization?

What is the tradition of productive collaboration between such ofces and academic units? Is there a culture for cross-walks and partnerships between service and academic units? Among academic units, is the culture one of "stove-pipes" or cross-disciplinary collaboration? It is not so much that the support infrastructure for CI must mirror existing traditions but rather that the wider the departure from precedence, the less comfortable its implications may appear.

At the center of most discussions about organization and structure on campuses is whether there should be a centralized ofce to lead and coordinate internationalization, or whether decentralized models are best. Centralization is touted on some campuses as delivering more efec-tive coordination, greater efciencies, and focused drive toward strategic objectives. Others see centralization as creating excessive red tape, stifing creativity and initiative on the "shop foor," enforcing "cookie-cutter" rules and regulations onto an extremely heterogeneous set of departments and motivations, and ultimately, destroying ownership of internationalization at the departmental and college levels.

Actually, to centralize or to decentralize is a false dichotomy. A middle ground rests in thinking about matrix organizational structures that have elements of hierarchy, decentralization, and significant direct collaborative crosswalks among contributors. Versions of a matrix organizational structure characterize how some of the largest and most complex institutions are organized to support CI.

4. What are the roles of senior international ofces and ofcers?

Ofces of international programs and senior international ofcers (SIOs) stand at the nexus of CI. These ofces vary greatly, though, from institution to institution in terms of responsibilities—from study abroad only; to that plus support for international students and scholars; to variously being responsible for English language centers, foreign languages, area study centers, and sources of support for research and project activity abroad or internationalization of the on-campus curriculum. The backgrounds of SIOs vary too. Some move into the administrative position from the faculty ranks, others from one of the functional international support units, and others from careers outside (e.g., former ambassadors).

As a result of such variations in ofce responsibilities and SIO backgrounds, the degree to which SIOs can exercise leadership and infuence to help coordinate CI difers greatly from campus to campus. That said, the impediments to successful comprehensive internationalization are substantial without campus-wide leadership and coordination at some efective level. Indeed, the notion of CI without any point leadership seems absurd.

Regardless of scope of responsibility, if ofces of international programs are seen by others on campus as solely or even greatly responsible for internationalization, the concept of "collective" engagement and collective responsibility for internationalization is weakened. CI requires international ofces to be fully engaged with academic, support, and service units in the process of internationalization, sometimes in a leadership role but always in a role of supporting and facilitating broad-based engagement and responsibility.

5. Is there a commitment to allocate resources strategically?

Insofar as resource allocation is driven by the institutional strategic plan, it is vital that internationalization is a core element in that strategic plan. Internationalization requires significant reallocation of institutional funds and efort. Adequate funds are the barometer of institutional commitment. Some new resources will be essential, but it is most improbable that internationalization can be accomplished without substantial reallocations of existing resources, or at the least "piggybacking" on other existing priorities. For example, will the process of introducing international content and perspective into the curriculum have access to and be able to shape existing majors, general education requirements, and faculty research priorities? If internationalization is seen as a new and freestanding commitment, as an "add on" to current priorities and not integrated with them, CI is almost certain to be underfunded. This is defnitely the case if the objective is to efect mainstream access for all students and faculty to international content and experience. Integration of internationalization into other institutional priorities is essential to access sufcient resources by piggybacking on, and sharing use of, existing resources. The chances of this happening increase if internationalization is prominent in the institution's mission statement, and especially if it is in its strategic plan.

Widening Engagement of Institutional Service Units

As cross-border student mobility increases, along with collaborative degree programs, the role of registrar offces in assessing credentials and awarding recognition for work done under systems with differing instructional contact hours, methods of measuring and counting, and pedagogies becomes more complex. To both support and respond to successful comprehensive internationalization, a larger portion of registrar workload and staff time will have to be assigned to it, but it will also require greater policy- and decisionmaking fexibility across systems and cultures in a global higher education environment (for example, across three- and four-year baccalaureate systems; K–12 systems that end with "11;" nonnumerical grading systems). Facilitating faculty research abroad impacts policies and practices of university travel offces, personnel and payroll systems, risk assessment, copyright and security protections, intellectual property regulations, contracts and grants administration, insurance, and accounting and record-keeping practices, to name a few. It is one thing for faculty to live and work within U.S. legal, political, and cultural boundaries and quite another to support faculty living and working abroad—negotiating differing features of law, regulation, and customs in foreign settings, some of which fundamentally confict with U.S. laws and regulations.

Rigid university housing contracts will stife study abroad. A residence hall environment unable to adapt its housing and food practices to requirements imposed by differing cultures will create unfriendly environments for international students and scholars.

Student support offces (e.g., for developing learning skills, counseling, housing, and clubs) need to think and behave in more varied ways to support international students coming from far differing learning environments who are far away from home and their normal support structures and who are simultaneously negotiating living and learning in a radically different environment. These issues apply not only to international students on U.S. campuses but U.S. study abroad students as well.

Academic advisers will not only have to attend specifcally to the needs of international students often largely unfamiliar with U.S. systems, but to the academic preparation of students who intend to study abroad and their reentry following.

From Periphery to Mainstream

By considering how institutional strategy, implementation plans, and people and processes interact and support each other, each institution can craft its particular approach to internationalization. CI, by defni-tion, seeks to impact all, involve all, and become a core feature of institutional missions, values, and ethos. Mestenhauser suggests that, "international education is not a feld of specialization for the few, but its own feld for the many." A commitment to "mainstreaming" seen in this way will have massive implications regarding who is expected to participate and contribute, what resource will be allocated, how the institution approaches collaboration, and what measures for performance will be employed.

A commitment to efecting truly comprehensive internationalization is a commitment to widen access and participation, to widen the client pool for internationalization, and to widen the set of contributors to its realization and success.

A commitment to mainstream involvement is not an excuse to disband central leadership, coordination, and programs that specialize in delivering and supporting components of comprehensive internationalization. An institutional commitment to study abroad without a study abroad ofce is nonsense and likely hazardous. Equally, a commitment to CI without some form of appropriate campus-level leadership and coordination helping to drive it is also nonsensical.

Creating an Organizational Culture for CI

Successful CI requires an organizational culture that gives it strength, purpose, adaptability, and sustainabil-ity. A CI culture is shaped by institutional leadership and sustained by eforts to extend its saliency throughout the organization. An institutional culture supporting international engagement and campus internationalization is an essential prerequisite for success.

The driving culture for CI is the product of an institutional vision that defnes its missions, values, and service not just in local or national terms but also in global terms, and sees all three levels interconnected. It encourages the involvement of everyone, not just a few, and it involves all institutional missions (teaching, research, and service). An efective culture for CI is institutionally pervasive and results in a broadly shared vision, up and down and throughout, about the necessity of internationalization.

Culture and commitment are not the product of an action checklist that when completed allows moving on to another institutional priority. Rather, a sustaining culture drives an ongoing and evolving set of actions that fow from a continuous sensing of the global environment of opportunities and constraints and the interaction of those with the local environment and internal institutional dynamics.

Evidence is clear that ongoing attention to internationalization characterizes the most successful institutions, including those receiving the NAFSA Senator Paul Simon Award for Campus Internationalization and ACE's "Promising Practices" as examples. A sustaining culture keeps CI at the center of institutional missions, values, and actions, and makes it programmatically adaptable.

A CI culture is not defned by input or output measures such as dollars allocated to international activity, numbers of students studying abroad, numbers of international students and scholars on campus, numbers of internationally focused centers and institutes, or research. Although these are indicators of the impact of a powerful guiding culture for CI, the real force and meaning of a CI culture for higher education is defned by the goals it pursues and the learning, research, and problem-solving outcomes achieved. Leadership helps to shape and prioritize these, but it is the collegium as a whole imbued with a common guiding culture that is needed to efectively pursue them.

Numerous factors infuence the success of CI. Some have already been noted. Four additional deserve particular mention: leadership and messaging, internationalization of the faculty, persistence and adaptability, and accountability to achieving measurable goals.

1. Clear and Consistent Leadership from the top

Although ultimately internationalization must be supported by those who will deliver and consume it (e.g., faculty, staf, students, clientele, and academic and service units), the importance of senior institutional leadership to igniting an institution-wide and systemic commitment to it is undeniable. Clear, consistent, and frequent messaging from the president and provost are particularly essential—messaging that goes to all institutional clientele including students, faculty and staf, alumni, and other external clientele. So, too, the role of academic deans is critical for catalyzing discussion and action in academic programs and in facilitating development of supporting academic programs.

Leadership and messaging need to continuously reinforce a culture of CI and an organizational dynamism in support of it. Trough its messaging, leadership also help to drive action consistent with desired outcomes

Leadership and messaging need to move beyond general rhetoric (e.g., "we will become a great internationally engaged institution," or, "we will internationalize our curriculum"). The messaging needs to identify spe-cifc programmatic thrusts (e.g., study abroad, general education, curricula in the majors, language learning, engagement abroad, the minimum expected of each student prior to graduation) and be tied to clear goals and outcomes.

2. Faculty and Academic Unit Engagement Internationally

CI cannot occur without majority faculty support and engagement. Faculty hiring and reward systems can signal institutional commitment to internationalization and an expectation that faculty will engage in and contribute to the efort through their instruction and their research in appropriate ways. The importance of faculty engagement is clear and has begun to receive needed attention in the literature. Faculty need support to build their own capacities where insuf-fcient. Merit systems that reward internationally engaged faculty and staf in promotion, tenure, and salary are essential. Institutional recognition and rewards for units that contribute successfully to internationalization (and accountability for those who do not) are also critical.

3. Persistence and Adaptability

Comprehensive internationalization is not a project with an end date, or completion of an action checklist; it requires an institutional commitment and staying power over the long run. It needs to survive changes in organizational leadership. In part, this is because the potential scope and scale of comprehensive internationalization can only successfully unfold in manageable stages over the longer run. But, it is also because institutions are dynamic entities with changing priorities and methods, and globalization itself is continually evolving. These factors mean that the efort to internationalize will require continual evaluation and adjustment to changing needs and infuences. The mix of resource allocations and programs at any point in time is a response not only to a general culture for international engagement but to the present social, political, economic, and global environments. As these environments change, so will the institution's responses in resource allocations and program thrusts and priorities need to change.

4. Clear and Measurable Goals

Successful internationalization, like any significant institutional thrust, needs measurable goals and mileposts. Goals identify what is important, defne "intentions," provide the basis for accountability, and drive behavior. Tey set markers to drive toward and put all on notice regarding not just intentions, but how success will be defned. Of course, the goals must be known, clear, and accepted, and there must be accountability for goal achievement across the institution.

Motivations are the basis for forming goals. Defning goals, therefore, starts with the motivations for internationalization. At a general level, institutional motivations can include combinations of:

- advancing institutional reputation domestically and internationally
- student learning and other student-centered outcomes (e.g., employment)
- revenue and markets
- research and scholarship
- service and engagement
- and global bridge building.

One approach to defning goals is to use a "systems" logic, where inputs, outputs, and outcomes are diferenti-ated. Examples of indicators that could be employed by institutions to measure progress along multiple CI mission dimensions are included :

There are reasons for measuring all three types of indicators. Input measurement provides an indicator of the level of investment made to create capacity to achieve a given set of outputs and outcomes (e.g., without study abroad programs there is no capacity for participation and no opportunity for learning outcomes). Likewise, outputs measure that there is activity, not just capacity to act or do things (e.g., the numbers of students who enroll and complete programs). Outcomes measure what happens as a result—ultimately, for example, on student learning, abilities, careers, and so forth.

Some goals may be instrumental as in building capacity (e.g., ofer-ing x programs, in y locations, for as many as z students). Other goals may be refected in participation levels (for example, as implied by the core of Open Doors data tables). Other goals measure valued end products or outcomes. There is an assumed causal relationship among the three.

Issues, Barriers, and Challenges

Comprehensive internationalization is driven by a set of internal and external motivations and by connection to institutional missions, values, and clientele. It does not occur in a vacuum. CI cannot divorce itself from wider parameters and constraints placed on higher education institutions, and it needs to avoid contributing unintended complications to higher education.

Avoiding Homogenization and Inappropriate Use of Global Rankings

A potential challenge arising from the globalization of higher education and the emergence of systems that help rationalize the fow of people, ideas, and credentials across academic systems (e.g., Bologna Process) is the risk that these may lead to a global homogenization of higher education. This may be reinforced by growing and overreliance on the outcomes of global ranking schemes.

Knight reports findings from a 2005 survey conducted by the International Association of Universities in which university respondents indicated they believed homogeniza-tion was among the least "important" risks of internationalization. However, the summary of findings did not specify whether respondents thought homogenization was inherently a good or bad thing. Also, as we are at the front end of the practical impacts of the globalization of higher education, it is reasonable to speculate that many of the responses were based on limited experience.

An often-touted strength of U.S. higher education is its size and diversity. Some would argue that diversity is protected by limiting the federal role in higher education. Whether this is true or not, the culture of U.S. higher education is one that does not support command and control systems that impose a rigidity and homogeneity. For example, accreditation bodies have moved away from prescribing highly detailed standards and expectations, and toward guiding principles that permit diverse institutional responses.

It may be that homogenization will never materialize, but there are emerging realities that will encourage it. For example, global ranking schemes such as those by the Times Higher Education or Shanghai Jiao Tong University force a common and limited set of criteria to which institutions will play if they are sensitive to their ranking. Counting courses and credits across systems requires developing some unit of exchange currency. Central authorities may be developed to manage rankings and rationalizations, and too easily diversity can be squeezed out in the interest of manageability.

There is the risk too that comprehensive internationalization, if driven by top-down systems alone, can overly homogenize the responses of individuals and programs to internationalize. Just as there is no single best model of internationalization for higher education as a whole, there is no such model for schools, departments, and curricula within individual institutions. As the institution-level model chosen needs to match the mission and clientele of the entire organization, so must it be matched to the mission, organizing intellectual paradigms, and clientele of individual academic units and programs.

Difculties arise when attempts are made in cookie-cutter fashion to specify a particular method or way to make internationalization operational. Semester-length immersion study abroad will not meet the needs of or be possible for all students in all majors; programs of difering lengths, design, pedagogy, and location will be needed. Countries and regions of interest will vary by discipline and program. Degree collaboration can take many forms, from dual or joint degrees to collaborations on parts of the degree program (e.g., feld research, a particular course, semester exchange, etc.)

A commitment to comprehensive internationalization does not threaten homogenization per se. But, the risk increases the more that operational detail is specifed. Some accreditation bodies, particularly in professions such as business and engineering, include international engagement criteria in their guidelines and standards for assessment. Yet, to avoid homog-enization, they leave it to individual programs to defne scope and modes of engagement and criteria for assessing their success. This is one example of an attempt to efectively balance of the need for guidelines with the necessity of avoiding one-size-fts-all methods.

There is growing evidence that institutions use global ranking schemes to choose global institutional partners, either seeking to "partner up" with those higher in rankings, or avoiding those seen as in a lower "reputational class." Ignored may be whether there is a ft in institutional "cultures" or the strengths of individual disciplines and programs within an institution where the real value resides. More problematic is the potential to ignore a kind of aggregate fallacy where the overall ranking of a potential partner institution is high but the disciplines and programs that will drive the substance of the partnership are not. For example, students choose both an institution and a major. What if the institution is strong but the target major is weak? The same is true with faculty and research collaborations being driven by the aggregate of institutional rank but ignoring unevenness in the disaggregate of programs and majors.

Good and Model Practices

The term "best" practice assumes a particular approach or method is best. This is rarely if ever the case in complex areas such as CI and across the multiplicity of higher education institutions. We can more readily defne "good" or "model" practices that have produced success in individual institutional settings and that may be transferable to other institutions with similar circumstances.

Over time, the list of good or model practices will grow because there is almost no limit to innovative ways of thinking about and engaging internationalization. But this will only be the case if we resist conceptualizations of internationalization that are labeled "best" or policies and standards that narrowly proscribe what counts and what doesn't.

An exemplar of diversity in approach and success can be seen in the composite of annual NAFSA Senator Paul Simon Award winners and précis of individual institutional winners.

Commercialization and Quality

From the same 1995 survey results cited earlier, Knight reports that respondent institutions are most concerned about the potential impacts of burgeoning market opportunities presented by rapid growth in global demand for higher education. Among these are concerns about "degree mills" that respond to opportunity and demand but pay little heed to quality, and global systems of quality control that do not develop fast enough to monitor, report on, and control such eventualities.

Although real, the risk of decreasing quality is less a matter of internationalizing higher education per se than it is a matter of not attending to quality while internationalizing. Risk also rises from globally exploding demand for higher education seats and the inability of established mechanisms to meet the demand. There is a potential risk if institutional motivations for internationalization are driven primarily by revenue potential. Cost, revenue, quality, and surplus are inherently interconnected issues. In the effort to internationalize, higher education institutions need to closely assess revenue motivations against other institutional values and motivations.

Barriers and Barrier Reduction

A pervasive and significant challenge on campus to the spread of CI is preservation of the status quo. James Duderstadt, former president of the University of Michigan, variously characterizes U.S. higher education as " increasingly risk averse, at times self-satisfed, and unduly expensive." He also feels that it has often ignored the changing environment, and failed to respond to the globalization of higher education markets. In his view, past achievement lulls U.S. higher education into complacency about its future. Two themes are of particular note in Dud-erstadt's thinking: the drag of mature enterprise and globalization. The two are linked.

Truly believing that one is "best" discourages time and energy spent looking outward. Self-satisfaction is a powerful narcotic creating a lethargic attitude toward change. However, if economic challenges continue, both public and political dissatisfaction with higher education increase, and challenges from the globalization of higher education grow, the days of lethargy are numbered. So, the barrier imposed by the status quo may be self-correcting.

Commentators looking more broadly at impediments to innovation in higher education have pointed to the absence of consequences for failing to achieve desirable outcomes—e.g., state appropriations based on headcount instead of measureable outcomes; inadequate market information to drive responsiveness to changing market conditions; and the fear of being the fisrt to head in a new direction. Tucker writes that, based on his experience facilitating innovation in higher education, "the fisrt question college presidents ask me in the context of discussing a specifc innovation is, 'who else is doing that?' If the answer is, 'no one, you can be the fisrt,' the discussion is over." In its October 25, 2009 edition, in the midst of fears about the "great recession," The Chronicle of Higher Education reported, "College leaders may be thinking strategic change but few are engaging it." One reason ofered was the fear of being fisrt.

The good news is that there are few college presidents and provosts today who don't at least in their rhetoric espouse the necessity and virtues of internationalization. The bandwagon is big and loud. A casual review of the publications of the higher education presidential associations based in Washington, D.C., The Chronicle of Higher Education, and numerous reports of associations such as NAFSA, AIEA, and IIE will convince anyone of the breadth and consistency of the rhetoric.

So, in one sense we may have reached a tipping point of acknowledgment in that "everybody" is at least talking about it. Internationalization is not a new idea. A review of publications over the last decade by NAFSA (e.g., institutional profles of Senator Paul Simon Award winners) and ACE (e.g., Promising Practices) will also point out actions taken by others to internationalize.

There are many robust examples of institutions engaging internationalization so that no one need fear being fisrt. Moreover, there is increasing "buzz" about pegging appropriations to outcomes, not headcount.

Faculty

Arguably, the most important variable in comprehensive internationalization is the faculty. Tey control the curriculum and decisions to award academic credit, they drive the research (along with graduate students), and they determine whether standards and criteria have been met for promotion and tenure. Tey are among the most powerful elements in the governance of an institution.

As CI seeks to significantly widen the circle of those involved, a large number of faculty will be challenged to broaden their knowledge and experience base for both classroom and research purposes. If they are not brought into the process efec-tively, they may see this variously as an inconvenience, as interference in academic freedom, a challenge, and something distasteful. Of course, many faculty willingly embrace internationalization in their work on intellectual and practical grounds (and the numbers are growing). Yet, there are systemic barriers that have to be addressed or goodwill will not be enough.

An institution cannot really engage CI without the active and agreeable participation of a majority of its faculty. A faculty barrier is potentially the most constraining.

Dealing with Barriers

There are no magic solutions to dealing with barriers to internationalization except institutional commitment and persistence in doing so across a number of variables.

The core strategy for success and overcoming barriers is imbedded in the old adage that "nothing breeds success like success." In Everett Roger's terms, the strategy for innovation and change is to create the conditions for "early innovators" who are subsequently rewarded for their success, then to create the conditions and rewards for "early adopters" who spread the innovation, and then to build toward a majority. Strategies:

- Small start-up or incubator funds (preferably with unit match) can be powerful motivators to undertake pilot projects. Unit match helps to internalize unit commitment.
- Institutional recognition through awards or additional funding for units achieving institutional priorities will reinforce and spread the saliency of the innovation.

Faculty Incentives

Like everyone, faculty need incentives. Funding is a significant inducement to internationalization, but it is not a sufciently powerful inducement on its own, particularly for sus-tainability. More important may be whether institutional reward systems for faculty and staf reinforce an internationalization efort and whether accommodations are made to support faculty engagement abroad.

- Is international engagement in various forms recognized as valuable in tenure and promotion criteria? It is one thing to signal that it is permissible to include international activity in a tenure package (e.g., internationalizing a course, invited speaker at an international conference, collaborative research and publication with colleagues abroad) but is another to suggest that it carries added or special weight, and quite another to say that it is expected or required).
- Regardless of what is written on papers and forms, the critical issue turns on what criteria are applied de facto by department promotion and tenure committees and administrators. If international engagement in varying ways is given low status in the process of "departmental counting," regardless what the forms say, this will significantly depreciate faculty international efort. What actually happens is usually a matter of department culture, priorities, and interpretations of national disciplinary standards.
- What gets counted counts. More to the point, when international engagement is seen as getting in the way of doing things that count, it will be actively discouraged. A typical example is discouraging junior faculty from leading study abroad programs or engaging in research abroad because it will distract them from doing the things necessary to meet requirements for tenure and promotion. This last point signals, perhaps, the most important foundational barrier to faculty engagement,

and that is whether international activity is seen as a core part of academic unit priorities. This is why integration of internationalization into core missions is so critical.

Faculty international engagement is also shaped by a number of practical considerations in connection with the need or expectation to be abroad (read: away from campus and home): teaching schedules, family obligations, and access to travel support. Flexibility and innovation in how various obligations are balanced becomes the key. Some examples include:

- Team-teaching courses so that part of the semester can be spent abroad on research, teaching, and presenting.
- Half-semester courses (this requires institutional fexibility in academic calendars and course schedules).
- Assisted-teach models where courses can be covered for short periods (e.g., one or two weeks during a semester) by others. Sandwich course designs that include a period of active learning engagement led by and through student teams.
- Use of technology to keep faculty engaged with students on campus while they are abroad.
- Travel funds to support faculty engaged in valued activities abroad: for example, presenting an invited paper at an international symposium, ofering intensive seminars abroad at partner institutions or for the home institution's programs abroad.

In sum, reducing faculty barriers to international engagement requires that it be seen as an important criteria in promotion, tenure, and other reward decisions; that actual departmental decisions on these matters give adequate recognition; and that international engagement is seen as a core function not only at the institutional level but at the unit level.

Unit-Level Inducements

For some departments, there is a natural afnity between unit priorities and internationalization (e.g., language and humanities departments, units specializing in global or comparative content). In other instances, particularly where the discipline has been domestically focused, strategies to induce change will be needed:

- Encouragement to include international engagement activities in unit tenure and promotion guidelines.
- Including international interest or experience in unit job qualifcation postings.
- Institutional assistance in identifying or providing funding opportunities for international activities.
- Requests for units to address their international engagement priorities and accomplishments as part of the annual budget planning process and as part of institutional strategic planning.
- Institutional awards and funding to reward unit contributions to institutional priorities such as internationalization.

If overall institutional funding and recognition systems reward unit international engagement, then conditions improve dramatically to induce faculty engagement. The keys are communicating internationalization's centrality to core missions, fexibility and accommodation to depart from current practice, and to adaptation of budget and personnel practices that facilitate. The options for doing so are endless to the creative and the willing.

Overarching Pressures for Change

Higher education faces a number of challenges, many of which are likely to force structural change over the long run. If the core of the enterprise begins to change in fundamental ways, it seems only prudent to expect opportunities for change to spread throughout. Budget crises are an opportunity for change—or to put it less elegantly, the "cover" to take actions that otherwise might not have been feasible. Although funding and budgets are powerful change motivators, many of the most salient of likely changes predate the current budget crisis and have support for other reasons as well. What might be the most prominent of pressures for change that could impact CI?

Funding, Accountability, and Stature based on Outcomes

There is growing pressure for higher education to document outcomes and impacts (e.g., what students actually learn, what they can do, what jobs they get, or the reputation and applications of faculty research). The widening interest in measuring outcomes will spread to internationalization and its components such as study abroad. Those advancing higher education CI will need to be able to demonstrate the achievement of desired outcomes with hard data.

Strategic and Full-Cost Financial Analysis and Cost/beneft Analysis

As available funds tighten, pressure builds to "de-fund" lower priority activities and to engage in cost/ beneft analyses that have the beneft of "full-cost" information. Full-cost modeling looks not only at direct attributable costs, but indirect costs and softer ones in the form of unbudgeted or unallocated time and energy of staf and the costs of foregone opportunities. The last, foregone opportunities, is particularly problematic if people see domestic versus international allocations of time as a zero-sum game. Can the benefts of internationalization survive its full-cost modeling? It will be difcult unless internationalization is integrated into the wider core of institutional missions.

Cost Control, Access, and Innovation

Cost control, access, and innovation will be core challenges in U.S. higher education for at least the coming decade, and very likely beyond. CI cannot proceed efectively in the present and future budget climates if it adds huge cost burdens. The problems of higher education cost, cost control, and value added increasingly apply in much of the world.

Innovation will have to occur in the way that expands access to international content and learning, and this will require creativity in what is taught and how subject matter, courses, and programs are delivered. This will of necessity include jettisoning some traditional modes of delivery and content. Further advances in CI will be inextricably tied to creativity and innovation in its def-nition and delivery. Can campus CI leadership be innovative in expanding access and delivery? Merely scaling up existing methods is not a practical solution.

Speed Time to Degree

Pressure and commentary is growing to increase substantially the number who complete postsecondary education as well as to reduce their time to degree. This is occurring at a time when U.S. completion rates have fallen from fisrt globally to well outside the top ten among OECD countries. Will internationalization of the curriculum, particularly language learning and study abroad, delay time to degree by adding requirements? What are the wider innovations and reforms necessary to avoid having CI delay time to degree?

From "Add on" to Integration into the Core

When budgets tighten, organizations of all kinds seek to defne their core and to distinguish what they "must do" from the "nice to do" and the "don't need to do." If CI is viewed in a tight budget climate as an "add on," it will be "subtracted of" when things get tough. Integration of internationalization into the academic core is vital. For example, integration of international content into existing degree requirements (e.g., general education as well as majors) is one strategy. Championing adoption of more fexible academic calendars and learning modules can increase the ease with which international content is included during the degree. Internationalization may itself have to become a catalyst for change, but at the very minimum it cannot aford to be aloof of the need for change. Will a commitment to CI include its integration into the core of campus priorities?

Review of Curricula, the Academic Core, and Governance structures

There are calls for a complete review of the academic core in response to a variety of challenges, including budgets, globalization of higher education, dissatisfaction with apparent outcomes, and national needs. Whether such systematic review occurs, the speed with which cutting-edge knowledge emerges now and the decreasing half-life of cutting-edge knowledge requires ongoing and reduced cycle time for curricular revisions. In the interest of being competitive, decisionmaking and governance systems must reduce their own cycle time.

Reduced Cycle Time for Change

Responsive change, including that for internationalization, requires efcient governance and decisionmaking. Can institutional governance systems become more responsive than the reputation they have? Will advocates of CI be at the core of ongoing change in curricula and governance deliberations, or will they and the elements of internationalization be on the periphery and an afterthought in governance and decisionmaking? If the latter, marginalization is nearly guaranteed.

Partnerships and Collaborations

Some calls for structural reform focus on building bridges across disciplines, institutions, and borders. There are long-standing calls for increased interdisciplinary programs and subject matter in higher education (e.g., environmental studies); internationalization can contribute to such eforts.

The rapidity of political and socio-economic changes worldwide ofers many challenges to higher education's ability to respond fexibly and swiftly to opportunities. Justin-time, project-based responses using various combinations of faculty across disciplines and other assets scattered across the higher education institution become essential. This also requires institutional investment in an infrastructure that can quickly assemble and support cross-disciplinary teams because so many problems with origins in globalization require interdisciplinary defnition as well as interdisciplinary solution.

Calls to reduce programmatic duplications across institutions or to close programs with low enrollment will force greater attention to inter-institutional partnerships (both domestic and international) to deliver content and programs cooperatively.

The literature of internationalization has begun to tackle the problem, common at many institutions, of fling cabinets full of inter-institutional memoranda of understanding (MOU). Many of these, signed during visits of colleagues from abroad, promised rich partnership and collaboration but rarely amounted to anything of worth. Sutton, for example has written and spoken extensively on what she refers to as "transformational partnerships". These arrangements are driven by multiple institutional missions and seek to establish long-term, in-depth, synergistic, and multifaceted partnerships.

The idea and intent is that transformational or strategic partnerships build win-win synergies between institutions as a major outcome, with mutual capacity building and value added to each institution extending well beyond what either could accomplish by going it alone (e.g., in study abroad, faculty and student exchanges, field research opportunities, collaborative research, joint submissions for funding). Transformational or strategic partnerships should have the impact of dramatically reducing the number of well intentioned but fruitless MOUs in favor of having a few very good ones.

Internationalization advocates need to have a prominent role in prioritizing and defning the features of cross-border collaborations to build transformational partnerships.

Broadening of Internationalization

Institutional research and outreach problem solving increasingly crosses borders, and broadens the reach of CI. Although, arguably, all institutions of higher education engage to some degree in both knowledge creation and knowledge dissemination, there is tremendous diversity in the attention and priority given instructional, research, and outreach service missions across institutions (from liberal arts, four-year institutions to the big research institutions).

With allowances for such difer-ences in emphasis among types of institutions, CI will be prompted at many institutions to move beyond its curricular and instructional foci. This will remap the campus leadership of internationalization, bringing new voices from the research side of the institution. What role will they have, and how will their interests and those more traditionally associated with internationalization result in a blended conversation and outcome?

Cross-Mission Synergies

Budget constraints prompt interest in investments that produce "two-fers" and "three-fers." Tis, too, will challenge CI to be more mission holistic in its orientation. In a more synergistic environment, for example, the choice of institutional partners is not simply a matter of finding a good study abroad site, but one that might serve institutional research and outreach missions as well. CI will increasingly have to become intertwined with all relevant institutional missions (teaching, research, and outreach problem solving to the extent relevant at a given institution). Are there dialog mechanisms and cross-walk structures on campus to accomplish this? The internationalization of learning, research, and outreach will require their interconnection.

Responding to Nontraditional Students

The so called "nontraditional" student has become the norm. Students who work, students with families, part-time students, older and adult learners, a diverse and multicultural student body, are all characteristics of the new traditional student body. How will internationalization facilitate access to this far-more diverse student client pool with differing needs and constraints from those of the "old traditional" student?

Global Competition for the Best Faculty and Students

Institutional stature is significantly, if not wholly, a product of its faculty and students. Research capacity is critical in a knowledge society. Faculty and their graduate students are the research engines of higher education and society. Will global recruitment of faculty and students expand to attract and to become the best? There seems little doubt that the American higher education system will have far greater competition for the best than it has had for decades.

From Concept and Rhetoric to Institutional Action

Common elements of orientation, Mindset, and Action

1. An enabling First step: Making the Case

The starting mindset to make CI even possible is a widespread campus belief that institutional aspirations and values will be fundamentally advanced by internationalization. The fisrt step for many institutions will be a dialog among key stakeholders that moves the campus mindset from seeing CI as having little or no value (or it being marginalized by mere tolerance for it) to seeing CI as essential. A parallel mindset needs to be built among key elements of the institution's external environment (e.g., constituents, alumni, donors, political arenas). Education and advocacy for CI is important both internally and externally.

Even though it seems nearly everyone gives at least lip service to the value of internationalization, one cannot assume that a deep understanding of and commitment to needed action necessarily follows—particularly in an environment of resource constraint and strong competition for institutional resources, time, and attention.

Even when internationalization is universally acknowledged as fundamental to the mission of the institution, it is not automatically clear what actions should follow and who should take them. Many of the rhetorical statements made in support of internationalization are sound bites that lack understanding of the underlying breadth and depth of CI that need to drive action.

Building a solid case for CI and a culture for it should be among the fisrt steps taken and is a matter of leadership, consistent messaging, and deep and wide campus dialog reinforced by action and documented desirable outcomes.

The requisite mindset for action begins with a campus-wide discussion and understanding of the rationale, motivations, and options to engage internationalization. Successful CI is not the product of well-meaning but heavy top-down decisionmaking by presidents and provosts. Neither is it only the result of bottom-up populism. It is the product of top down and bottom up acting in concert to pursue consensus. Useful actions to achieve consensus include:

- A dialog involving campus leadership, governance, and internal and external clientele culminating in a shared understanding of the compelling rationale for CI, and its meaning, goals, program priorities, and the outcomes sought. What should this institution look like if it becomes comprehensively internationalized?
- Clear and consistent messaging from the president, provost, and academic leadership on the importance of CI to institutional missions and values, and on their expectations for participation by all students, faculty, staf, and administrators—each in ways beftting their unique roles and responsibilities.
- Ongoing information and education programs to sustain widespread awareness and understanding throughout the campus of the dimensions of CI and that encourage all to consider why they should participate and how they can contribute, as well as beneft.
- Support of pilot and demonstration projects that ofer successful examples of payofs from widening international engagement.
- Regular reporting of internationalization engagement actions and outcomes and meaningful institutional recognition and rewards for units and individuals successfully engaged.

2. Long-range Commitment and Audacious Goals

Broad acceptance of the importance of CI is necessary, but insufcient. A necessary additional enabler is to set goals and expectations that shift thinking from viewing CI as relevant only for some and as a peripheral institutional commitment to seeing CI as a core commitment impacting all. Democratization of access and action to mainstream participation and benefts is at the heart of implementing comprehensive internationalization.

"Stretch goals" tied to CI serve not only to signal intended breadth and depth, but are preconditions for comprehensiveness. Some may view such goals as audacious, but in the audacity is the stretch needed to make CI comprehensive. Examples include the following:

- Every undergraduate student given significant exposure to international, comparative, and global content as part of their degree programs. General or liberal education requirements can provide a component of such exposure with the majors providing additional components. Defnitions of "significant exposure" and operational means are defned using campus-wide governance and curriculum processes.
- Learning outcomes established for internationalization, incorporating knowledge, attitudes, and skills outcomes. Institutional and departmental governance processes should defne intended outcomes and modes of measuring achievement and make them operational.
- All students have opportunity to engage learning through education abroad. Enhancing study abroad options, identifying and minimizing barriers to participation, and incorporating such experiences into degree programs are needed strategies.
- All faculty encouraged to enhance international, comparative, and global perspective in their teaching and scholarship. Faculty should not abandon their existing teaching and research agendas, but are encouraged and supported to incorporate ideas and perspectives from other systems and cultures as relevant. Support can take many forms such as encouraging visiting appointments at institutions abroad, faculty exchange programs, travel support for conferences, funding for study/research abroad, access to language programs, workshops on internationalizing curricula, and grant writing to support international activity.
- The integration of all international students and scholars into the campus living and learning environment. Every international student

and scholar is encouraged and supported to contribute measurably to campus understandings and appreciation for global diversity, to international izing the on-campus environment, and to maximizing the contact and cross-learning of both domestic and international populations.

- All graduate students given understanding of the practice of their profession and discipline in other cultures. Components and methods could include classroom learning, the use of technology for discussions or team projects with similar students abroad, and opportunities for professional engagement abroad (visits, student exchanges, feld work/ research) relevant to their programs.
- Routine institutional support of research and of research collaborations abroad. Institutional policies, mechanisms, and support ofces need to be oriented to encouraging and supporting faculty and student research on global and comparative topics, facilitating collaborations with institutions and colleagues abroad, and facilitating faculty and student work in other countries.
- Community engagement that routinely includes connection of local constituencies to global opportunities and knowledge. This is a two-way connection: fisrt, connecting institutional capacities to community needs in, for example, helping to develop global linkages for business and cultural purposes; and second, connecting community capacities to campus needs—tapping into the diversity of local resources for languages and culture, or contacts abroad to support internationalization.

Not all institutions will pursue all of these stretch goals, in part because of fundamental diferences in mission mix and priorities. However, whether some or all are actively pursued, a commonality running throughout the list is a commitment to internationalization touching all aspects of the institution.

Given the "stretch" nature of many of these goals, a long-range commitment to pursuing them will be essential.

3. A Mindset of Shared Responsibility and Collaboration

Institutional dialog and leadership needs to build a culture for cross-unit collaboration in both mindset and action. This may be a tough sell in an environment where priorities are governed by organizational and intellectual silos and by narrow disciplinary standards that depreciate attention given to cross-cutting institutional objectives. Yet, it is the collaboration of many not just a few that is needed if CI is to be successful.

CI cannot occur without the willing and meaningful collaboration of academic departments. Additionally, productive collaborations formed between academic departments and international programming units is essential. Education abroad in its various forms provides the experience component of international learning; together, the on-campus curriculum and education abroad are partners in internationalizing curriculum and learning. Internationalized curriculum and learning require an internationally engaged faculty. Language departments provide access to the communication tools supporting internationalization, and area study provides the core knowledge required to function globally and within world regions. International students and scholars enrich and internationalize the on-campus learning environment and can significantly enhance campus research capacity and outcomes. Engagement in development activity abroad connects the institution to global applications and solutions and provides invaluable feld experience for faculty and students.

It is the potential synergies among these elements that makes the whole greater than the sum of its parts and the "comprehensive" part of CI possible. To accomplish this, the leadership and staf of individual departments and ofces must locate and build upon the connections that lead to synergies and be governed by a collaborative mindset. The collaborations need to be expanded throughout the campus enterprise and across academic units, international program units, and general campus support and service units. Some examples of such behavior are in the sidebar.

4. Collaborative and Coordinating Leadership

The success of CI depends on a mindset where components of internationalization are driven not just for their own purposes but for their contribution to overall CI goals. For example, study abroad or language learning can be strengthened by conscious connection to other components of CI such as internationalizing the on-campus curriculum. This has been the experience of several campuses that have consciously sought to integrate study abroad into the curriculum of majors; language study has been enhanced through programs of "languages across the curriculum."

A failure to connect and integrate the eforts and programs of individual ofces into the larger CI efort guarantees less than ideal results in both. Tinking and behaving departmentally tends to focus attention on inputs (size of the ofce budget) and outputs (clientele head counts), rather than on outcomes relating to overall CI objectives (e.g., graduates who are workforce ready for a twenty-fisrt century environment). Study abroad and learning a second language may well be goods independently, but have even greater impact when connected to and reinforcing larger institutional objectives.

SIO Leadership Roles. The absence of overall leadership and coordination of the CI efort almost guarantees its fragmentation and sub-optimization. Although it is understood that not all senior international ofcers (SIOs) are strategically placed to provide such leadership and coordination and that scale and scope of the CI efort will depend on institutional mission and size, leadership and coordination will enhance CI eforts in any campus setting.

Building a coherent institutional strategy for internationalization across the work of either a few or numerous internationally engaged ofces and programs requires leadership that is (a) senior and infuential enough to promote development of an institutional consensus and strategy for CI as a whole, and (b) leadership that can help facilitate development of synergies across the programming components of internationalization. Some key questions that may help SIOs begin the thinking-through process and the starting point include:

- What are the scope, consistency, and strength of institutional rhetoric for CI?
- Do actions (policies, programs, resources, outcomes) align with the rhetoric?
- What are strengths, weaknesses, synergies, and conficting realities of the institution's CI eforts?
- What should be the strategic action plan and priorities for strengthening CI?

SIOs can have important leadership roles on their own as well as supporting presidents and provosts and other academic leaders in:

- Building the case for CI throughout the campus and developing a campus mindset for CI.

- Promoting a sense of shared role, responsibility, and collaboration across campus to achieve CI.
- Gaining campus acceptance and follow-through to achieve universal opportunity for students and faculty to engage internationalization.
- Helping to shape an adaptive bureaucracy to the needs of CI and enhance campus academic and support/service unit assistance for CI.

Leaders of International Program Components. Depending on the campus, there can be a few or many ofces or programs that specialize in aspects of international engagement: e.g., education abroad, international students and scholars, English language centers, language departments, area study centers, international thematic centers such as in business, to name some of the possibilities. If individual ofces and programs are to contribute efectively to internationalization as well as maximize achievement of their own internal goals, efective "outward-looking" leadership of these ofces and programs is important.

Equally important is a leadership style in these ofces that looks for collaboration and win/wins in dealings with other stakeholders. The types of questions that provide a start for looking outward, connecting actions of a particular ofce or program to CI, and for building synergies include:

- Knowing the institution's overarching objectives for CI.
- Identifying how the program can or should contribute to achieving CI objectives.
- Identifying principal clients and their needs.
- Knowing who or what ofers barriers for the program to meet its objectives.
- Identifying collaborations that would enhance achieving program objectives.
- Assessing what the program does not do well, for which collaborations with others would help.

There are a myriad of ways in which these issues and their answers can play out across ofces and programs; but leadership consciously attuned to answering them provides a basis for synergy and connecting individual international program activities to CI.

5. Integration into Institutional Policies and Processes

Core institutional documents such as mission and value statements provide direction and a sense of priorities. Bureaucracy sets the rules of the game, provides order and orientation, but it also constrains and can stife fexibility and adaptation. CI is weakened or rendered inefec-tive if not appropriately recognized and supported by core institutional documents and policies. Adapting core institutional documents and the bureaucracy to govern both domestically and internationally is a core leadership issue. Some of the specifc issues to address include:

- Declaring where the institution is headed and what is important.

  These are answered publically in institutional mission statements and companion statements about institutional values. Tey are given further detail in institutional strategic plans. Is CI a prominent part of such institutional direction-giving documents?

- Reinforcing the message. Change is, in part, the product of consistent and frequent messaging. It is reinforcing to give prominent attention and placement to CI and its activities and successes on the university Web page; in institutional brochures and recruitment materials in job postings; and in college, department, and alumni newsletters and magazines. What are the institutional priorities, outlets, and frequency for reinforcing the institutional CI message?

- Defne and reward what counts. What is counted counts. The integration of international dimensions into curricula and degree requirements signals what counts for students. The inclusion of international activity and accomplishments into promotion, compensation, tenure, and related decisionmaking signals what counts for faculty and staf. A requirement that departments and units identify their intended contributions to CI as part of their annual planning activity, followed by the fow of institutional resources to departments and units contributing to CI, underscore what is important to the institution and for departments and units. Is internationalization a core part of the curriculum, institutional recognition and reward systems, planning processes, and resource allocation decisions?

- Recruit and employ for CI. Organizations are defned in important ways and success dictated by whom they seek to attract. Important institutional CI messages are sent by signaling eforts to recruit (a) students who have strong global interests; (b) faculty with international backgrounds, experience, or interests; (c) staf who see the importance of international engagement and who will work creatively to actively support it; and (d) administrative leaders who see a significant part of their leadership role creating the vision and support for achieving CI. Does the institution seek broadly to recruit and attract the internationally interested and engaged?

- Commitment to human resource development. Whereas curriculum and pedagogy are the human resource development tools applied to students, education and training in the form of (for example, professional development workshops, access to language training, or experience abroad) are components of institutional personnel development processes. Is there an institutional commitment to developing the international knowledge, skills, and abilities of existing faculty and staf?
- Designing adaptive bureaucracy and service units. Rules and regulations designed to support a community and domestic base of operation often don't easily sustain cross-border mobility or "doing business" abroad—and sometimes are powerful barriers to doing so. Diferent cultures, practices, and legal systems intervene in a myriad of ways only some of which can be anticipated— afecting for example, institutional travel regulations, risk assessment, insurance requirements, intellectual property expectations, translating standards across cultures, contractual practices, regulations, and resolving conficts among regulations from having to deal with multiple governmental entities. An important mindset for successfully acting on CI is fexibility to adapt necessary rules and procedures to new environments. Is there a mechanism to identify bureaucratic barriers to CI and for acceptably resolving them? How hidebound and resistant is institutional bureaucracy to changes in procedures and practices?

Goal: Expansive and Pervasive Internationalization

A comprehensive approach to internationalization is all encompassing. Globally informed content is integrated into the vast majority of courses, curricula, and majors. Comparative and global perspectives are integrated into research and scholarship of faculty. The benefts of cross-cultural and comparative understanding are extended through outreach to citizens, businesses, and public ofcials.

The prerequisites for action and success in pursuing the expansive and pervasive CI agenda require fully engaged leadership from the top of the institution to academic deans, heads of academic and support units, academic governance, faculty, and key support stafs. Among the fisrt steps of leadership is the need to engage campus dialog and consensus building on the importance of CI, engagement around a "stretch" set of goals, building a campus-wide mindset of shared responsibility and coordination of efort, and commitment to fashioning administrative, organization, and policy structures that will facilitate support and facilitate CI.

References

Altbach, Philip G., Liz Reisberg, and Laura Rumbley. 2009. *Trends in Global higher Education: Tracking an Academic Revolution.* Paris, France: UNESCO

Green, Madeleine F. 2005. *Internationalization of U.S. Higher Education: A Student Perspective.* Washington, D.C.: American Council on Education Mestenhauser, Josef A. 1998. "International Education on the Verge: In Search of New Paradigm." *International Educator* VII, 2-3:68–76.

Olsen, Christa L., Madeleine F. Green, and Barbara A. Hill. 2005. *Building a Strategic Framework for Comprehensive Internationalization.* Washington, D.C.: American Council on Education.

Rogers, Everett M. 2003. *Diffusion of Innovations.* New York: Free Press.

Ruby, Alan. 2010. *The Uncertain Future for International Higher Education in the Asia-Pacific Region.* Washington, D.C.: NAFSA: Association of International Educators.

Bibliography

Adelman, C. 2009. *The Bologna Process for U.S. Eyes: Re-learning Higher Education in the Age of Convergence*, Institute for Higher Education Policy, Washington

Agarwal, P., Said, M.E., Sehoole, M., Sirozi, M. and de Wit, H. 2008. H. de Wit (ed.), *The Dynamics of International Student Circulation in a Global Context*, Rotterdam, Sense Publishers. 223-261

Altbach, P.G. Levy D.C. (eds.), 2005 *Private Higher Education: A Global Revolution*, Rotterdam, Sense Publishers. 1-12.

Altbach, Philip G., Liz Reisberg, and Laura Rumbley. 2009. *Trends in Global higher Education: Tracking an Academic Revolution.* Paris, France: UNESCO

American Council on Education. 2003. *Internationalizing the Campus. A User's Guide.* ACE, Washington.

Arafeh, S. 2004. *The Implications of Information and Communications Technologies for Distance Education: Looking Toward the Future*, Arlington, VA, SRI International.

AVCC. 1998. *Code of Ethical Practice in the Provision of Education to International Students.* Australian Universities of the Australian Vice-Chancellors Committee.

Barrow, C. 2008. *Globalization, Trade Liberalization, and the Transnationalization of Higher Education.* 18 November 2008 presentation at Boston College,

Bashir, S. 2007. *Trends in international trade in higher education: Implications and options for developing countries*. Washington, DC: World Bank.

Ben-David, J. and Zloczower,A. 1962. Universities and academic systems in modern societies. *European Journal of Sociology*, Vol. 3, No. 5, pp. 45-84.

Bray, M.; Packer, S. 1993. *Education in small states: Concepts, challenges and strategies*. Oxford, UK: Pergamon Press.

Cao,Y. 2007. *Chinese Private Colleges and the Labor Market*, Ph.D.

Castells, M. and Hall, P.G. 1994. *Technopoles of the world: the making of twenty-firstcentury industrial complexes*. London and New York, Routledge.

Chen, D.A.C.; Dahlman, D.J. 2004. *Knowledge and development: A cross-section approach*. Washington, DC: World Bank. (World Bank policy research working paper, No.°3366.)

Chestnut Hill, MA. Canton, E. and Blom,A. 2004. *Can Student Loans Improve Accessibility to Higher* Education and Student Performance: An Impact Study of the Case of SOFES, *Mexico*, World Bank, Washington DC.

Clark, B.R. 1987. *The Academic Life. Small Worlds, Different Worlds*. Princeton, NJ, Carnegie Foundation for the Advancement of Teaching.

Crocombe, R.; Crocombe, M.T. 1994. *Post-secondary education in the South Pacifi c*. London: Commonwealth Secretariat.

D'Antoni, S. 2008. *Open Educational Resources: The Way Forward*, UNESCO, International Institute for Educational Planning, Paris.

Daniel, J. 2006. *The reality of cross-border delivery in higher education: Challenge, myth and opportunity*.

Etzkowitz, H. and Leydesdorff, L.A. 1997. *Universities and the Global Knowledge Economy: A Triple Helix of University-Industry-Government Relations*. London and New York, Pinter

Fallis, G. 2007. *Multiversities, Ideas and Democracy*. Toronto, University of Toronto Press.

Finn, M.G. 2003, "Stay Rates of Foreign Doctorate Recipients from US Universities, 2001", Oak Ridge Institute for Science and Education, URL: *www.orau.gov/orise/pubs/stayrate03.pdf*.

Florida, R.L. 2002. *The Rise of the Creative Class: And How It's Transforming Work, Leisure, Community and Everyday Life*. New York, Basic Books.

Green, Madeleine F. 2005. *Internationalization of U.S. Higher Education: A Student Perspective.* Washington, D.C.: American Council on Education Mestenhauser, Josef A. 1998. "International Education on the Verge: In Search of New Paradigm." *International Educator* VII, 2-3:68–76.

Gupta,A., Levy, D.C. and Powar, K.B. 2008. *Private Higher Education: Global Trends and Indian perspectives*. New Delhi, Shipra Publications.

Guri-Rosenblit, S. 2009. *Digital Technologies in Higher Education: Sweeping Expectations and Actual Effects*. New York, Nova Science

Hallak, J.; Poisson, M. 2007. *Corrupt schools, corrupt universities: What can be done?* Paris: IIEP-UNESCO.

Herbst, M. 2007. *Financing Public Universities: The Case of Performance Funding*. Dordrecht, The Netherlands, Springer.

Institute of International Education (IIE). 2007. *Atlas of student mobility*. New York, NY: IIE.

International Labour Offi ce (ILO). 2004. *Promoting employment: Policies, skills, enterprises*. Geneva, Switzerland: ILO.

Johnstone, S.M. 2005. Open educational resources serve the world. *EduCause Quarterly*, Vol. 28, No. 3, pp. 15.

Kerr, C. 2001. T*he Uses of the University*. Cambridge, MA, Harvard University Press Marton, F., Hounsell, D. and Entwistle, N.J. 1997. *The experience of learning*. Edinburgh, Scottish Academic Press.

Knight, J. 2006. *Higher Education Crossing Borders: A Guide to the Implications of the General Agreement on Trade in Services (GATS) for Cross-border Education*. Vancouver, BC, Commonwealth of Learning.

Knight, Jane. 2008. *Higher Education in Turmoil. The Changing World of Internationalisation.* Rotterdam, the Netherlands: Sense Publishers.

Larsen, K. and S. Vincent-Lancrin. 2002, *"International Trade in Educational Services: Good or Bad?", Higher Education Management and Policy*, Vol. 14, No. 3, OECD, Paris.

Levy, D.C. 2006. The private fit in the higher education landscape. J.J.F. Forest and P.G. Altbach (eds.), *International Handbook of Higher Education*, Dordrecht, The Netherlands, Springer. 281-292.

Mabizela, M. 2007. Private surge amid public dominance in provision of higher education in Africa. *Journal of Higher Education in Africa*, Vol. 5, No. 2 & 3, pp. 15-38.

Marton, F., Hounsell, D. and Entwistle, N.J. 1997. *The experience of learning*. Edinburgh, Scottish Academic Press.

Maurrasse, D.J. 2001. *Beyond the Campus: How Colleges and Universities Form Partnerships with their Communities*. New York, Routledge.

Mclntosh, C. and Varoglu, Z. 2005. *Perspectives on Distance Education. Lifelong Learning & Distance Higher Education*, Paris, UNESCO and Commonwealth of Learning.

Mclntosh, C. and Varoglu, Z. 2005. *Perspectives on Distance Education. Lifelong Learning & Distance Higher Education*, Paris, UNESCO and Commonwealth of Learning.

Obasi, I.N. 2006. New private universities in Nigeria. *International Higher Education*, No. 45, pp. 14.

OECD. 2006, *The Challenge of Capacity Development: Working towards Good Practice,* DAC Guidelines, OECD, Paris, available for free download at: www.oecd.org/dac/governance/capacitydevelopment

OECD/World Bank. 2007, *Cross-Border Tertiary Education: A Way towards Capacity Development,* OECD, Paris.

Olsen, Christa L., Madeleine F. Green, and Barbara A. Hill. 2005. *Building a Strategic Framework for Comprehensive Internationalization.* Washington, D.C.: American Council on Education.

Ramos, A., Trinona, J. and Lambert, D. 2006. Viability of SMS technologies for nonformal distance education. J. Baggaley (ed.), *Information and Communication Technology for Social Development*, Jakarta, Indonesia, ASEAN Foundation.

Rogers, Everett M. 2003. *Diffusion of Innovations.* New York: Free Press.

Ruby, Alan. 2010. *The Uncertain Future for International Higher Education in the Asia-Pacific Region.* Washington, D.C.: NAFSA: Association of International Educators.

UNESCO. 2009. World Conference on Higher Education: The New Dynamics of Higher Education and Research For Societal Change and Development, 5 8 July 2009. COMMUNIQUE (8 July 2009), Paris.

Van der Wende, Marijk C. 2001. Internationalisation Policies: About New Trends and Contrasting Paradigms.*Higher Education Policy* 14 (3): 249-259.